MYTHS OF THE ENGLISH

Myths of the English

Edited by
Roy Porter

Polity Press

This edition © Polity Press 1992
Introduction © Roy Porter; chapter 1 © 1991 Nyrev, Inc.;
chapter 2 © Marina Warner; chapter 3 © David Cressy;
chapter 4 © M. A. Crowther; Chapter 5 © Clive Emsley; chapter 6 © Bob
Bushaway; chapter 7 © Margaret Kinnell; chapter 8 © Reba N. Soffer;
chapter 9 © Iain Pears; chapter 10 © Gertrude Prescott Nuding.

First published in 1992 by Polity Press
in association with Blackwell Publishers

First published in paperback 1993
Reprinted 1994

Editorial office:
Polity Press
65 Bridge Street
Cambridge CB2 1UR, UK

Marketing and production:
Blackwell Publishers
108 Cowley Road
Oxford OX4 1JF, UK

238 Main Street
Cambridge, MA 02142, USA

ISBN 0 7456 0844 2
ISBN 0 7456 1306 3 (pbk)

A CIP catalogue record for this book is available
from the British Library and the Library of Congress.

Typeset in 10½ on 12 pt Sabon
by Hope Services (Abingdon) Ltd.
Printed in Great Britain by
T.J. Press (Padstow) Ltd

This book is printed on acid-free paper

CONTENTS

ACKNOWLEDGEMENTS

I am very grateful to Peter Burke and to the enthusiastic editors at Polity for originally suggesting the theme of this book and inviting me to edit it. Since then, many historians have been generous with advice in helping to clarify and confirm its themes; and I have been fortunate indeed in the team who kindly agreed to contribute. I thank them all for their keenness, co-operation and promptitude in producing their stimulating and original essays. As always, Frieda Houser has supplied the administrative skills which made editing a pleasure.

R. P.

Notes on the Contributors

BOB BUSHAWAY's doctoral thesis for the University of Southampton was published as *By Rite: Custom, Ceremony and Community in England, 1700–1880* (1982). He published several articles on English rural customs and collective ritual before turning to the popular culture of the Great War. He works as a university administrator and is an associate member of the Department of Modern History at the University of Birmingham. He is married with three children.

DAVID CANNADINE is Professor of History at Columbia University. His books include *The Pleasures of the Past* and *The Decline and Fall of the British Aristocracy*.

DAVID CRESSY is an English historian, educated at Cambridge, who has taught in California for twenty years. His books include *Bonfires and Bells: National Memory and the Protestant Calendar in Elizabethan and Stuart England* (1989); *Coming Over: Migration and Communication between England and New England in the Seventeenth Century* (1987); and *Literacy and the Social Order: Reading and Writing in Tudor and Stuart England* (1980). He is currently interested in social ritual and rites of passage in early modern England.

M. A. CROWTHER is Reader in the Department of Economic History at the University of Glasgow. Her research interests include the history of social policy, poverty and crime, and she is the author of *The Workhouse System 1834–1929* and *British Social Policy 1914–1939*.

CLIVE EMSLEY is Professor of History at the Open University. He was educated at the University of York and Peterhouse, Cambridge. He has taught at the University of Calgary and the University of Paris VIII. His main area of interest is the history of crime and policing; his publications include *Policy and its Context, 1750–1870, Crime and Society in England 1750–1900* and *The English Police: A Political and Social History*.

MARGARET KINNELL teaches children's literature in the Department of Information and Library Studies at Loughborough University and is managing editor of the *International Review of Children's Literature and Librarianship*. She is currently researching childhood and children's literature from the seventeenth to the nineteenth century.

IAIN PEARS is author of *The Discovery of Painting: The Growth of Interest in the Arts in England, 1680–1760* (1988). He is currently working on a history of nineteenth-century Paris.

GERTRUDE PRESCOTT NUDING is an art historian (Princeton and Austin/Texas). She came to London as a Fulbright Fellow in 1982, then held a curatorial position in the Iconographic Collections of the Wellcome Institute for the History of Medicine. Since 1985 she has lectured on the history of prints and on the history of photography and collecting at Richmond College and has given guest lectures in Sotheby's and Christie's educational programmes as well as at the Wellcome Institute, The Royal Institution, Leicester University and at Art Historians' Association conferences. Her published articles include 'Portraits for the Nation', *History Today* (1989); 'Faraday: Image of the Man and the Collector', *Faraday Rediscovered* (1985; 1989); articles on the market for Irish art in *Irish Arts Review Yearbook* (beginning 1990–1). She has written for *Apollo, Art and Auction* and, more recently, the *Art Newspaper*. She is currently preparing a book analysing the art market from the 1970s to the 1990s.

REBA N. SOFFER has written on ethics and society; on the relations between the social sciences, social theory and social practice; on the origins of history as a discipline; on the universities; and on history and religion. Her book *The Modern University and National Values: The Making of an Elite, 1850–1930* will be published in 1992.

MARINA WARNER was formerly Tinbergen Professor at Erasmus

University, Rotterdam, where she was writing a study of fairytale. Her studies of female symbolism include *Alone of All Her Sex: The Myth and Cult of the Virgin Mary* (1976); *Joan of Arc: The Image of Female Heroism* (1981); and *Monuments and Maidens: The Allegory of the Female Form* (1985). She has written three novels; *The Lost Father* (1988) was awarded the PEN Silver Pen Award, and was regional winner of the Commonwealth Writers' Prize, 1989. She reviews for the *Times Literary Supplement, The London Review of Books, The Independent on Sunday* and other papers, and broadcasts regularly on radio and television. The English National Opera have commissioned a libretto for a children's opera, *The Queen of Sheba's Legs*, and a new novel, *Indigo*, was published in spring 1991.

LIST OF ILLUSTRATIONS

INTRODUCTION
Roy Porter

This volume aims to look afresh at taken-for-granted aspects of the world in which we live, by exploring the historical meanings of things.

'All the past's a stage.' The words Shakespeare so easily might have put into Jaques's mouth ring especially true today. We are living not just at the end of a century but at the finale of a millennium; and so the customary nostalgic hankerings of the *fin de siècle* are increased tenfold. Over the 1980s, much-trumpeted 'opportunity capitalism' has translated relics of the British past – stately homes, factories and furnaces, village vistas – into 'heritage'; and history has thereby become valuable, precisely because past time is money, and the magic of the immemorial big money indeed. Mrs Thatcher was herself fond of commending 'Victorian values' as codes of right conduct. Of course, as many have leapt to point out, the values the former Prime Minister upheld – that 'society' was a fiction, and home was where you went when you had nothing better to do – are norms no Victorian ever dreamt of espousing;[1] but this merely confirms the commonplace that those who appeal to bygone ages for the way, the truth and the life, are often those who know least about them. The past thus seems to be up for grabs, a chest of props and togs ready-to-wear in almost any costume drama, available to fulfil all manner of fantasies; and it is no accident that a crop of books has been appearing with titles like *The Invention of Tradition* (1983), *The Enchanted Glass: Britain and its Monarchy* (1988), *Patriotism: The Making and Unmaking of British National Identity* (1989) and, in France, Pierre Nora's *Les Lieux de Mémoire* (1984) – explorations of what Raphael Samuel and Paul Thompson have elsewhere dubbed *The Myths We Live By*.[2]

The authors of such volumes have aimed to peel away the mythic patinas gilding such institutions as the monarchy or the City, and to expose 'tradition' as an invention often designed to confer spurious sanctity and cover multitudes of sins. And, in so doing, they have reflected upon the processes whereby our 'sense of the past' comes to be not just a datum, an innocent snapshot, but the product of cultural negotiation, expressive of present needs. As Peter Burke emphasized twenty years ago in his *The Renaissance Sense of the Past*, the very invention (or discovery) in the sixteenth century of a feeling for history – the perception that classical times were essentially *different* from modern times – arose from the ideological struggles of humanist intellectuals to ground their own identity in the role models of antiquity, while advancing the claims of their own princely patrons and flowering civilizations to independent glory.[3]

Since the Renaissance, the entrenchment of a 'sense of history' has brought, one would hope, authentic intellectual gain, sharpening our curiosity and enlarging our sympathies for alien cultures, creeds and customs. But in Britain today, a historical cast of mind also reflects the depressing fact that ours is a dangerously fossilized civilization, one embalmed in ever more antiquated artefacts. The bulk of the infrastructure, the bricks and mortar, of Britain today – its street plans, sewers, railway tracks, prisons and schools – is over a century old. We are perhaps more surrounded, choked even, by the past than any earlier generation. And if the conservationist urge is often generous, it is equally true that many prefer to live in 'ye olde past' (or at least to daydream about it) than in the present, basking in bygone glories in a museum-land conserved by the National Trust, marketed by Heritage, and tailor-made for tourists, however unsuited it may be to meet the challenges of modernity.[4] British historians are thus in the peculiar position of living in a culture highly preoccupied with the past, but fascinated with it for all the wrong reasons; out of nostalgia, rather than the urge to understand the present and forge the future.[5]

Historians are in a somewhat uncomfortable position. They relish demystifying the 'pasts' vaunted by others, exposing these as self-serving ideological constructs. Yet they must also, willy-nilly, apply these insights or strictures reflexively to themselves. Are historians just myth-mongering too, peddling fantasied pasts of their own? And if so, is this not a far more culpable kind of intellectual treason, executed with a cynical awareness of 'telling tales'? Or, alternatively, might the profession's much-prized commitment to scholarly objectivity afford some rock upon which the edifice of Scientific History may continue to rise, safe from the swirling eddies of prejudice, false consciousness and overheated fancies?[6]

There is no doubt that various intellectual fashions in recent years have sharpened our awareness that 'the world we have lost' may be but another landscape of the imagination, rather like the realms of gold paraded before our eyes in glossy holiday brochures. For one thing, the synchronic/diachronic mental polarity espoused by 1970s structuralists suggested that the past was less a reality 'back there', over our shoulder, as it were, than a mode of mental sorting, just another method of cataloguing experience and structuring discourse. After all, we were endlessly scolded, only hopelessly benighted empiricists still thought there were such things as authors; and the 'history' of ideas, of literature – of anything! – was, in truth, just a shelf of intertextually related texts, and temporality but a taxonomic construct.[7] Then again, certain tendencies in French thought in particular – currents associated with Roland Barthes, Jean Baudrillard and Pierre Bourdieu – insistently drew attention to the unquenchable need of consumer capitalism to generate and appropriate meaning-laden symbols for its proliferating discourses.[8] A show of history was grist to the mill for the sign systems of advertisers, politicians and other patterers in a modern telecommunications universe desperate for eligible, authority-bearing images. Ironically, the ultra-modern present has been able to take comfort in the myth of the past because history is, in some sense, like a bottomless well, incapable of running dry, indeed, like knitting, growing all the time.

Meanwhile, historians themselves, locked in professional polemics, began to pay heightened attention to the ideological undertow of rival versions of the past, revealing how contested readings served as stalking-horses in current political debates, and invoking the maxim: to understand the history, first study the historian. Yet, by a paradoxical stroke, even as they did so, historians found their new fancy-clothes being snatched by a younger generation of literary critics, espousing a 'new historicism' that purported, on the strength of sophisticated critical textual hermeneutics, to uncover deeper layers of meaning, complexity and irony in the past than conventional historians had found.[9]

Under such circumstances, it is not surprising that historians have grown abnormally introspective and self-critical. For one thing, they have been asking searching questions about their own craft. What is history? Science or art? The harvest of rigorous methodologies, or the brainchild of imagination and flair? At bottom, fact or fiction? In consequence, numerous historians – Theodore Zeldin and Michael

Ignatieff, to mention just two – have tried their hand at the novel; and Simon Schama has spliced fact and fiction into a 'novella', *Dead Certainties: Unwarranted Speculations*, boldly claiming that solid information and imaginative projection are alike integral to that resurrection of the dead, that art of memory, which is the act of historical re-creation.[10]

Historians have also been putting their working concepts to the question. We speak of revolutions; the industrial revolution, or the scientific revolution; but what weight should such metaphorical terms actually carry? What hidden agendas are they hawking around?[11] We talk, far too loosely, about death and sex as though these were unproblematic biological events: but, as recent scholarship has been insisting, the meanings of birth, copulation and death have been immensely culture-bound, time- and place-dependent.[12] The same applies to childhood, to gender and to all manner of other historical categories and entities.[13] To enhance our historical understanding, and gain better insight into taken-for-granted realities, the objects and institutions, the concepts and assumptions comprising our intellectual furniture must constantly be questioned. How are meanings generated? Whence does intellectual authority arise?

Exploring such problems is the aim of this present volume. Its ten essays – most of them by academic historians, British and American, but including others by writers with different fields of expertise – pose unfamiliar questions to familiar aspects of our environment, tangible, mental and emotional. Two annual British rituals are examined: Guy Fawkes' Night and Armistice Day. A brace of institutions is addressed: Oxford and Cambridge. Two readily recognizable 'types' come under the microscope: the tramp and the 'bobby'. Other essays investigate the media responsible for creating images and communicating identities.[14] In particular, two literary genres are explored: the Aesopian fable, and school stories for children. Myths of greatness, and of the 'grit' long associated with stereotypes of English character, are analysed through accounts of military heroes and discussion of the distinctively British preoccupation with portraiture. And, as in some ways the epitome of the whole volume, the comic operas of Gilbert and Sullivan are evaluated, as multi-messaged celebrations of the peculiarities of the English themselves.[15]

These essays share much common ground. All deal with institutions or types which, alongside their everyday, bread-and-butter history, radiate meanings and mythologies supportive of the English way of life (even when, occasionally, they seem disparaging or satirical) . The emblem of the bobby, discussed by Clive Emsley, and the policeman's parallel, the schoolmaster, examined by Margaret Kinnell, both bolster the myth that authority is a benign presence.[16] Being a freedom-loving people, the English naturally need a symbolic libertarian counterweight to the long arm of the law; and, as M. A. Crowther shows, the perfect exemplar of this lies in the somewhat anarchic but ultimately innocuous figure of the tramp, a licensed outsider, less a rebel than an oddball luxuriating in that idiosyncrasy that is another supposed hallmark of Englishness.[17]

Such symptoms of the English disposition – individuality, a certain unbiddability – find echo in Iain Pears's analysis of the fabrication of the rhetorical opposition between the Duke of Wellington and Napoleon Bonaparte: characterized as cruel and impulsive, the Corsican forms a fine foil to the representation of the Iron Duke as steady, reliable, and superabundantly blessed with British 'bottom'. It is such 'ordinariness' that is the prime feature of the face that Gertrude Prescott Nuding shows to be the cardinal feature of the portrait beloved by the English. Preoccupied with continuity, the English love facial likenesses because they are the elevation of genealogy and pedigree into visual art.[18] The myth of the common also pervades Bob Bushaway's analysis of Armistice Day. The Cenotaph is the emblem of the English soldiery *en masse*; the Tomb of the Unknown Warrior commemorates, in a parallel manner, not some dazzling hero, but each and every fighting man.[19]

Myths play on varied registers, and their semiotics are subject to shift.[20] If the bonfires of Guy Fawkes' Night were originally warnings against Catholic conspiracy, in course of time, as David Cressy demonstrates, the meanings the authorities broadcast on the Fifth of November emphasized the deliverance of Parliament itself as the guarantee of constitutional freedom – though, on occasion, Bonfire Night could be used by agitators to fan the flames of anti-Irish feeling.[21]

These essays furthermore show how one myth reinforces another, all of them serving as particular pieces in the entire jigsaw of significations. Reforming themselves in the nineteenth century, the ancient universities assumed a new self-image as the training ground for that ineffable 'character' judged so indispensable for the manning of the Civil Service and the administration of the Empire.[22] But what when women's colleges began to be founded at Oxford and Cambridge? Clearly ladies were not to be permitted to go off and govern colonies. Nevertheless, as Reba Soffer makes clear, Newnham and the other female colleges established themselves upon the same teachings of comradeship and duty as all-male Balliol. A distinctive ethos among the women's colleges might have proved unacceptably ideologically subversive.[23]

Some institutions are, of course, created specifically for broadcasting and perpetuating mythologies. That might be said of the fables – they are so much more than children's stories – surveyed in Marina Warner's account of the Mother Goose *oeuvre*. The repeated juxtapositions of children and adults in these allegories, these cautionary tales of the bad endings awaiting those who step out of line through pride or ambition, provide entertaining instantiations of the norms taught to children to guide their adult lives. Tales of the imagination thereby provided inner repertoires of archetypal experience anticipating experience itself, memories before the event.[24]

If the folk story was a kind of mental memory museum, it is no accident that, over the last couple of centuries; the state has invested in national museums. The British Museum was invented in the mid-eighteenth century just when British nationalism was coming of age; by contrast, the Victoria and Albert Museum, founded out of the proceeds of the Great Exhibition at the height of British power, was a device for countering Arnoldian fears of rampant philistinism.[25] For the museum, the school, the university, and the art gallery all figure as agents in the transmission of the myth of civilization itself.[26] Victorians conceived the march of mind; they grew convinced that future glory depended upon manufacturing a philosophy of progress no less than buttons and battleships. Such was the homily of history, and they would teach its moral through cultural missionary activities. As evidenced in Carlyle's *Sartor Resartus*, Victorians possessed an acute awareness of the symbolic regalia of identity. It was they, not surprisingly, who invented anthropology, that supreme science of iconography, designed to supplement the Christian faith they perceived to be on the wane.[27]

In other words, the Victorians took to worshipping themselves, though, fearful of possible impiety and hubris, they did so through decorous self-mockery: John Bull, *Punch*, and, as David Cannadine shows, above all, the D'Oyly Carte operettas permitted self-veneration without vanity, pride through parodic pantomime. If Nuremberg Rallies were soon to broadcast Nazism in propaganda extravaganzas which ultimately proved to be 'self-consuming artifacts',[28] Gilbert and Sullivan were able to invent a very English way of glorifying Englishness through sending it up. A talent for self-mockery was evidently part of the English genius, reinforced by pulling the legs of unfortunate foreigners who took themselves too seriously. Rather as with the public-school myth in the *Billy Bunter*

stories, such jollities were effective means of masking social problems and class tensions.[29]

This book is not offered in the D'Oyly Carte spirit, as a Festival of
Britain in disguise. Nor is it intended as an earnest exercise in self-
flagellation. It is rather presented as a collection of illuminating, original and entertaining essays examining the functions of public
parable, the authority of the past in fabricating such myths and, we
hope, the role of historians in defamiliarization and deconstruction.[30]

NOTES

1 See Eric Sigsworth (ed.), *In Search of Victorian Values* (Manchester, 1988).
Many of the contributors to that volume, not least the editor, seek to disabuse
the Prime Minister of her rose-tinted vision of the Victorian age.

2 Eric Hobsbawm and Terence Ranger (eds), *The Invention of Tradition*
(Cambridge, 1983); Tom Nairn, *The Enchanted Glass: Britain and its Monarchy*
(London, 1988); Raphael Samuel and Paul Thompson (eds), *The Myths We
Live By* (London, 1990); Pierre Nora, *Les Lieux de Mémoire* (Paris, 1984–6);
J. Le Goff and P. Nora (eds), *Faire de L'histoire*, 3 vols (Paris, 1974).

3 Peter Burke, *The Renaissance Sense of the Past* (New York, 1970).

4 The Australian historian, Donald Horne, has thus characterized Britain –
indeed, Europe in general – in his *The Great Museum: The Re-Presentation of
History* (London, 1984), which perceptively views the valuing of history as a
ploy designed to legitimize mainstream features of British society: Parliament,
the monarchy, the aristocracy, the Anglican Church, Oxbridge, the literary
establishment, and so forth. I am writing this introduction at a time when
British politicians, faced with the prospect of a federal Europe, seem capable
only of harking back to earlier centuries of British independence (when Britain
ruled the waves), and hence capable only of talking in terms of what would be
'lost' by federalism. See also Patrick Wright, *On Living in an Old Country*
(London, 1985).

5 These views are set out in Juliet Gardiner (ed.), *What Is History Today . . . ?*
(London, 1988); *The History Debate* (London, 1990).

6 I do not intend further to raise the questions of historical objectivity and historical method. These have never been better discussed than in E. H. Carr,
What Is History? (London, 1961).

7 There is no end of writing on structuralism and all subsequent
related literary and philosophical movements. For lucid introductions, see
Jonathan Culler, *On Deconstruction* (London, 1983) and *Framing the Sign:
Criticism and its Institutions* (Norman, 1988).

8 Roland Barthes, *Elements of Semiology*, trans. Annette Lavers and Colin Smith
(London, 1967), *Mythologies*, trans. Annette Lavers (London, 1972), *The
Fashion System*, trans. Matthew Ward and Richard Howard (New York, 1983)
and *Elements of Culture* (Cambridge: Cambridge University Press, 1986;
Cambridge: Polity, 1989); Jean Baudrillard, *Le Système des Objets* (Paris, 1968),
La Société de Consommation (Paris, 1970), *The Mirror of Production* (St Louis,

1975) and *For a Critique of the Political Economy of the Sign* (St Louis, 1981); Mark Poster (ed.), *Baudrillard: Selected Writings* (Cambridge, 1989); Pierre Bourdieu, *Distinction: A Social Critique of the Judgement of Taste*, trans. R. Nice (London, 1984) and *Questions of Culture* (Cambridge, 1989).

9 For instances see Stephen Greenblatt, *Shakespearean Negotiations: The Circulation of Social Energy in Renaissance England* (Berkeley, Oxford, 1988; Jonathan Dollimore and Alan Sinfield (eds), *Political Shakespeare: New Essays in Cultural Materialism* (Ithaca, 1985).

10 Simon Schama, *Dead Certainties: Unwarranted Speculations* (London, 1991).

11 See, for conceptual discussion, the essays in Roy Porter and Mikuláš Teich (eds), *Revolution and History* (Cambridge, 1986).

12 See, for instance, Philippe Ariès, *Western Attitudes Towards Death: From the Middle Ages to the Present* (Baltimore, 1974; London, 1976) and *Images of Man and Death*, trans. J. Lloyd (Cambridge, 1985); Clare Gittings, *Death, Burial and the Individual in Early Modern England* (London, 1984, 1988); John McManners, *Death and the Enlightenment* (Oxford, 1981, 1985); Ralph Houlbrooke (ed.), *Death, Ritual and Bereavement* (London, 1989); and, on sex, Michel Foucault, *Histoire de la sexualité*, vol. 1: *La volonté de savoir* (Paris, 1976), trans. by Robert Hurley as *The History of Sexuality: Introduction* (London, 1978), vol. 2: *L'usage des plaisirs* (Paris, 1984), trans. by Robert Hurley as *The Use of Pleasure* (New York, 1985) and vol. 3: *Le souci de soi* (Paris, 1984), trans. by Robert Hurley as *The Care of the Self* (New York, 1987); and the new *Journal of the History of Sexuality*. Foucault insisted that historians must study not 'sex' (i.e. the biological drive) but 'sexuality' (i.e. the cultural expression).

13 For childhood, see Philippe Ariès, *Centuries of Childhood: A Social History of the Family* (New York, 1962); L. DeMause (ed.), *History of Childhood* (London, 1975); Ivy Pinchbeck and Margaret Hewitt, *Children in English Society*, 2 vols (London, 1969, 1973); Linda Pollock, *Forgotten Children: Parent–Child Relations from 1500 to 1900* (Cambridge, 1983) and *A Lasting Relationship: Parents and Children over Three Centuries* (London, 1987). For gender, see Ludmilla Jordanova, *Sexual Visions: Images of Gender in Science and Medicine between the Eighteenth and Twentieth Centuries* (London, 1989); Lynne Nead, *Myths of Sexuality: Representations of Women in Victorian Britain* (Oxford, 1988); Cynthia Eagle Russett, *Sexual Science: The Victorian Construction of Womanhood* (Cambridge, Mass., 1989).

14 For the notions of national difference implied here, see B. Anderson, *Imagined Communities: Reflections on the Origin and Spread of Nationalism* (London, 1983); Linda Colley, 'Whose Nation? Class and National Consciousness in England, 1750–1830', *Past and Present*, 1986, no. 113, pp. 96–117.

15 E. P. Thompson, 'The Peculiarities of the English', *The Poverty of Theory and Other Essays* (London, 1978), pp. 35–91; Philip Dodd and Robert Colls (eds), *Englishness* (London, 1987); J. H. Grainger, *Patriotisms: Britain 1900–1939* (London, 1986); H. MacDougall, *Racial Myth in English History: Trojans, Teutons and Anglo-Saxons* (Montreal, Hanover and London, 1982).

16 For histories and mythologies of the police and the law, see Clive Emsley, *The English Police: A Political and Social History* (Hemel Hempstead, 1991); J. M. Beattie, *Crime and the Courts in England, 1660–1800* (Oxford, 1986); V. A. C. Gatrell, 'Crime, Authority and the Policeman State', in F. M. L. Thompson (ed.), *The Cambridge Social History of Britain 1750–1950*, vol. 1:

Regions and Communities; vol. 2: *People and their Environment*; vol. 3: *Social Agencies and Institutions* (Cambridge, 1990), vol. 3, pp. 243–310; Douglas Hay and Francis Snyder (eds), *Policing and Prosecution in Britain 1750–1850* (Oxford, 1989); Douglas Hay et al. (eds), *Albion's Fatal Tree: Crime and Society in Eighteenth-Century England* (London, 1976); J. Innes and J. Styles, 'The Crime Wave: Recent Writing on Crime and Criminal Justice in Eighteenth Century England', *Journal of British Studies*, 1986, vol. 25, pp. 380–435.

For the idea of the child in his or her relation to pedagogical authority, see M. J. M. Ezell, 'John Locke's Images of Childhood: Early Eighteenth Century Responses to *Some Thoughts Concerning Education*', *Eighteenth Century Studies*, 1983/4, vol. 17, pp. 139–55; Isaac Kramnick, 'Children's Literature and Bourgeois Ideology: Observations on Culture and Industrial Capitalism in the Later Eighteenth Century', *Studies in Eighteenth Century Culture*, 1983, pp. 11–44; Samuel F. Pickering Jr, *John Locke and Children's Books in Eighteenth-Century England* (Knoxville, 1981); Joyce Whalley, *Cobwebs to Catch Flies: Illustrated Books for the Nursery and Schoolroom, 1700–1800* (Berkeley, Los Angeles, 1975); Susan Pederson, 'Hannah More Meets Simple Simon: Tracts, Chapbooks, and Popular Culture in Late Eighteenth-Century England', *Journal of British Studies*, 1986, vol. 25, pp. 84–113; John R. Gillis, *Youth and History: Tradition and Change in European Age Relations, 1770–Present* (New York, 1981); Bette P. Goldstone, *Lessons to be Learned: A Study of Eighteenth-Century English Didactic Children's Literature* (New York, Berne, Frankfurt-am-Main, 1984); Victor Neuberg, 'The Penny Histories', in *Milestones in Children's Literature* (New York, 1968).

17 The myth of pastoral is perfectly designed to accommodate the tramp or wanderer as a romantic solitary who distracts attention from the real poor. See John Barrell, *The Idea of Landscape and the Sense of Place, 1730–1840: An Approach to the Poetry of John Clare* (Cambridge, 1972), *The Dark Side of the Landscape: The Rural Poor in English Painting, 1730–1840* (Cambridge, 1983) and *English Literature in History, 1730–80: An Equal, Wide Survey* (London, New York, 1983); Roger Sales, *English Literature in History, 1780–1830: Pastoral and Politics* (London, 1983); Denis Cosgrove and Stephen Daniels (eds), *The Iconography of Landscape: Essays on the Symbolic Representation, Design and Use of Past Environments* (Cambridge, 1989). For the vagrant as emblem of the outsider, see H. Mayer, *Outsiders: A Study in Life and Letters* (Cambridge, Mass., 1984). For the real situation of vagrants, see A. L. Beier, *Masterless Men: The Vagrancy Problem in England 1560–1640* (London, 1985). For ambiguities in responses to 'rebels', see Stephen Humphries, *Hooligans or Rebels? An Oral History of Working-Class Childhood and Youth 1889–1939* (Oxford, 1981).

18 It is noteworthy, of course, that in reality English heroes were not solid, steady types. See the unmasking of James Wolfe in Schama, *Dead Certainties*. For portraits, see David Piper, *The English Face* (London, 1957); John Barrell, *The Political Theory of Painting from Reynolds to Hazlitt* (New Haven, 1986); Benedict Nicolson, *Joseph Wright of Derby: Painter of Light*, 2 vols (London, 1968). For painting as pedigree, see David Cannadine, *The Decline and Fall of the British Aristocracy* (New Haven, 1990); Lawrence Stone, *The Crisis of the Aristocracy 1558–1641* (London, 1965); Lawrence Stone and Jeanne C. Fawtier

Stone, *An Open Elite? England 1540–1880* (Oxford, 1984). On the propaganda importance of such images, see A. Leith, *The Idea of Art as Propaganda in France, 1750–99* (Toronto, 1965). Caricature and cartoons serve more ambiguous functions. See James Cuno (ed.), *French Caricature and the French Revolution, 1719–99* (Los Angeles, 1989); Ronald Paulson, *Representations of Revolution 1789–1820* (New Haven, 1983); David Kunzle, *The Early Comic Strip: Picture Stories and Narrative Strips in the European Broadsheet ca. 1450–1826* (Berkeley, 1973) and *The History of the Comic Strip: The Nineteenth Century* (Berkeley, 1989); M. Dorothy George, *English Political Caricature 1793–1832* (Oxford, 1959) and *Hogarth to Cruikshank: Social Change in Graphic Satire* (London, 1967); Michael Duffy (ed.), *The English Satirical Print, 1600–1832*, 7 vols (Cambridge, 1986).

19 See also David Cannadine, 'War and Death, Grief and Mourning in Modern Britain', in Joachim Whaley (ed.), *Mirrors of Mortality* (London, 1981), pp. 187–242; Linda Colley, 'The Apotheosis of George III: Loyalty, Royalty and the English Nation', *Past and Present*, 1984, no. 102, pp. 94–129. For the type of the military hero, see Leo Braudy, *The Frenzy of Renown* (Oxford, 1987). For notions of immortality, see Charles B. Paul, *Science and Immortality: The Eloges of the Paris Academy of Science (1699–1791)* (Berkeley, 1980).

20 G. S. Kirk, *Myth: Its Meanings and Functions in Ancient and Other Cultures* (Berkeley, 1970).

21 For wider discussion of calendar rituals as creators of licensed identity, see David Cressy, *Bonfires and Bells* (London, 1989). For the Irish dimension, see Roger Swift and Sheridan Gilley (eds), *The Irish in Britain 1815–1939* (London, 1989).

22 Myths of antique virtue were valuable here. See G. W. Clarke, *Rediscovering Hellenism* (Cambridge, 1988); F. M. Turner, *The Greek Heritage in Victorian Britain* (New Haven, 1983).

23 For the university background, see S. Rothblatt, *The Revolution of the Dons: Cambridge and Society in Victorian England* (Cambridge, 1981); Lawrence Stone (ed.), *The University in Society*, 2 vols (Princeton, 1975); John Gascoigne, *Cambridge in the Age of the Enlightenment: Science, Religion and Politics from the Restoration to the French Revolution* (Cambridge, 1989).

24 For the lasting power of symbols see Marina Warner, *Monuments and Maidens: The Allegory of the Female Form* (New York, 1985) and *Alone of All Her Sex: The Myth and the Cult of the Virgin Mary* (London, 1976, 1985); Jack Zipes, *Breaking the Spell: Radical Theories of Folk and Fairy Tales* (Austin, 1979); Bruno Bettelheim, *The Uses of Enchantment: The Meaning and Importance of Fairy Tales* (New York, 1977).

25 Gerald Newman, *The Rise of English Nationalism: A Cultural History, 1740–1830* (New York, London, 1987); H. Cunningham, 'The Language of Patriotism, 1750–1914', *History Workshop Journal*, 1981, vol. 12, pp. 8–33; Matthew Arnold, *Culture and Anarchy* (Cambridge, 1869). On the rise of nationalist feeling, see Eric Hobsbawm, *Nationalism* (Cambridge, 1990) and *Nations and Nationalism since 1780* (Cambridge, 1990).

26 For the development of the display of art, see Trevor Fawcett, *The Rise of English Provincial Art: Artists, Patrons and Institutions Outside London, 1800–1830* (Oxford, 1974); Louise Lippincott, *Selling Art in Georgian London: The Rise of Arthur Pond* (London, New Haven, 1983); Iain Pears, *The*

Discovery of Painting: The Growth of Interest in the Arts in England 1680–1768 (New Haven, 1988); R. D. Altick, *The Shows of London: A Panoramic History of Exhibitions, 1600–1862* (Cambridge, Mass., 1978).

27 For the creation of history in the nineteenth century as the ideological support for national, progressive and 'civilizing' missions, see S. Bann, *The Clothing of Clio: A Study of Representations of History in Nineteenth Century Britain and France* (Cambridge, 1984); Peter J. Bowler, *The Invention of Progress: The Victorians and the Past* (Oxford, 1989); J. W. Burrow, *A Liberal Descent: Victorian Historians and the English Past* (Cambridge, 1981); Philippa Levine, *The Amateur and the Professional: Antiquarians, Historians and Archaeologists in Victorian England, 1838–1886* (Cambridge, 1986); J. Kenyon, *The History Men: The Historical Profession in England since the Renaissance* (London, 1983). As has been widely observed, it was at this time that the notion of (high) culture was developed: see C. Geertz, *The Interpretation of Cultures* (New York, 1973); Raymond Williams, *Culture and Society, 1780–1950* (London, Harmondsworth, New York, 1958), *Keywords: A Vocabulary of Culture and Society* (London, 1976, 1988), *The Long Revolution* (London, 1961, 1975), *The Country and the City* (London, New York, 1973, 1985) and 'Common Culture' and 'Culture is Ordinary', in *Resources of Hope* (London, 1989); A. Kuper, *The Making of Primitive Society* (London, 1988).

28 S. Fish, *Self-Consuming Artifacts* (Berkeley, 1972).

29 For the ambiguities of popular culture – a culture of the people, or a culture which papers over social cracks? – see Patrick Joyce, *Visions of the People: Industrial England and the Question of Class, c.1848–1914* (Cambridge, 1991); John M. Golby and A. W. Purdue, *The Civilization of the Crowd: Popular Culture in England. 1750–1900* (London, 1984). For the ironies of Gilbert and Sullivan, see Eric Sigsworth, 'W. S. Gilbert: The Wisest Fool', in Sigsworth, *In Search of Victorian Values*, pp. 179–94.

30 In making these formulations, I am much indebted to David Cannadine, *The Pleasures of the Past* (London, 1989).

1

GILBERT AND SULLIVAN: THE MAKING AND UN-MAKING OF A BRITISH 'TRADITION'

David Cannadine

Gilbert and Sullivan were self-made products of the Victorian era who, for all their wit, humour and lightheartedness, might have stepped straight from the pious pages of Samuel Smiles's book, *Self-Help*.[1] They were both born in unpromising circumstances, but their ascent to the high peaks of fame and fortune was even more successful than that of such renowned Gilbertian social climbers as the judge in *Trial by Jury* and Sir Joseph Porter in *HMS Pinafore*. This was very largely the result of the series of comic operas which they created together. Their partnership began tentatively, with *Thespis* (1871), *Trial by Jury* (1875) and *The Sorcerer* (1877), but it was only with the production of *HMS Pinafore* (1878) that they effectively established themselves. During the next decade, they produced a rapid succession of new works: *The Pirates of Penzance* (1879), *Patience* (1881), *Iolanthe* (1882), Princess Ida (1884), *The Mikado* (1885), *Ruddigore* (1887), *The Yeomen of the Guard* (1888) and *The Gondoliers* (1889). But then Gilbert and Sullivan fell out (ostensibly over the costs of new furnishings for the Savoy Theatre), and their last two operas – *Utopia Limited* (1893), and *The Grand Duke* (1896) – were not a success.

Taken as a whole, however, their remarkable partnership is unique in the history of popular entertainment, far surpassing either Rodgers and Hammerstein or Lerner and Loewe in its duration and productivity. For over one hundred years, their operas have been enhancing the gaiety of nations, with their 'innocent merriment', their 'ballads, songs and snatches', and their 'magic and spells'. Mr Gladstone went to see *Iolanthe*, and happily acknowledged 'the great pleasure which the entertainment has given me'. Queen Victoria commanded a performance of *The Gondoliers* at Windsor, and found it 'quite charming' throughout.[2] More recent admirers have ranged from Winston Churchill via Franklin D. Roosevelt to Harold Wilson. In the summer of 1980, *The Pirates of Penzance* was so successfully re-staged in Central Park, New York, that it was transferred to Broadway and London's West End. And six years later, Jonathan Miller's audacious and innovative production of *The Mikado*, for the English National Opera, was greeted with widespread acclaim. As Gilbert boasted to Sullivan in 1887, 'we are world-known, and as much an institution as Westminster Abbey' – a self-satisfied verdict which English-speaking posterity has enthusiastically endorsed.[3]

For many of the Savoy Operas' most ardent and appreciative admirers, this is a state of affairs so self-evidently 'right as right can be' that it requires no detailed explanation. Gilbert and Sullivan, it is argued, were uncommonly gifted individuals, whose latent genius flowered only in their harmonious, if ultimately discordant, collaboration. Together, they produced works which were so original in form and so sparkling in content as to be 'timeless' in their appeal and 'universal' in their significance.[4] But all genius – especially collaborative genius – requires the aid of luck and circumstance to come to full flower. The purpose of this essay is to let a little daylight in on the Savoyards' magic by setting Gilbert and Sullivan in the broader context of nineteenth- and twentieth-century British history. What were the circumstances and conventions of the mid-Victorian theatre, in which Gilbert served his apprenticeship, and against which the Savoy Operas deliberately but indebtedly reacted? How did the operas themselves reflect (or deny) the contemporary concerns of their original, late-Victorian, middle-class audiences? And how was it that they soon established themselves as a British 'tradition', which has survived virtually unaltered almost down to our own time?

I

However venerated and venerable they have since become, the fact remains that in their own day Gilbert and Sullivan were theatrical innovators so deliberate and so successful that they might almost be called revolutionaries. But like all revolutionaries, their achievement was significantly determined by the world they were trying to change: in this case the unrespectable nineteenth-century stage, patronized primarily by members of the working classes, who sought fun, laughter, excitement and escape from the dreary monotony of their humdrum lives.[5] Theatre owners were generally regarded as shady characters, and their living was decidedly precarious. Writers were ill-rewarded, and could only make ends meet by maintaining parallel careers as actors or as journalists. The stage was neither an honourable nor a disciplined profession, and actresses were regarded as being little better than prostitutes. Not surprisingly, the upper and middle classes, who had delighted in the eighteenth-century theatre of Garrick and Sheridan, had effectively withdrawn their patronage altogether. There were occasional attempts to raise the tone and standard, as when Squire Bancroft and his wife staged Thomas Robertson's comedies at their Prince of Wales's Theatre in the 1860s; but this was very much the exception which proved the rule.

For the most part, the works that were produced on the London stage were singularly lacking in distinction or refinement. Tragedy, comedy and satire had effectively disappeared by the early nineteenth century, and had been replaced by a variety of inferior genres. The most popular was melodrama, with its stories of murder, torture, haunted castles and wicked baronets, such as Douglas Jerrold's *Black Ey'd Susan* (1829), and Dion Boucicault's *The Corsican Brothers* (1851). Almost as appealing was burlesque: the deliberate travesty of classical plays and characters, as in the works of James Robinson Planche, which included *Olympic Revels* (1831) and *The Golden Fleece* (1845). Pantomime and extravaganza were also highly popular with their emphasis on magic, love and the supernatural. And there was ballad opera: a genre which began with John Gay's *The Beggar's Opera* (1728), but which was by this time much debased and was now devoid of satiric edge or musical merit. To this uninspired *mélange* was added imported comic opera: Offenbach's works reached the London stage in the 1860s, and Strauss's *Die Fledermaus* was first performed in 1875. But the libretti were often poorly translated, the music was badly performed and the tone of the productions was vulgar, slapdash and risqué.[6]

It was in this unsavoury theatrical world that W. S. Gilbert learned his craft, appropriately moving, in his early years, between the law, journalism and the stage. Although trained as a barrister, he soon turned to writing, and produced a series of satirical verses eventually published as the *Bab Ballads* (1869), which brought him to the attention of theatre managers. Inevitably, many of his early plays were in the prevailing style of burlesque, pantomime and extravaganza, and these were the forms which were later parodied and mimicked in the

Savoy Operas. *Thespis* was actually performed at the Gaiety – a theatre renowned for burlesque – and in its Greek gods and acting troupe contained two essential elements of that genre. *The Sorcerer* was based on *Dulcamara*, Gilbert's earlier burlesque of Donizetti's *L'Elisir d'Amore*. Both *HMS Pinafore* and *The Pirates of Penzance* owed much to nautical melodrama, while *Iolanthe*, with its fairies and final transformation scene, clearly harked back to pantomime. And with *Ruddigore*, Gilbert once more returned to Gothic blood-and-thunder melodrama, complete with haunted house and wicked baronets.[7] Throughout his libretti, Gilbert's delight in disguise and mistaken identity, in topsy-turveydom, and in the last minute restoration of order by essentially implausible means, showed his indebtedness to this mid-Victorian tradition, just as his ageing and unattractive women – Ruth, Kathisa, Lady Sophy – preserved memories of transvestite dame parts in earlier burlesque.[8]

Even though the Savoy Operas were designed for the middle classes of late Victorian England, allusions to this older, more vulgar theatrical tradition would have been understood and appreciated – at least during the early years of the collaboration. And it was also from this same mid-Victorian theatrical world that the impresarios emerged who became the midwives to the Gilbert and Sullivan partnership. Thomas German Reed and his wife sought to raise the moral tone of the stage at their euphemistically entitled Royal Gallery of Illustration, where they put on one-act comic operas, imported from France, but shorn of their customary vulgarity, in a large drawing room, with piano and harmonium, which had more in common with a chapel than with a theatre. Both Gilbert and Sullivan worked for them, writing libretti and scores for comic operas and musical plays, not yet in partnership, but with different collaborators. John Hollingshead, a self-made journalist, opened the Gaiety Theatre in 1868, made it an established home of burlesque and brought Gilbert and Sullivan together for *Thespis* in 1871. And Richard D'Oyly Carte, who persuaded them to join forces again four years later for *Trial by Jury*, was himself a theatrical agent, manager of the Royalty Theatre and minor composer of operetta.

But Carte's main ambition was 'the staging of English comic opera in a theatre devoted to that alone', and he saw in Gilbert and Sullivan the perfect vehicle for realizing his objective.[9] In 1876, he formed the Comedy Opera Company, which was exclusively devoted to the production of their work, and in 1881 he opened the Savoy, the most modern and glamorous theatre in London and the first to be lit by electricity. He made the first night of a Gilbert and Sullivan opera into one of the social highlights of the 1880s, inviting Oscar Wilde himself to the premiere of *Patience*, and Captain Shaw to the opening of *Iolanthe*. Also he zealously promoted official performances in the provinces and overseas, especially in the United States. But above all, he enabled Gilbert and Sullivan to establish their own permanent repertory company, which effectively institutionalized the production of their works, and which included principal performers who themselves soon became famous – George Grossmith, Rutland Barrington and Jessie Bond. In short, it was Carte's revolution in theatrical management which made possible Gilbert and Sullivan's revolution in theatrical entertainment.

On the stage of the Savoy, Gilbert and Sullivan were left by Carte in 'absolute control', and they wielded their authority over the company with a dictatorial sway that had been almost entirely absent from the mid-Victorian theatre.[10] Sullivan drilled and disciplined the orchestra, refusing to tolerate slap-dash attendance or lacklustre playing, while Gilbert exercised complete dominion over the casting, dressing and staging of the operas. He planned his productions on a model theatre at his home, down to the very last detail. He took endless trouble over the design of the costumes and the scenery. He rehearsed the chorus and the principals until they were exhausted with fatigue. And he insisted that his words and stage directions be followed to the letter: ad libbing, interpolations, slapstick humour and cheap laughs were absolutely forbidden, and offenders were severely reprimanded. The essence of the Savoy style, as Gilbert once explained, was treating 'a thoroughly farcical subject in a thoroughly serious manner'. The success with which he accomplished this meant that he became the first author–producer to dominate the Victorian stage.

In addition to showmanship, glamour and discipline, the Savoy operas provided wholesome and respectable entertainment. The dialogue was devoid of offence, there was no transvestism and the women's costumes were entirely decent. Men and women changed in rooms on opposite sides of the stage; their morals were expected to be – like the Mikado's – particularly correct; and on more than one occasion, Gilbert came to the defence of female members of the cast whose honour had been wrongly impugned. Not for nothing was D'Oyly Carte's company once re-christened 'The Savoy Boarding School'.[11] Above all, the presence of Sir Arthur Sullivan's illustrious name on the programme conferred unrivalled prestige and reassurance. He had studied music in Leipzig, was the composer of hymn tunes and oratorios and was widely regarded as the greatest English musician since Purcell. He was the close friend of the Prince of Wales and the Duke of Edinburgh, his music was much admired by Queen Victoria and he was knighted in 1883. That such a paragon should grace the orchestra pit of a theatre was a virtual guarantee of respectability. For all their gaiety and laughter, it was once remarked that the performance of a Gilbert and Sullivan opera at the Savoy, with a rapt audience following every word in their programme, and turning the same page at the same time, was reminiscent of a prayer meeting in a church or chapel.[12]

But it was the content of the operas themselves which most powerfully signalled their departure from earlier theatrical tradition. For Gilbert's libretti were of vastly superior quality to anything that had recently been played on the London stage. His complex plots were carefully and economically crafted. He created a series of memorable, outsize characters: the Lord Chancellor in *Iolanthe*, Poo-Bah in *The Mikado*, Jack Point in *The Yeomen of the Guard*. He brought back political satire, which had been absent from the theatre since the eighteenth century. His dialogue was witty and epigrammatic in a way that had last been heard on the stage in the days of Sheridan. He assumed that his audiences were well-educated and well-informed: the plots of *Trial by Jury* and *Iolanthe* are unintelligible without some knowledge of the law; *Patience* took for granted an understanding of contemporary developments in the arts; and *Princess Ida* presupposed a familiarity with recent trends in higher education for women. And the word-play in his verses was astonishingly varied in its metre and rhythm, from the profusion of syllables and elaborate rhymes in the patter songs to the genuine vein of poetry which suffuses the verses in *The Yeomen of the Guard*, as in this quatrain, which was later chosen by Gilbert as the inscription for Sullivan's memorial in London:

> Is life a boon?
> If so, it must befall
> That death, when e're he call,
> Must call too soon.

And Sullivan's music was as clever, as humorous and as versatile as Gilbert's words. When the libretto required it, he composed a hornpipe, a waltz, a march, a gavotte, a cachucha, a madrigal, an aria or a love duet: indeed, Nanki-Poo's opening song in *The Mikado* is, by turns, a sentimental ballad, a patriotic march, a sea shanty and a lullaby. Sullivan poured out many memorable melodies: 'The sun whose rays' in *The Mikado*, 'Take a pair of sparkling eyes' in *The Gondoliers*. He could illuminate character in a phrase, as with the ponderous double bass passage that introduces the policemen in *The Pirates of Penzance*. He pointed up the contrasts between the different social groups portrayed in the operas: the soldiers and the aesthetes in *Patience*, the Spanish nobility and the Venetian citizens in *The Gondoliers*. And he was unrivalled as a parodist and pasticheur. Mabel's song, 'Poor wand'ring one' in *The Pirates of Penzance* is a Gounod-esque waltz, full of coloratura trills and cadences. The finale to Act I of *The Mikado* is strikingly reminiscent of Verdi. 'All hail great judge' (*Trial by Jury*), and 'This helmet I suppose?' (*Princess Ida*) are both exuberant parodies of Handel. And the scene when the banished Iolanthe is raised from the bottom of the stream recalls the opening of *Das Rheingold*.

This was the measure of the revolution in theatrical taste for which Carte, Sullivan and Gilbert were jointly responsible. They deliberately sought to make their works appealing to the well-edu- cated middle classes, and they triumphantly succeeded. They created a new form of entertainment, precisely pitched between the music hall and the concert hall, which was intelligent but not intellectual, tasteful but not pretentious, tuneful but not cloying. They took the theatrical conventions of the lower classes, and made them acceptable to the bourgeoisie. As their confidence grew, Gilbert and Sullivan gradually left behind the old traditions of farce, pantomime, melo- drama and burlesque, and in their later operas, *The Mikado*, *The Yeomen of the Guard* and *The Gondoliers*, they created self-sufficient dramas and extended scores which seemed to hold out the prospects of limitless creative possibilities. As *The Times* noted in 1887, 'the middle classes, and even the working classes, which had no opportu- nity of appreciating either art or music fifty years ago, cannot com- plain that these wholesome enjoyments are now monopolised by a fashionable aristocracy.'[13] And for these developments, the Savoy Operas themselves were significantly and self-consciously responsible.

Of course, Gilbert, Sullivan and Carte were not alone in bringing about this transformation of the late Victorian theatre: while they were making comic opera respectable at the Savoy, Henry Irving was achieving very similar results with Shakespeare and melodrama at the Lyceum. And for Gilbert and Sullivan, their very success brought with it its own dangers. In part, this was because, even in their own unrivalled hands, it proved impossible to reproduce comic opera indefinitely. The 'carpet quarrel' of 1890 effectively ended their long run of collaborative triumphs, and neither Gilbert nor Sullivan found another partner with whom he could happily work. But it was also because the new theatre audience which they had done so much to call into being soon began to look elsewhere for less demanding and less cerebral amusement. The long-running successes of Alfred Cellier's *Dorothy* (1886), and Sidney Jones's *A Gaiety Girl* (1893) and *The Geisha* (1896), signalled the arrival of a new form of light entertainment: musical comedy. Its lyrics were less intellectual, there was no satire, the melodies were simpler, the humour was broader and there was a greater stress on romantic entanglement and lavish spectacle.[14] In *The Gondoliers* and *Utopia Limited*, Gilbert and Sullivan made some attempts to adjust their style to this new fashion, with more elaborate staging and greater stress on dancing and display. But by then, they were too old and too disenchanted to change their ways. 'What the public want,' Carte lamented, 'is simply "fun" and little else.'[15]

II

Although one essential context for understanding the Savoy Operas is their place in the history of theatrical entertainment, there is a broader perspective that must not be lost sight of. For the years of Gilbert and Sullivan's collaboration, between 1871 and 1896, were for the British among the most crowded, tumultuous and disturbing of the nineteenth century.[16] They saw a deepening economic depression, with well-grounded fears that Britain's industrial pre-eminence was being lost. They saw growing international rivalry between the great powers of Europe, the scramble for colonies in Africa and the murder of Gordon at Khartoum. They saw an unprecedentedly popular and venerated monarchy, and an increasingly impoverished and insecure aristocracy. And they saw a middle class bewildered by Irish Home Rule, worried by the depression of prices, profits and interest rates, and concerned about a working class which was better educated and partially enfranchised, yet sometimes seemed ominously discontented. What aspects of this changing world did Gilbert and Sullivan consider fit material for the moral, middle-class audiences of their operas?[17]

In the context of such international and domestic turmoils, it is especially significant that the Savoy Operas were a paean of praise to national pride and to the established order.[18] Whatever their ostensible location, all Gilbert and Sullivan's operas are in fact about

England. There is nothing disingenuous about the chorus 'For he is an Englishman' in *HMS Pinafore*. In *Ruddigore*, the Union Jack is described as 'a flag that none dare defy'. The claim, in *Utopia Limited*, that Britain 'occupies a pre-eminent position among civilized nations' is not made ironically. And the prevailing assumption of all the operas is that foreigners – whether Japanese or Spanish or German or Venetian – are mildly comical and profoundly unfortunate. There are schoolboyish satires on the army, the navy and the peerage. But while Sir Joseph Porter, the First Lord of the Admiralty in *HMS Pinafore*, is teased for being a landsman, the skill of Captain Corcoran and the steadfastness of his crew are never doubted – well, 'hardly ever'. In *The Pirates of Penzance*, Major General Stanley may not be the most up-to-date commander in his knowledge of military strategy, but the 'soldiers of the queen' in *Patience* are glamorous, robust, fearless and patriotic. And the most barbed song remaining in *Iolanthe* – 'When Britain really ruled the waves' – was set by Sullivan to a broad, stately, majestic tune, which soothes the simple satire into affectionate mockery.

Within this robustly patriotic setting, the operas were obsessed with the personnel and the rituals of monarchy. 'Because with all our faults we love our Queen' applied as much to Gilbert and to Sullivan personally as it did to the pirates of Penzance. But the image of royalty underwent important changes during the Savoy opera cycle, exactly mirroring the transition in the British monarchy from secluded unpopularity and republican protests in the middle of the queen's reign to popular symbol and ceremonial splendour by the end.[19] In the early pieces, the pirate king in *The Pirates of Penzance* and the Fairy Queen in *Iolanthe* owe much to the older tradition of melodrama, burlesque and pantomime: they are not credible as real rulers. But the later sovereigns – in *The Mikado*, *The Gondoliers*, *Utopia Limited* and *The Grand Duke* – are much more elaborate and individual creations. In the same way, the pageantry surrounding the monarchy reaches its grandiose climax at the gondoliers' court of Barataria, and at the elaborately staged Drawing Room in *Utopia Limited*, which was an almost exact rendition of a royal reception at Windsor Castle or Buckingham Palace. And in *The Gondoliers*, produced only two years after Victoria's Golden Jubilee, and in the centenary year of the French Revolution, it is republicanism, not monarchy, which is ridiculed and mocked.[20]

In depicting the British aristocracy, Gilbert was no less sensitive to changing circumstances. The pirates of Penzance are 'no members of

a common throng; they are all noblemen who have gone wrong' –
but who in the end go right again. There are peers and notables in
Iolanthe, The Mikado, The Gondoliers and *The Grand Duke.* There
is a whole dynasty of baronets in *Ruddigore,* and there are titled
principals in *The Sorcerer.* In *Patience,* Bunthorne is a landed gentleman (albeit dressed in aesthetic costume), and in the same opera, the
Duke of Dunstable is a lieutenant in the Dragoon Guards. In other
operas, Major General Stanley, Captain Corcoran and Colonel
Fairfax all possess landed estates or patrician relatives. But unlike the
monarchy, these 'tremendous swells' are not as secure as they once
were. During the early 1880s, the power and composition of the
House of Lords were widely attacked by radicals, who were enraged
by the way in which the second chamber consistently obstructed
Liberal legislation, and this provides the essential background to
Iolanthe, with its chorus of haughty peers who vainly believe that the
upper house 'is not susceptible of improvement'. And in the same
decade, when landed incomes were hard hit by agricultural depression, many peers were obliged to search for additional income by
selling their status for money, and becoming ornamental directors of
commercial ventures, in the undignified manner of the Duke of Plaza-
Toro in *The Gondoliers.*[21]

In treating the army and the navy, the Savoy Operas were equally
up-to-date and essentially well-disposed. Gilbert was the son of a
naval man, and adored sailing, and Sullivan's father was a military
band conductor: both were respectfully admiring of the armed services. The Royal Navy – not just in *HMS Pinafore,* but also in
Ruddigore and *Utopia Limited* – is depicted as the greatest fighting
force in the world, 'the bulwark of England's greatness'. At the very
time when the era of inexpensive British naval mastery was suddenly
drawing to a close, the Savoy Operas offer a robust celebration of
the age of unchallenged fighting sail.[22] In the same way, the British
army was very much in vogue. Cardwell's reforms at the War Office,
carried out between 1868 and 1870, had abolished the system of purchasing commissions and sought to remedy the inefficiencies and
abuses made plain at the time of the Crimean War. And in making
fun of Sir Garnett Wolseley as Major General Stanley in *The Pirates
of Penzance,* Gilbert was in fact gently mocking one of the most progressive new commanders, who led the British forces in the Ashanti
Wars of 1873, and was sent out to relieve Gordon at Khartoum in
1885. Moreover, by giving the army such attention (it also appears
in *Patience, Ruddigore, The Yeomen of the Guard* and *Utopia Limited*), he was also acknowledging its importance in those many late

nineteenth-century imperial conflicts quaintly known as 'Queen Victoria's little wars'.[23]

The other two professions on which Gilbert lavished his attention were conerned with domestic order rather than international security: the law and the police. Since Gilbert had himself trained for the bar, it is hardly surprising that *Trial by Jury* was set in a courtroom, and that solicitors, barristers, judges and even the Lord Chancellor himself make repeated appearances in the operas.[24] Moreover, this was the very period that saw extensive legal reform, beginning in the late 1870s with the establishment of the Central Criminal Courts and ending with the creation of the Bar Association in 1894.[25] And it was also at this time that the police force established itself in the popular imagination as the avuncular representative of state authority. Even as late as the 1870s, the constabulary was still much disliked by the working classes, as licensed snoopers, as symbols of repressive authority, as agents of an intrusive state: they were widely regarded as the 'plague of blue locusts'.[26] Only at the very end of that decade, and during the early 1880s, was the force transformed in the popular imagination into a friendly, familiar and well-disposed organization. The affectionate image so vividly conveyed in *The Pirates of Penzance* was not a long-established convention but a very recent development. Indeed, Gilbert and Sullivan may not just have reflected this change in popular attitudes: they may actually have helped to create it.

This, in essence, is the social universe of the Savoy Operas: a universe selectively but perceptively modelled on the real and recognizable Britain of the years 1871 to 1896. There is monarchy on the way to apotheosis, and there is aristocracy on the way to decline. There are those great professions most concerned with domestic security and international peace. But, apart from Dr Daly in *The Sorcerer*, there are no clergymen; significantly, Gilbert abandoned his original idea of constructing the plot of *Patience* around two rival curates because both he and Sullivan feared it would offend contemporary sensibility. In the same way, the commercial and entrepreneurial bourgeoisie hardly appears at all, apart from the gentlest references to middle-class social climbing in *The Mikado*. Indeed, Mr Goldbury, the unscrupulous company promoter in *Utopia Limited*, is satirized for not embodying those quintessential middle-class virtues of honesty and decency. As for the working class, they are invariably picturesque and dutiful: rustic maidens, country bumpkins, jolly jack tars. And the settings are almost always pastoral and sylvan: country houses and villages predominate, and apart from Titipu (which is a Japanese town) and the Palace of Westminster (significantly bathed in mellow moonlight in Act II of *Iolanthe*), the press and pace of urban life hardly intrude.

So, in terms of their contemporary resonance, the Savoy Operas were as important for what they left out as for what they put in. The international anxieties generated by Irish Home Rule, the scramble for Africa and economic depression are not just ignored: the patriotic presumptions of Gilbert and Sullivan are that they do not even exist. And the same was true in the domestic sphere. In London, in particular, the 1880s were a decade of real-life melodrama. There were the revelations of appalling poverty contained in Andrew Mearns's book, *The Bitter Cry*, and in Charles Booth's early social surveys; there was 'Bloody Sunday' and the great dock strike; and there were the terrible 'Jack the Ripper' murders.[27] But the only extended and explicit allusions to such contemporary social problems – Strephon's savage song 'Fold your flapping wings' in *Iolanthe*, and Princess Zara's final, bitter speech in *Utopia Limited* – were both cut out after adverse public reaction on the first night. At a more refined level, these late Victorian operas offered essentially the same invitation to the middle classes that the mid-Victorian burlesques and pantomimes had held out to the proletariat: they were encouraged to laugh rather than to think. In so far as there was satire it was carefully trimmed to the tastes of an increasingly conservative public.[28]

But it is in this broader context of *fin de siècle* apprehension and dissolving certainties that the ostensibly innocent topsy-turveydom of the Savoy Operas takes on its real significance.[29] For within their own world of make-believe, they repeatedly hold out the prospect of the established social and political order being overturned and subverted – the very danger which, in reality, so many comfortably-off contemporaries genuinely feared. In *The Sorcerer* and *HMS Pinafore*, it is because love may level ranks. In *The Pirates of Penzance*, it is because the police are defeated by vagabonds. In *Princess Ida*, it is because the dominance of men is rejected by women. In *Iolanthe*, it is because the fairies subdue the House of Lords, and take over Parliament. And in *The Gondoliers*, it is because the two temporary monarchs are in fact armchair republicans. But in every case – with the exception of *Iolanthe* – order is eventually restored. Of course, the sheer absurdity of the inversion, and the preposterous artificiality of the means whereby everyone lives happily ever after, deliberately invited incredulous laughter. But in the context of the time, the boundary line between humour and anxiety was very narrow indeed.

In all these ways, the Gilbert and Sullivan operas were perfectly judged productions for their targeted audience: the London middle classes, especially of the 1880s. Between them, the court composer and the court jester blended fact and fantasy, realism and escapism, satire and sweetness, 'patriotic sentiment' and 'innocent merriment', comforting reassurance and ludicrous subversion, in a heady and resonant mixture. But their congruence with that particular decade runs even closer. Beginning with the last great fling of Gladstonian reform, it ended with Lord Salisbury's Unionists firmly in power, and witnessed a major shift in middle-class opinion from mid-Victorian Liberalism to late Victorian Conservatism. Gilbert himself seems to have followed a similar path, from the savagely irreverent versifier of the *Bab Ballads* to the Harrow country gentleman of the 1890s. And the Savoy Operas trace what is recognizably the same trajectory. It is not just that they gradually leave burlesque, pantomime and melodrama behind, and become more self-confident and self-conscious works; it is also that the satire gets weaker, the locations become more exotic, and the importance of spectacle increases.[30] To some extent, these developments may be explained by changing attitudes on the part of the audience and changing theatrical conventions. But they also mirror very closely the broader political developments of the decade.

III

Because the Savoy Operas were so much the product of this particular theatrical milieu and historical generation, they quickly began to show distinct signs of their age. By the time of *Ruddigore*, Gilbert's continued preoccupation with melodrama and pantomime was clearly anachronistic. The many contemporary allusions in the libretti – to W. H. Smith, Captain Shaw, the aesthetics movement, Parliamentary trains and company promoters – inevitably lost their topicality, while Sullivan's references to Offenbach and Gounod, Wagner and Verdi, remained recognizable only to people who knew something of classical music. By the 1890s, the operas seemed altogether too sophisticated and too cerebral, compared with the light musical comedies which George Edwardes was staging at the Gaiety Theatre. And in the early years of the new century, these were followed by the sensational successes of Lehar's *The Merry Widow* (first seen in London in 1907), Frederic Norton's *Chu Chin Chow* (1916) and Harold Fraser Simpson's *The Maid of the Mountains* (1917). When Sullivan died in 1900, his reputation as a serious composer entered a sudden and seemingly irretrievable decline. Gilbert, who lived on until 1911, expected no better: 'Posterity', he once remarked, 'will know as little of me as I shall know of posterity.'[31] Yet however harshly posterity has dismissed their non-collaborative endeavours, their joint works soon bloomed and blossomed anew. As *The Times* explained in 1948, unconsciously echoing Gilbert's remarks of sixty years before, the Savoy Operas had 'become a national institution'. But how, exactly, did this quite unexpected development occur?[32]

Part of the answer undoubtedly lies in the zeal with which the D'Oyly Carte family exploited their exclusive rights of professional performance in Britain – rights which they retained until the 1950s. After Richard D'Oyly Carte's death in 1901, his widow Helen took charge of the company, and she was followed from 1911 to 1948 by her stepson, Rupert. The first major Gilbert and Sullivan revival took place in London between 1906 and 1908, the productions being superintended by W. S. Gilbert himself. Between the wars, Rupert D'Oyly Carte sponsored a succession of London seasons and provincial tours, and gramophone recordings were made of many of the operas. And in the late 1920s and early 1930s, the company returned to the United States once more.[33] The result was that while most works that had been staged during the 1880s, 1890s and 1900s disappeared without trace after their initial London run, the support provided by the D'Oyly Carte Company ensured that Gilbert and Sullivan survived. Moreover, the operas themselves were produced 'precisely in their original form, without any alteration in their words, or any attempt to bring them up to date', and when permission was given to amateur societies to perform them, it was on the same exacting condition that Gilbert's stage directions must be slavishly followed.[34] As a result, the operas soon ceased to be topical, and by firmly resisting any changes, became renowned instead for being unapologetically and proudly 'traditional'.

But this deliberate and very successful cultivation of anachronism also suggests a deeper reason for their recovery and survival. For many aspects of British life which by the inter-war years were regarded and revered as 'traditional' had in fact been invented only during the last quarter of the nineteenth century: the splendid public spectacles of monarchy, the Royal Tournament, the Henry Wood Promenade Concerts, the old school tie, the Wimbledon tennis championships, Test Match cricket and Sherlock Holmes, to name but a few.[35] And to some extent at least, the Gilbert and Sullivan operas themselves survived because they had been, and thereafter remained, an integral part of this remarkably enduring late Victorian world. Their pageantry, their stirring marches, their gorgeous costumes, and their robust loyalty to crown and nation made them an essential and appropriate adjunct to the recently apotheosized monarchy. Sullivan's music was regularly played on state occasions at Buckingham Palace. The revived procession of Knights of the Garter, held at Windsor Castle, was a real-life version of the peers' entrance and march from *Iolanthe*. And when Henry Channon noted that there was a 'Gilbert and Sullivan atmosphere' about Queen Elizabeth II's unprecedentedly lavish coronation, he was essentially describing one invented British tradition in terms of another.[36]

A similar close relationship existed between the reality of aristocratic life and the picture conveyed in the Savoy Operas. During the 1880s, Gilbert and Sullivan had depicted the gentry and peerage in novel terms, as picturesque yet fading. But it was right for the time, and it became even more valid during the next half century. In 1909, the peers foolishly behaved as they had threatened to do in *Iolanthe*: they 'interfered in a matter which they did not understand', and threw out Lloyd George's 'People's Budget', with the result that their powers were drastically reduced. Although 'competitive examination' was never suggested, a variety of schemes to reform the composition of the upper house were put forward intermittently from the 1880s to the 1930s. And many noblemen, impoverished by renewed agricultural depression during the 1920s and 1930s and forced to sell some or all of their estates, were compelled to seek remunerative employment in the manner of the Duke of Plaza-Toro.[37] Not surprisingly, P. G. Wodehouse's inter-war aristocratic world is recognizably the same as Gilbert's: indeed, the Duke of Dunstable appears both in the Savoy Operas and in his novels. And Noel Coward's song, 'The Stately Homes of England', is very much the spirit of *Iolanthe*, fifty years on.[38]

Likewise, the great professions remained as central to British life as they had been in the time of Gilbert and Sullivan. In the case of the armed services, subsequent developments meant that Gilbert's affectionately satirical creations became suffused with an unexpected (and unintended) nostalgic glow. As the cult of Nelson and his flagship *HMS Victory* gathered force, and with the centenary of the Battle of Trafalgar in 1905, *HMS Pinafore* became a worthy sister ship, appropriately anchored nearby, off Portsmouth.[39] In the era of the Dreadnought, the Battle of Jutland and the Washington Treaty, Gilbert's old-fashioned Royal Navy became a comforting reminder of the time when Britannia really had ruled the waves. Admiral Lord Fisher, who had modernized the navy during the 1900s, and was First Sea Lord on the outbreak of the First World War, greatly admired

HMS Pinafore, and regularly attended D'Oyly Carte performances. And in terms of nautical patriotism, it was a very short step from *HMS Pinafore* to Henry Wood's *Fantasia on British Sea Songs*, and even to Noel Coward's wartime film, *In Which We Serve*. In the same way, as the commanders of the British army became more middle class, and as the humiliations of the Boer War were followed by the horrors of the trenches, Gilbert's 'soldiers of the queen' picturesquely recalled the time when officers had indeed been gentlemen, and when the only wars were (to the British) relatively minor colonial skirmishes.

By contrast, Gilbert's portrait of the forces of law and order retained, and even increased, its essential topicality. The structure of the legal profession as reformed during the last quarter of the nineteenth century remained fundamentally unaltered down to the Second World War. British politics were dominated during the ensuing decades as never before by a succession of lawyer-politicians: Asquith, Lloyd George, Lord Reading, Lord Simon and Lord Birkenhead (who knew many of the Lord Chancellor's songs from *Iolanthe* off by heart). And in the lawyer-humorist A. P. Herbert, it almost seemed as if Gilbert himself had been re-incarnated. Herbert wrote a succession of articles in *Punch*, entitled 'Misleading Cases', which amusingly satirized the law and its anomalies, and from the 1920s to the 1940s, he produced a series of plays, operettas and musical reviews for the London stage. Between the 1880s and the 1930s, crime decreased in Britain, and the police consolidated their position as a force, not just for order, but also for good.[40] Like Gilbert's reluctant heroes in *The Pirates of Penzance*, they were regarded as (and respected for) being decent, dutiful, well-meaning and incorruptible – even if not over-bright. And it was precisely this Gilbertian image of the constabulary that was carried on in the detective stories featuring Sherlock Holmes, Lord Peter Wimsey and Miss Marple, in such songs as 'If you want to know the time, ask a policeman', and in early television programmes like *Dixon of Dock Green*.

The result was that although the Savoy Operas were specifically written for the well-educated middle classes of late Victorian England, they successfully captivated a much broader national audience during the first half of the twentieth century. As the music halls went into decline during the inter-war years, the unabashed patriotism of Gilbert and Sullivan found a ready response among the many members of the 'flag-saluting, foreigner-hating, peer-respecting' working classes.[41] Their undemanding tunefulness appealed with equal success to the increasingly philistine members of the upper classes, produced by the public schools from the late nineteenth century onwards. Their determined refusal to address social problems, and their light-hearted escapism, which had made them such a tonic during the gloomy decade of the 1880s, were of even greater value at the time of the inter-war depression. And their disdain for 'abroad', their inability to take foreigners seriously, and their determination not to bow down to continental dictators, or endure 'the tang of a tyrant's tongue', gave them a new and reassuring relevance during the First World War – and again during the 1930s.

So, as the specific circumstances of their original performances were gradually forgotten, the Savoy Operas gradually began to acquire all the ahistorical trappings of a national 'tradition'. It was entirely fitting for Englishmen to laugh at themselves in this gentle, self-regarding way, a viewpoint reinforced by the fact that Gilbert's puns, jokes and elaborate rhymes could not be easily translated into foreign languages. The productions of the D'Oyly Carte Company remained essentially unchanging, and the audiences were reassured that this was so. Age could not wither them, nor custom stale their infinite monotony. In 1930, the D'Oyly Carte principal, Henry Lytton, was knighted, specifically for his work in 'Gilbert and Sullivan'. Three years later, he dedicated his autobiography, appropriately entitled *A Wand'ring Minstrel*, 'to Rupert D'Oyly Carte, the worthy upholder of a great tradition'. In 1934, he celebrated his golden jubilee on the stage, and received a national testimonial, signed by past and present Prime Ministers of all three parties: Ramsay MacDonald, Lloyd George and Stanley Baldwin.[42] And at almost exactly the same time, the supplement to the *Oxford English Dictionary* officially recognized the adjective 'Gilbertian' as a fully accredited word in the English language. The incorporation of Gilbert and Sullivan into national 'tradition' was complete. In celebrating British institutions, with the gentlest of satire and the greatest of affection, they had become a British institution in themselves.

IV

In an almost Gilbertian fashion, therefore, the Savoy Operas had thus assumed three very different historical guises: they were the audacious expression of a nineteenth-century theatrical revolution; they were perfectly judged entertainment for the late Victorian middle class; and they became a national institution, an 'ethnic folk right', during the first half of the twentieth century.[43] Since the

Second World War, however, they have gradually been emancipated from the thraldom of British 'tradition'. This is in part attributable to the ending of the D'Oyly Carte monopoly. With the expiration of Sullivan's copyright in 1950, and of Gilbert's eleven years later, the family lost its rights of exclusive professional performance, and could no longer insist that Gilbert's stage directions must be precisely followed in all amateur productions. Thereafter, the D'Oyly Carte Opera Company continued to perform, but its finances grew precarious, and its performances seemed increasingly lacklustre and outmoded. In 1982, the Arts Council refused the company a government subsidy because of its staid and unimaginative productions, and after more than one hundred years as the creator, upholder and embodiment of the Savoy 'tradition', the D'Oyly Carte Company closed down.[44] And in 1985, the death of Dame Bridget D'Oyly Carte, who had managed the family business since 1948, and was the last direct descendant of the original impresario, effectively brought to an end this phase in the history of Gilbert and Sullivan opera.[45]

But it is not just that this unique institutional support and controlling influence has finally fallen away. For in the radical and confrontational Britain of the 1980s and early 1990s, the operas themselves seem less comfortingly and relevantly 'traditional' than they did in what seem by contrast to have been the more emollient and consensual inter-war years. Today, it is Mrs Thatcher rather than Elizabeth II who has most in common with the Fairy Queen in *Iolanthe*. The House of Lords is very largely a political irrelevance, the aristocracy are the proprietors of safari parks or photographers' studios, and life peerages are given out to members of all social classes. With Britain no longer an imperial power, the army and the navy seem increasingly tangential to national life. The legal profession is on the brink of the most systematic reform since the time of Gilbert and Sullivan themselves; and with rapidly rising crime rates, and countless allegations of police corruption and brutality, the constabulary are no longer as appreciatively or as affectionately regarded as once they were.

But while traditionalists may regret these changes, the effect in many ways has been both salutary and liberating. There have been new and vigorous performances of the operas, both on television and in the theatre. Joseph Papp's production of *The Pirates of Penzance* in New York took many liberties with Sullivan's score, but it also presented the Pirate King as an authentic swashbuckling hero, and in so doing pointed up the close connections between the early Savoy Operas and Victorian melodrama. Even more audaciously, Jonathan

Miller's *Mikado* removed Gilbert's Japanese façade altogether, setting the opera in inter-war England, and suggested that its true identity was as a comedy of manners and a satire on social and political ambition. Just as the operas have been revitalized by these imaginative new productions, so their creators have become historically credible beings for the first time. Sullivan's recently opened diary shows that he was far from being the pious paragon of popular legend: he loved wine, women and gambling, and there was little sign in his own life of the ponderous religiosity of his sacred music.[46] And the latest interpretation of W. S. Gilbert suggests that he was not so much the crusty but good-humoured uncle so implausibly beloved of Savoyard mythology: on the contrary, his wit and satire were the outward expressions of a coarse, aggressive, ill-tempered and litigious nature.[47]

The result of these recent developments is that the operas and their creators have been emancipated from what had increasingly become the stultifying encrustations of a century-old British 'tradition'. Viewing Gilbert and Sullivan in their proper historical context means, paradoxically, that the Savoy Operas themselves are being produced more freely and more adventurously than ever before. It may well be that for Gilbert, for Sullivan and, above all, for their works, the most fascinating and exciting time in their history is yet to come.

NOTES

1 This essay originated as a lecture, given at a symposium on 'Gilbert and Sullivan: A Window on the Victorian World', held at the Pierpont Morgan Library in New York on 16 and 17 November, 1989, and was subsequently published, in a revised and augmented form, in the *New York Review of Books*, 7 March 1991, pp. 38–43. I am most grateful to Mr Frederic Woodbridge Wilson, the Curator of the Gilbert and Sullivan Collection at the Morgan Library, for his expert help and encouragement, and to the editor of the *New York Review of Books* for permission to reprint my essay (with footnotes added) here.
2 C. Brahms, *Gilbert and Sullivan: Lost Chords and Discords* (London, 1975), p. 123; L. Baily, *Gilbert and Sullivan and Their World* (London, 1973), p. 104.
3 H. Pearson, *Gilbert: His Life and Strife* (London, 1957), p. 128.
4 C. Hibbert, *Gilbert, Sullivan and their Victorian World* (New York, 1976), p. 279.
5 For the essential background, see G. Rowell, *Theatre in the Age of Irving* (Blackwell, 1981), chs 1, 2, 4; M. R. Booth, 'The Metropolis on Stage', in H. J. Dyos and M. Wolff (eds), *The Victorian City: Images and Realities*, 2 vols (London, 1973), vol. 1, pp. 211–26.

6 R. Traubner, *Operetta: A Theatrical History* (New York, 1989), pp. 11–13, 19, 36–40, 113–18; C. Hayter, *Gilbert and Sullivan* (New York, 1987), pp. 24–42.

7 For the relation between Gilbert's early work and the Savoy Operas, see J. Stedman, *Gilbert Before Sullivan* (Chicago, 1967), pp. 1–52.

8 J. Stedman, 'From Dame to Woman: W. S. Gilbert and Theatrical Transvestism', *Victorian Studies*, 1970, vol. 14, pp. 27–46.

9 G. Smith, *The Savoy Operas: A New Guide to Gilbert and Sullivan* (London, 1983), p. 39.

10 Smith, *Savoy Operas*, pp. 48–9.

11 Hibbert, *Gilbert, Sullivan and Their Victorian World*, p. 152.

12 Rowell, *Theatre in the Age of Irving*, p. 88.

13 Baily, *Gilbert and Sullivan*, p. 92.

14 Traubner, *Operetta*, pp. 187, 195–201.

15 A. Hyman, *Sullivan and his Satellites: A Survey of English Operetta, 1860–1914* (London, 1978), p. 116.

16 For the general background, see N. Stone, *Europe Transformed, 1878–1919* (London, 1983), pp. 13–73; E. J. Hobsbawm, *The Age of Empire, 1875–1914* (London, 1987), esp. chs 2–7.

17 For two pioneering discussions, see I. Bradley, 'Gilbert and Sullivan and the Victorian Age', *History Today*, 1981, vol. 31, no. 9, pp. 17–20; E. M. Sigsworth, 'W. S. Gilbert . . . The Wisest Fool', in E. M. Sigsworth (ed.), *In Search of Victorian Values: Aspects of Nineteenth-Century Thought and Society* (London, 1988), pp. 179–94.

18 E. P. Lawrence, '"The Happy Land": W. S. Gilbert as Political Satirist', *Victorian Studies*, 1971, vol. 15, pp. 180–3.

19 D. Cannadine, 'The Context, Performance and Meaning of Ritual: The British Monarchy and the "Invention of Tradition", *c*.1820–1977', in E. J. Hobsbawm and T. Ranger (eds), *The Invention of Tradition* (Cambridge, 1983), pp. 108–38.

20 Baily, *Gilbert and Sullivan*, p. 100.

21 F. M. L. Thompson, *English Landed Society in the Nineteenth Century* (London, 1963), pp. 305–8; D. Cannadine, *The Decline and Fall of the British Aristocracy* (London, 1990), pp. 406–17.

22 P. M. Kennedy, *The Rise and Fall of British Naval Mastery* (London, 1976), pp. 177–9.

23 B. Bond, 'Recruiting the Victorian Army, 1870–92', *Victorian Studies*, 1962, vol. 5, pp. 331–2.

24 A. Goodman, *Gilbert and Sullivan at Law* (London, 1983), pp. 178–94.

25 D. Duman, *The English and Colonial Bars in the Nineteenth Century* (London, 1983), pp. 55–70.

26 R. D. Storch, 'The "Plague of the Blue Locusts": Political Reform and Popular Resistance in Northern England, 1840–1857', *International Review of Social History*, 1975, vol. 20, pp. 61–90; J. E. King, '"We Could Eat the Police!": Popular Violence in the North Lancashire Cotton Strike of 1878', *Victorian Studies*, 1985, vol. 28, pp. 439, 468–71.

27 See W. J. Fishman, *East End* (London, 1988); J. R. Walkowitz, 'Jack the Ripper and the Myth of Male Violence', *Feminist Studies*, 1982, vol. 8, pp. 542–74.

28 R. Allen (ed.), *The First Night Gilbert and Sullivan* (London, 1975), pp. 203–4, 413.

29 P. M. Kennedy, 'Continuity and Discontinuity in British Imperialism, 1875–1914', in C. C. Eldridge (ed.), *British Imperialism in the Nineteenth Century* (London, 1985), pp. 32–3.

30 Hayter, *Gilbert and Sullivan*, pp. 45, 118–19.

31 Pearson, *Gilbert*, p. 229.

32 *The Times*, 13 September 1948.

33 R. Wilson and F. Lloyd, *Gilbert and Sullivan: The D'Oyly Carte Years* (London, 1984), pp. 90, 121–8.

34 Hibbert, *Gilbert, Sullivan and their Victorian World*, p. 272.

35 E. J. Hobsbawm, 'Introduction: Inventing Traditions' and 'Mass Producing Traditions: Europe, 1870–1914', in Hobsbawm and Ranger, *Invention of Tradition*, pp. 1–14, 263–308.

36 R. Rhodes James (ed.), *'Chips': The Diaries of Sir Henry Channon* (London, 1967), p. 470.

37 Cannadine, *Decline and Fall*, pp. 48–54, 417–20, 458–71.

38 For the influence of Gilbert and Sullivan on Wodehouse and Coward, see S. Morley, *A Talent to Amuse: A Biography of Noel Coward* (Harmondsworth, 1974), pp. 4, 9, 28; B. Green, *P. G. Wodehouse: A Literary Biography* (London, 1981), pp. 13, 18–19, 26, 49, 95–8.

39 C. F. Behrman, *Victorian Myths of the Sea* (Athens, Ohio, 1977), pp. 104–7.

40 V. A. C. Gatrell, 'The Decline of Theft and Violence in Victorian and Edwardian England', in V. A. C. Gatrell, B. Lenman and G. Parker (eds), *Crime and the Law: The Social History of Crime in Western Europe since 1500* (London, 1980), pp. 240–1, 280–6, 290–3.

41 G. Best, 'The Making of the English Working Classes', *Historical Journal*, 1965, vol. 8, p. 278.

42 L. Ayre, *The Gilbert and Sullivan Companion* (New York, 1972), p. 207.

43 Brahms, *Gilbert and Sullivan*, p. 14.

44 Wilson and Lloyd, *Gilbert and Sullivan*, p. 208.

45 *The Times*, 3 May 1985.

46 A. Jacobs, *Arthur Sullivan: A Victorian Musician* (Oxford, 1984).

47 D. Eden, *Gilbert and Sullivan: The Creative Conflict* (London, 1986).

2

SPEAKING WITH DOUBLE TONGUE: MOTHER GOOSE AND THE OLD WIVES' TALE

Marina Warner

Mother Goose is a drag role; like Widow Twankey or the Wicked Stepmother, she was played by a pantomime dame in the first dramas to pluck her from the pages of children's collections of tales or rhymes and put her on stage.[1] *Harlequin and Mother Goose; or, the Golden Egg* opened at Drury Lane just after Christmas in 1806. The panto was written by Thomas Dibdin, who had conflated various familiar fairytale motifs to produce a story about a certain young and venturesome Jack. With the help of a goose that lays golden eggs, Jack succeeds in winning the hand of the ogreish squire's lovely daughter. Mother Goose is Jack's fairy godmother, and she provides him with the marvellous bird; she appears astride a gander and may have even flown down on to the stage in a goose-shaped *machina*; she performs further wonders, whistling up a wind and raising the dead. In the impresario Joseph Grimaldi's production that year, Samuel Simmons played her as an ancient hag;[2] in 1902, nearly a hundred years later, at the same theatre, the much-loved music-hall performer Dan Leno wore periwig, jewels, ostrich feathers, frills and furbelows in a less gothic interpretation of the traditional figure of Mother Goose.

The transvestism of the pantomime part sharpens the comedy: Mother Goose becomes a figure of fun, like others among the nursery population who had appeared between the covers of anthologies that actually bore her name.[3] Mother Hubbard, Old Dame Trot, Dame Wiggins of Lee and other characters of eighteenth-century ditties and verses share Mother Goose's crone features – her chapfallen jaw, the toothless bight of chin and nose in profile, the Punch-like proboscis, the stick, the conical hat, and the apron and petticoats. Most of these

Dan Leno as Mother Goose, Drury Lane, 1902
Photography by Davey; Theatre Museum, London
Source: Victoria and Albert Museum, London.

nursery characters also have a special relation with animals: bears, dogs, cats, storks, monkeys and mice play their part as familiars to the old beldames of nursery lore in their cottages and kitchens, and the illustrations that accompanied the printed rhymes frequently inspired the artists to delightful mischief: the Dalziel Bros in particular drew a richly waggish series of dogs capering and clowning for

'Old Mother Hubbard and her Dog' in the bumper compendium of 1892, *Mother Goose's Nursery Rhymes and Fairy Tales*.

Mother Hubbard was a contemporary of the pantomime Mother Goose, for her high-spirited antics were first committed to paper in the now familiar verse form by Sarah Martin in 1805.[4] The same decade saw the appearance of many titles attributed to Mother Goose and her consequent establishment in Britain as the figure of female wisdom, the repository and mouthpiece of traditional lore and children's entertainment. Her works can be sifted into two loose and separate piles: nonsense rhymes on the one hand, begun around twenty years earlier by the London printer John Newbery's enterprising but not widely disseminated anthology, *Mother Goose's Melody*; and on the other, books inspired by Charles Perrault's famous collection of fairytales, containing the familiar and much loved stories of 'Cinderella', 'Puss in Boots', 'Bluebeard', 'The Sleeping Beauty' and so forth. The earliest English translation had been published in 1729, but different versions began to appear regularly after the turn of the eighteenth century and were widely distributed by the mid-nineteenth century in a variety of editions, American and English.[5] Though different in content, the two kinds of works laid in Mother Goose's lap shared a common spirit, at once tongue-in-cheek and didactic, as if the absolute simplicity of the tale-teller's downhome wisdom could not be presented straight without embarrassment. Newbery's edition of *c*.1765 forestalls levity of response, poising the mock-serious tone quite neatly in the foreword: 'Let none therefore speak irreverently of this ancient maternity [of the rhymes] as they may be considered as the great grandmothers of science and knowledge . . .'[6] It asks the reader to be respectful while making it clear that everyone really knows at heart that the contents are stuff and nonsense.

Mother Goose had been only one of several contenders in the British nursery until the beginning of the nineteenth century. Marie-Catherine d'Aulnoy's tales, for instance, were published under the name of 'Mother Bunch' in 1790, and 'Nurse Lovechild' and 'Gammer Gurton', as well as Tom Thumb, were ascribed children's stories and verses. But by the time the pantomime opened in London, Mother Goose was gaining over her competitors as the most dependable hearthside source:

I think I have now amused you with some very entertaining Tales, which shew you what has been done in Past Times. You know the Fairy days are now over and . . . it is your duty, in whatever station you are placed, to labour honestly and diligently for your support in

life. No gifts are now bestowed upon us but what come from a
Superior Cause. Consequently you cannot expect to grow good, rich,
or opulent, without a proper use of those means which are most boun-
tifully given to all mankind. Study, therefore, to be useful, avoid cen-
sure and evil-speaking. Do good to all, and you may be assured that
the best of gifts will fall to your share, namely, present as well as
future happiness.[7]

Mother Goose the wonderful and benign crone had become a peda-
gogue; she was to preside over the educationalist task of sweetening
lessons in life by high jinks and hopeful romances; her double nature,
her masquerade were built into her role as a children's entertainer
who is at heart bent on moral instruction. In this the British incarna-
tion of Mother Goose continued her predecessor's role in France, 'la
mère l'oye', for there too, the fairytale writers insisted on their edifying intentions.

The phrase *Contes de ma mère l'oye* or 'Mother Goose Tales' first
appeared in print in 1697 as a title on the frontispiece of Charles
Perrault's collection *Contes du temps passé*;[8] not on the title-page,
but in a panel hanging on the wall behind the engraved image of a
crone telling stories to three children. *Contes de ma mère l'oye* were
referred to before this date, but in passing in earlier literature, as in
Loret's *La Muse historique* of 1650. The term was often coupled
with the phrase *contes de peau-d'âne*, or 'Donkeyskin tales', after the
heroine of another traditional story Perrault chose to retell. Cyrano
de Bergerac, for instance, called the works of his fellow poet Scarron
'a pot pourri of Donkeyskins and Mother Goose tales'; Scarron himself imagined the young Astyanax in Troy being entertained by his
grandmother Hecuba's tales, among which he also included
'Donkeyskin'.[9]

The *Dictionnaire* of the Académie in 1694 drew up a scornful
litany in its definition of the word 'conte': 'Le vulgaire appelle *conte
au vieux loup, conte de vieille, conte de ma mère l'Oye, conte de la
cigogne, conte de peau d'asne, conte à dormir debout, conte jaune,
bleu, violet, conte borgne*, des fables ridicules telles que celles dont
les vieilles gens entretiennent et amusent les enfants.'[10] In this learned
piece of lexicography, the vituperative labels collapse the distinction
between the tellers and their tales: old and young meet on the territory of folly.

The images of both the goose and the donkey convey a certain
flavour, subsequently sustained with remarkable consistency in the
proliferating material associated with Mother Goose in France and

across the Channel: they are proverbially foolish animals. Mme de Sévigné, writing to the King's sister in 1656, told her the story of '*la cane de Montfort*', an ancestor of Jemima Puddleduck, a ninny who forgot to go go church on Sunday, and was ever afterwards obliged on the feast of St Nicholas to leave her pond with her ducklings and offer them all up in expiation at the altar. Mme de Sévigné adds that this wasn't a Tale of Mother Goose, '*Mais de la cane de Montfort/Qui, ma foi, lui ressemble fort.*' 'But of the duck of Montfort who, upon my soul, indeed resembles her.'[11] She thus transposed, quite unconsciously, the character of the teller to the subject of the tale.

The folly of such creatures is allied to simplicity, and simplicity can also be understood as wisdom. It is the plight of the ass to bray, the fate of the goose to cackle, but the geese saved the Capitol from the Gauls in 390 BC, according to one of the best known legends about the bird, and a golden goose was carried there in procession to celebrate Rome's delivery every year afterwards until the custom fell away. Like various other birds (especially hens), geese appear in folklore about the dangers of women's noise. La Fontaine, a contemporary of Perrault, tells in one of his Fables, 'Les Femmes et le Secret', how a husband, as a test of his wife's discretion, cries out in the night that he's laid an egg; she immediately rushes to her neighbour and the egg grows four times the size, the neighbour runs on, and the eggs increase to three in number, and so forth, until the whole town knows that he's laid more than a hundred.[12] The metaphor of laying a giant egg, used here for telling a whopper, animates the image of the storytelling goose who believes the tall tales she passes on.[13]

Both animals are proverbially comic, too; the ass is stubborn, the goose giddy. In both French and English, the expressions 'silly goose' and 'silly ass' exist. The goose is low, associated with low functions: in French, the verb *cacarder* is used for the noise made by a goose, the result *caquet* or cackle. Not as onomatopaeic as the English 'honk', *cacarder* does catch the coprological side of infantile existence more than 'cackle'. 'To goose' also implies bottoms, as if geese were emblematic of the nursery stage, Freud's anal-retentive phase. However, the associations of geese do not end in the cradle, and like asses, they strike salacious resonances as well: the donkey, the mount of the satyr Silenus, was famed for his priapism; the goose was sacred to Isis and to Aphrodite, who rides most gracefully sidesaddle on one in a particularly beautiful kylix in the British Museum.[14] The 'goose-month' was a term used for a woman's lying-in before the birth of a child, while 'goose' was also a term for venereal disease in England in the seventeenth century. In France *la petite oie*, 'little goose' was used of favours begged and received between lovers.[15] Goose-feather beds are synonymous with luxury, while *oies blanches* is still used in France for 'convent girls', ripe for picking. It may be that buried deep inside comfy Mother Goose is the ancient goddess Porne, one of Aphrodite's aspects.

The off-colour tone conveyed by invoking Mother Goose's name places the seventeenth-century fairytale in direct line of descent from the fabulae, or fables, the late classical genre of comic folklore in which the classical unities are broken and humour, tragedy, the real and the marvellous spiritedly combined in defiance of classical proprieties. The presence of beasts in this literature – especially of lowly creatures, like asses or geese – seeks to establish a popular milieu for the written stories' origins as well as their reception. The animals communicate a claim that the tales' inspiration is untutored, unsophisticated, however consummately skilled their invention and execution, and the creatures' participation in the plot necessarily breaches the bounds of realism, to take the stories into the territory of the marvellous, where beasts can talk and change their shape. The animal in the story indicates the presence of magic and absurdity, leading to shivers, thrills and laughter, all vital effects in the fairytale too. By a kind of metonymy, the kind of character who appears in the tales is attributed their authorship – as with the pantomime Mother Goose, who is both a character in the story and the mind from which it springs. Mother Goose tales are presented as recorded experience, learned at first hand by the comical, enchanted tellers and their forebears. A certain symmetry is implied between the low humour of the animal, the lowness of the genre, and the lowness of the presumed audience: for children, as well as animals, are perceived as lesser creatures – like women, especially old women, of the lower class. The very use of the title 'Mother' when applied to an old woman strongly implies a member of an inferior social class; in the seventeenth and eighteenth centuries both Mother and *Mère* were used to address midwives, bawds and other slightly dubious and unattached characters, like *la mère maquerelle* (the Madam of a brothel), as well as the famed prophetess Mother Shipton and the witch Mother Red Cap. From goose to Mother Goose is thus a short step; even in classical Latin the word for old woman, *anus*, had a certain tone, veering from the awed to the contemptuous.

Charles Perrault was working consciously in the tradition of the fable in the last decade of the seventeenth century; before publishing the fairytales in 1697, he had written gallant allegorical exegeses of the animal fountains in the Labyrinthe at Versailles,[16] and in 1699 he translated Gabriel Faerno's animal fables from Italian into French.[17] In the preface to his *Contes de fées*,[18] he makes reference to Milesian tales, a late Latin branch of risqué literature mostly lost to us now, the most celebrated survivor being Apuleius's *The Golden Ass*, which begins, 'in this Milesian tale I shall string together divers stories [*varias fabulas*]'.[19]

One of these, the most famous precursor of the modern fairytale, is the story of 'Cupid and Psyche', which an old woman with hoary head tells to a distraught bride, Charite, who has been captured by pirates on the eve of her wedding. In her preamble the little old lady – *anicula* – promises Charite to 'put away all thy sorrow and to revive thy spirits with *anilibusque fabulis* – old wives' tales. She begins, with a very early first instance of the formula, '*Erant in quadam civitate rex et regina*' – [Once upon a time] in a certain city there was a king and queen . . .' But Perrault rather more disingenuously then disavows his affinity with the bawdy and gruesome and often outlandish levity of writers like Apuleius, saying that he could not divine the moral purpose of such a tale as Cupid and Psyche, whereas in the *Contes* he was publishing, the message was plain. He then explicitly drew a distinction between the native tradition of story on which he drew, and the romances and fables of the ancients: 'They were made to please without a thought for good behaviour,' he wrote. 'This is not the case with the tales that our ancestors invented for their children. They did not tell them with the elegance and the ornament with which the Greeks and Romans adorned their fables, but they always took the greatest care that their tales contained a praiseworthy and instructive moral.' Perrault thus produced references to Mother Goose's pedagogic probity, presented himself as a mere conduit of past wisdom, and vowed: 'I have imposed upon myself to write nothing which might wound either modesty or seemliness.' He appended, to corroborate his enterprise, a madrigal by a young relative, Mlle Lheritier de Villandon, herself a poet as well as a collector and writer of tales, who returned to the theme that such stories carried the seal of tradition, and that she had enjoyed this one as much as when her nanny had recounted it by the fireside when she was small.[20]

The Victorian progeny of Perrault's Mother Goose in Britain are far too numerous to list.[21] Throughout the century, and intensively in its last two decades, Mother Goose compendia were published, illustrated by the leading children's artists, including Kate Greenaway.

She was sometimes called 'Goody Goose' from the term 'goodwife', used for an old woman, and she was identified with nurses and aunts or other dependent members of a household, old retainers and relatives, not with its controllers, the housewife herself, or her mother, for instance. The frontispieces of collections adapted the illustration in Perrault's original edition of 1697; the old woman continued to spin, wearing the clothes of a servant, while the various children around her wore the lace caps and collars of the family.

Mother Goose's gooseyness was generally of the farmyard variety: domestic, and comical. She was sometimes even shown as a goose herself, in poke bonnet and spectacles and shawl, with a webbed hand lying in her lap, an eager tongue showing in her open beak and a twinkle in her eye. But there was a conflict between her cosiness (the pedagogic project) on the one hand and her magic (the entertainment) on the other. At times, the plump old storyteller seemed more of a wild goose, unruly and wilful and independent. Andrew Lang, for instance, the great folklorist and collector of tales, extended the metaphor of the bird to describe Perrault himself aloft on inspiration, flying 'for ever "vivu per ora virum" borne on the wings of the fabulous Goose, *notre Mère l'oye*'.[22]

The pantomime contained both aspects of Mother Goose, and one of its most interesting derivatives was the popular story, 'Mother Goose and her Son Jack', which appeared in various forms throughout the century.[23] The printer J. E. Evans around 1820 issued the verse tale of Jack and his goose (an early example of 'novelization') in which the splendid lines appeared:

> Old Mother Goose
> When she wanted to wander
> Would ride through the air
> On a very fine gander.[24]

Insecure social status, physiognomy, old age, magical powers, and not least, the ability to fly: it can come as a shock to pass beyond the panto jollity and the sermons of the edifying storytellers to recognize that Mother Goose indeed shares rather a lot in common with a witch, or at least with perceptions of witches in the demonology of the seventeenth century.

When Samuel Simmons or Dan Leno in drag in the pantomime gave a comic turn to these supernatural powers of an ugly old woman, were they drawing the teeth of an ancient fear? Were they reassuring the audience by their slapstick that they had nothing to

Title-page by Chester Loomis, *Familiar Selections from the Rhymes of Mother Goose with New Pictures* (London, 1888)
Source: Victoria and Albert Museum, London.

fear from old women like Mother Goose even if they could take off into the air and conjure up ghosts? The impersonating male would certainly have sent the spectators a long way down the road to laughter, the great undoer of belief, the shield against terror. How could they take Mother Goose seriously when she spoke and strode and acted like a man? (It is intrinsic to pantomime drag, as opposed to the cabaret variety, that the actor tips you the wink all the time that he's a man in petticoats.)

This mockery of possible beliefs in dangerous witchcraft and pooh-poohing of fears about horrible old women cannot, however, be ascribed to a new robust scepticism, or to the prevailing rationalism of the times when the Mother Goose panto first appears, or to the distance between the Georgian and Jacobean ages. Much earlier, the

arts of the crone-like witch 'Mother Bunch' had also been treated
with levity: she was credited with the authorship of several 'jest-
books'.[25] But no amount of 'jesting' camouflages the fact that these
booklets appealed to existing beliefs in wisewoman magic, in the
potential of the love philtres, cures and other craft that 'Mother
Bunch' recommends; nor that they were published during the period

Cover, *Denslow's Mother Goose*, illustrated by W. W. Denslow (London, 1902)
Source: Victoria and Albert Museum, London.

'Old Mother Goose/When she wanted to wander/Would ride through the air/On a very fine gander.' From *Mother Goose's Nursery Rhymes and Fairy Tales* (London, 1892)
Source: Victoria and Albert Museum, London.

of intensive witch-hunting in England, Scotland and France. A comic touch does not automatically signify disbelief.

Guying the crone might reflect some deeper relation between the old woman with imagined powers and the people she threatens (or helps); it might fulfil another function besides simply making fun of past foolishness and superstition. It is possible that the pantomime

dame's clowning disguises continuing belief and maintains it all the
more persistently by appearing to make light of magic. Like court
jesters, who could dare to say aloud what no-one else could, on the
pretext that they were fools who spoke only nonsense, the old mothers of nursery rhyme can get away with more when they are presented as ridiculous. They can use their powers, their magic, if they
seem to be foolish. In a vivid anonymous Dutch painting of around
1500, for instance, the Fool peeps through his fingers as he laughs: he
sees what is forbidden, and humour defends him against its power,
and also protects him from the transgression he commits by seeing it.
It is pertinent that fools in iconography sometimes wear spectacles
(sometimes, even, blazoned on their bottom), to stress their far-sight-
edness; Mother Goose frequently appears bespectacled too. Such
clowning covers up her power. The nonsense rhymes she tells about
other beldames of folklore, like Mother Bunch and Mother Hubbard,
also draw the sting of the magic they perform. Another hag, for
instance, who makes an appearance in *Mother Goose's Melody*,
shares something of her witch-like character:

> There was an old lady toss'd in a blanket,
> Seventeen times as high as the moon;
> But where she was going no mortal could tell,
> For under her arm she carried a broom.
> Old woman, old woman, old woman, said I?
> Whither, ah whither, ah whither so high?
> To sweep the cobwebs out of the sky,
> And I'll be with you by and by.[26]

By telling tales against herself, Mother Goose cuts the ground from
under her and circumvents suppression.

For joking, like cursing, can be used as a means of self-defence: the
procuress, like the clown a stock character from antique comedy,
uses a bawdy tongue like a weapon. Cathérine Clément, in her
influential manifesto of the late 1970s, 'La Jeune née', invokes Baubô,
also known as Iambe, the old bawd whom the grieving Demeter
meets in her search for her abducted daughter Persephone. Nothing
can alleviate the mother's misery – except the old creature, who
clowns for her, telling her dirty jokes and and even 'mooning'
(exposing her bottom). 'All laughter is allied with the monstrous,'
writes Clément. 'Laughter breaks up, breaks out, splashes over . . . it
is the moment at which the woman crosses a dangerous line, the cultural demarcation beyond which she will find herself excluded.'[27] The

obscene jest, made in a spirit of good humour, staves off hostility in a way that the obscene curse cannot; the vituperative hag risks her life, but the ribald old woman, the pantomime dame, saves her skin, and her speech – her wisdom – is not silenced.

In the pantomime, however comic and exaggerated the antics of her interpreter, Mother Goose's claims to supernatural power cannot be wholly invalidated; after all, the plot depends on her effectiveness: it is she who manages the union of Jack and his beloved, as well as providing the all-important golden egg in the first place. The plot directs the audience to trust in her, even as the performance directs them to laugh at her. She is a kind of fate, an all-seeing all-powerful crone who must not be crossed, and she answers to the wish fulfilment that drives most fairytales, reflecting the fatalism of the genre, its romantic message that something will come out of the blue to reward the virtuous and punish the wicked. This is of course a superstitious position, upheld, reinforced and rendered thoroughly appealing, by the pantomime itself or by the fairy story in the telling.

The drag that the dame wears may therefore not be ludicrous at all deep down, it may rather correspond to the raiment of officiating priests, the cross-dressing of the Hopi or Hindu shaman. If panto can be seen as a Christmas rite, the dame's drag may symbolize the central celebrant's necessary robes as he makes a bid to assimilate the powers with which Mother Goose is invested, on behalf not only of the other characters with him on stage, but on behalf of the audience too. Their pleasure, their sense of satisfaction at the end of the play will rise from the consummation of good fortune, the love and money Jack wins through Mother Goose's mediation.[28] We must not underestimate how deeply fairytale and popular stories appeal to audiences because of the fatalistic beliefs enshrined in them, that absolve individuals from responsibility and self-government and place happiness in the hands of all-powerful and capricious fairies.

Just as the male sexuality of priests must be effaced in their lives and appearance, so the female sexuality of the old witch figure becomes disturbingly elusive. The ambidextrousness of the sacred also informs the iconography of Folly, as for instance in Quentin Massys's portrait of a jester, in which the old fool could well be a crone, Mère Folle of the Feast of Fools.[29] Age abolishes the distinctions between male and female, and age and wisdom are conventionally related. When the pantomime dame is playing an older woman, Widow Twankey or Mother Goose, the role does not take on the codes of femininity as insistently as other roles in the drag artist's repertoire (the Ugly Sisters for instance). Just as the joke is on prettiness in

Cinderella pantos, when the Ugly Sisters prink and mince and squeal, but then it turns out that it is the pretty girl's wishes that come true, so the joke in the Mother Goose impersonation is on old hags, but in the end, it is still the old hag who has her way.

The tradition of male impersonation in the history of Mother Goose's development as the traditional eponym for a storyteller interestingly reproduces exactly the literary circumstances. 'Mother Goose' in print is a costume worn by male authors; she is a form of ventriloquist's dummy, or a kind of oracular mask through whom various fairytale writers since the seventeenth century have spoken. She must of necessity speak with double tongue since her tales are always mediated through another. By positing this aboriginal figure of wisdom, the pedagogues managed to put forward their own views.

The search for an original behind the primordial figure of Mother Goose, the desire to hear her speak her own lines, led historians to America. A certain Mrs Goose (or Vergoose) of Boston in the mid-seventeenth century was believed to be the authentic source of an American collection of Mother Goose rhymes. The rumour was she had driven her family and neighbours mad with her incessant singing and reciting to her grandson until her son-in-law, a printer, collected her ditties and published them in order to quieten her. Unfortunately, no evidence of this early Mother Goose collection, which would certainly predate Newbery's and even Perrault's, has ever come to light. Later, another Mrs Goose, who died in 1690 and was buried in the graveyard on Boston Common, was also put forward.[30] But she was an even less convincing candidate.

The pressing need people feel to find a real-life original author presents a noteworthy aspect of this historical search. Discussing the symbolic sides of Mother Goose, I have run into sceptics who still assume it is a proper name that once belonged to an individual storyteller and therefore dismiss my explorations of its possible further significance. Their position illuminates the passage from myth to memory that this volume explores: a symbol in popular lore sheds her mythical dimension – and all that entails in terms of shared prejudices and desires – in order to figure as a simple person in history, incompletely recorded, but otherwise remembered in the books and other works that bear her name. Thus false acts of memory are used to calm the turmoil of magic and myth; fantasies are turned into actualities in a piece of stagecraft that leaches them of meaning, and itself represents a thaumaturgic act of exorcism.

Fantasies of Mother Goose draw on experience, though hard evidence for the history of real-life Mother Geese, of female storytellers, is difficult to unearth. Nevertheless, examples recur of 'old wives' spinning tales, of balladeers and singers as well as storytellers like Marie de France; numerous writers have described women's circles, as in Boccaccio's *Decameron*, and Straparola's *Le Piacevoli Notti*. Since the nineteenth century authors have recalled their nurses', mothers' and grandmothers' stories – including Virginia Woolf, whose mother Julia Stephen wrote fairytales.[31] In George Eliot's *Felix Holt*, Mrs Transome says of her son, Harold, 'He will not even listen to me any more than if I were an old ballad-singer.'[32] Though ballads are not identical with stories, the remark testifies to the existence of old women who sang stories for their living. In Scotland and Brittany, where *veillées* or fireside sessions were customary, storytellers and balladeers were both men and women. In Holland, old women passed on oral traditions about historical events as well as tales and songs.[33] Oscar Wilde's father, in Merrion Square, Dublin, asked for tales in lieu of fees from his poorer patients, many of them women, which Speranza Wilde then collected in book form. The literary efforts of women in children's literature throughout the nineteenth century have not been fully documented and analysed, but Andrew Lang, in his copious collecting for the Blue, Green, Red (etc.) Fairy Books, was assisted by a team of editors and transcribers, led by his wife, Leonora Alleyne. Nurses, governesses and old women were engaged in educating children, as ample testimony shows, from medieval and Renaissance images of 'The Education of the Virgin', showing St Anne teaching Mary to read, to anecdotes like Gulliver learning languages from his giant nurse and his servant the sorrel nag, as Swift himself had been taught his letters by his nurse after his mother sent him to England for three years. Mother Goose was a recognizable type of figure to the children to whom her collections of tales were addressed.

Much more work needs to be done on the historical aspects of female storytelling, but when the pursuit of Mother Goose's individual identity and historical status is abandoned, she can still be historically analysed as a fascinating compound of many fantasies, about children, and women, and national identity; as a projection of a deep desire to discover origins and tap roots at source. Mother Goose as a cultural image reveals the tremendous power of atavism in the moral ambitions of children's educators.

In Perrault's book, the tablet *Contes de ma mère l'oye* on the wall behind the storyteller faces the named author on the title-page, Perrault's son Pierre Darmancour. It not only duplicates the collection's name, but also offers another origin of the stories: behind

Pierre Darmancour, Mother Goose is speaking: behind the child, the crone. In the preface Perrault confirmed this message, and renounced creating the stories in favour of a pristine source, in the nursery, among the servants, the nursemaids, the women and children. By making this claim, Perrault, a member of the Académie, was defending native literature against his fellow *académiciens*, who proclaimed the complete superiority of Greek and Latin over all things French. *Confrères* in the Académie, like Boileau, repeatedly savaged Perrault and the women writers of the time, such as Mlle de Scudéry and her fellow *précieuses*. The defence of fairytale in the 1690s takes place within this bitter Quarrel of the Ancients and Moderns; to the Moderns, like Perrault, the fairytale was a living shoot of national, vernacular, modern culture; to the Ancients, the genre was a bastard child of the vulgar crowd.[34]

The femaleness of the genre became crucial in the argument for the tales' aboriginal status. Nothing can be more home-grown than mother's milk; and milk here can be taken to mean language.[35] The feminine origin ascribed to the tales offered a warranty of their truthfulness as testimony from outside literary high culture; the claim is then recapitulated, again and again, by individual women who take up writing fairy stories: in seventeenth- and early eighteenth-century France, they were hardly peasants, but they saw themselves in contact with the people through their childhood memories. Women *raconteuses* outnumber men in *Le Cabinet des fées*, dominating this compendium of over forty volumes published when the fad had passeed its climacteric in France, at the end of the eighteenth century.[36] For different women fairytale writers in the circle in which Perrault moved, Mother Goose symbolized women's language, lore and speech, and these were in turn aligned, by force of social circumstance, with the people's wisdom. She came to personify an imagined, primordial body of home-grown knowledge which abolished the distinction between fact and fiction and returned readers and listeners to their childhood and, through childhood, to their roots.

Marie-Jeanne Lheritier de Villandon, Perrault's young cousin, developed an argument for the origins of fairytales far more fully than Perrault, and as she wrote her *contes* before him, possibly as early as 1692, it is likely that they exchanged ideas on the subject, and that the figure of Perrault's Mother Goose conceals not only his handiwork and thinking, but also hers.[37] Constantly referring to her own *gouvernante*'s stories, she has inspired one folklorist at least to identify Mother Goose with the Lheritier family nurse, who may have come from Normandy. This commentator waxed lyrical at the thought: she 'had gathered honey from the lips of nurses and mothers, [she] had drunk from the source in the hollow of her hand'.[38]

For Marie-Jeanne Lheritier proves as anxious as Perrault to renounce authorship in favour of an anonymous tradition: two of her fairy stories, 'Ricdin-Ricdon', an early version of 'Rumpelstiltskin' and 'La Robe de Sincérité', a predecessor of 'The Emperor's New Clothes', are embedded in her novel *La Tour ténébreuse* (the dark tower), where they are told by no less a hero than Richard the Lion Heart in order to while away his captivity.[39] His audience consists of the troubadour Blondel: he has smuggled himself in in disguise, and he then commits the stories to memory to recount them later. This frame carefully sets up Mlle Lheritier's theory of the national, Gallic matrix of the fairytale, in the middle ages, among the troubadours and storytellers of Provence. She propounded it fully in the preface to her most famous fairytale, 'L'Adroite princesse, ou les aventures de Finette' (known in English as 'The Discreet Princess'), which is often attributed to Perrault.[40] She declares that, like the *bourgeois gentilhomme*, she wants neither prose nor verse, but instead 'a tale told any how, and as one speaks'.[41] 'I'm not looking for anything except some moral of a sort . . .' she continues. 'You will see how our Forebears knew how to insinuate that one can fall into a thousand horrors.'[42] However, Mlle de Lheritier's style does not come out any old how, the way one speaks, but is the flowery and learned prose of a *précieuse* from the aristocratic salons of the Sun King's Paris, directed at the entertainment of her coevals, the group of friends who gathered together to dress up as characters in fairy stories while they improvised variations on the spot and awarded one another garlands for their efforts.[43] Mlle Lheritier admits that she has somewhat elaborated on the story, and excuses herself by saying that when she was a child, the telling of it by her *gouvernante* lasted 'une bonne heure', a good hour.[44]

The genealogy Mlle Lheritier puts forward differs from Perrault's; like him, she is concerned with improving morals and *bienséance* ('seemliness'), but for her, this entails disclaiming kinship with animal fables in favour of homespun proverbs, and putting a clear distance between all classical sources and the tales. She then begs her friend the Comtesse de Murat to follow her example:

L'antique Gaule vous en presse:
Daignez-vous mettre dans leurs jours
Les contes ingénus, quoique remplis d'adresse
Qu'ont inventé les Troubadours.[45]

The troubadours, epitomized by the romantic figures of Blondel and Richard the Lion Heart in the tower, are connected to Mlle Lheritier's *gouvernante*, and to Perrault's *nourrice*, the nurse and old woman, and to Mother Goose, through two aspects of the same essential element in the fairytale's self-image: oral transmission and its counterpart, native language. Mother Goose could be called Mother Tongue.[46]

At some point, which Mlle Lheritier is naturally unable to specify, the transmission of the stories passed underground, out of the hands of court poets, and their memory was then kept by children who heard them from the old; though she herself, their champion, was in her thirties in the 1690s, nobody in the romance she is composing about native fairytale literature and its diffusion is middle-aged. The simplicity of Mother Goose, the peasant *raconteuse*, matches that of a child in the aristocratic or bourgeois nursery; age and youth come full circle, the illiterate meets the preliterate. Beneath this image of the ancient old woman lies a preconception that simple folk are like children, and their stories, wisdom and morals suitable child's fare. History happens to prominent and active individuals in their prime; it bypasses the young and the old and the insignificant, who become the incorrupt repositories of tradition, outside time and circumstance. Just as natural mothers are conspicuously absent from the plots of many favourite fairytales, so mothers do not figure in the propaganda that sustained the first publication of Mother Goose tales. The stories' antiquity was somehow matched and verified by the teller's age, and their removal from the scene of activity, into the timeless zone where dotage meets infancy.

Mlle Lheritier drew certain distinctions: she put some distance between herself and the comic and possibly bawdy character of animal tales, and explained that the language in which these ancient stories were communicated had to be altered, had to be cleansed. For whereas, in the picture she paints of the genre's early days, the storytellers travelled from castle to castle 'chez les personnes de qualité' until no royal entertainment was complete without a troubadour, the transmission had sunk down the social scale, and bad characters and improper happenings and other unseemliness had befouled the tradition:

> These stories became filled with impurities as they passed through the mouth of the common people; in the same way as pure water always becomes defiled with rubbish as it passes through a dirty culvert. If the people are simple, they are also coarse: they do not know what propri-

ety is. Pass lightly over a licentious and scandalous event, and the tale they tell after will be filled with all the details. One tells these criminal deeds to a good purpose, to show that they always go punished, but the people, from whom we received them, report them with no veil to cover them, and indeed have tied them to the subject thus unveiled so tightly that it's a hard task to tell the same adventures and keep them concealed.[47]

The voice of experience sounds through this rather plaintive text, in which poor Mlle Lheritier, committed to believing in the virtuous simplicity and good faith and perfect manners of a pure French tradition, finds herself continually face to face with its vital and rude adulteration, and struggles to legitimize it again as courtly literature. Behind the mask of the nurse, the minstrelsy of a gracious and noble past still can be heard, she pleads. Her quandary as she both denies and confronts the character of the *gouvernante* or Mother Goose takes us to a deeper ambivalence in the fairytales that she and Perrault wrote, about magic and the people, about the grotesque and low life, about women's lore and men's, women's speech and men's.

Another tale Mlle Lheritier recounted she also attributed to tradition, transmitted in this case by a 'Lady very knowledgeable about Greek and Roman antiquities, but even more learned about Gallic antiquities, [who] told me this tale when I was a child'.[48] Thus Mlle Lheritier cannot quite bring herself to set aside classical learning altogether, in case she – and her source – might seem ignorant. Again, the fairytale is autochthonous, and thoroughbred: it is 'one of those Gallic fables which come in direct line from the Storytellers or Troubadours of Provence'.[49]

The pattern reappears: the near source is female, not aristocratic, but the origin is noble, French and male. Whether her contact with the past store of tales be a servant or an educated woman, they originate in what Mlle Lheritier calls *romans* – novels – or even, citing the Spanish term, 'Romances'. Their authenticity is confirmed by direct contact with a speaking woman to whom they are second nature; their nobility on the other hand is guaranteed by their birth. Like a fairytale heroine herself, the story on the lips of Mother Goose is somehow in disguise, and is, under the simple or even uncouth exterior, a radiant and well-born princess, like Cinderella, like Donkeyskin. Mother Goose is not only being played by a man, but conceals many ancestors beneath her skirts: troubadours, poets, national heroes of tradition. It is not surprising to find that counterfeit and masquerade lie at the core of many of Mlle Lheritier's tales.

'Marmoisan, ou l'innocente tromperie' ('Marmoisan or the innocent trick') is dedicated to Mlle Perrault, Perrault's daughter, by Mlle Lheritier, with a preface asking her to see that it is included in the family's collection of tales.[50] In the story, which Perrault did not take up for his book, after all, the heroine goes to war in the place of her twin brother after he has been accidentally killed in a shameful erotic adventure – he falls off a ladder trying to enter a girl's bedroom without permission, and is run through by her father. In her brother's shape, Marmoisan distinguishes herself and heaps honour on her household; she struggles not to be revealed, though many traps are set for her by jealous courtiers who suspect her of being a girl, and by the prince who has fallen in love with her and longs for her to turn out not to be a boy. She maintains feminine decorum throughout, too, refusing to join in the rough ribaldry of the court, at women's expense. In the end, she is wounded in the lists at a tourney, and her travesty uncovered – to rejoicing all round. The story of the amazon princess was adapted from a slightly older writer, the Comte de Prechac, whose book, *L'Héroine mousquetaire*, related the true exploits of Christine de Meirak, who fought disguised in the French army in 1675–6.[51]

In 'Finette, or the Discreet Princess', the heroine tricks the false suitor who has married both her sisters, and then evades death by placing a dummy in bed in her stead. Mlle Lheritier does not spare the details of its manufacture from straw, a stuffed bladder, sheep's blood, the lights of the animals they'd eaten at dinner, all dressed up in a nightcap and nightgown.[52]

The recurrence of imposture in Mlle Lheritier's stories might arise simply from the device's splendid narrative possibilities – but there could be more to it: as a woman writer, she identified with the travestied Marmoisan, she wanted to prove through her heroine that she could be a valiant knight and at the same time a completely feminine woman, who inspires love. Likewise, she could play a man's part in the world of letters and win approval and renown. Her fairytales tend to validate the inferior category against the superior, vernacular folk literature against the classics, oral tradition against book learning, the female against the male, by skilfully imitating the style of the dominant category, its learning and its refinement, in a successful masquerade.

Perrault is less defensive about adopting *le merveilleux national*, about calling in Mother Goose as it were as witness; as a man, as an establishment figure, Colbert's assistant in the Superintendency of the royal buildings for twenty years, a famous courtier in favour with the

King, Perrault did not need to feel quite so uneasy as his friend, colleague and relative Mlle Lheritier. As Virginia Woolf pointed out, it's all very well to spurn Greek when you've been given the chance to study it, to reject tradition when you have been raised in it. But the Quarrel of the Ancients and the Moderns affected men and women writers differently. Mlle Lheritier could not have composed a sonorous Latin ode or a canny epigram in Greek for the King's birthday even if she had wanted to. She had to be a Modern, on the side of the mother tongue willy-nilly; when Perrault began writing fairytales too – the first man in France to do so, and certainly the first *académicien* – he was making common cause with women as well as showing Gallic pride.[53]

Mother Goose, whatever her immediate guise, made the likes of Mlle Lheritier anxious; her haggard witchiness and her low social status did not make her an entirely comfortable alter ego. As a marginal type, and a speaking woman, such a figure would be an object of widespread suspicion and disapproval, and Mlle Lheritier longed, as her tales show, and as we all do perhaps, for recognition and praise. It is possible that one of the buried reasons for the vanishing mothers of fairytale is that perfection in a woman entails exemplary silence and self-effacement – to the point of actually disappearing out of the text. The strictures against women's speech have been fierce in our Judaeo-Christian culture, and the enemies of the Moderns in France in the 1680s and 1690s were also committed misogynists. Perrault republished his poem 'L'Apologie des femmes', a rather touching hymn of praise to conjugal love, with a new preface, as a *réplique* to Boileau's satire against women.[54] Boileau had been refused permission to publish this masterpiece of abuse when he first wrote it, because it attacked Mlle de Scudéry so plainly; but it contents were circulated. Molière, in two of his most brilliant comedies of the 1670s, *Les Femmes savantes* and *Les Précieuses ridicules*, had also made merciless fun of the salons where Mlle de Scudéry and her friends presided, and where conversation was the main pastime and the principal art. These were the circles in which Mlle Lheritier moved. Mlle Lheritier indeed wrote a eulogy of Mlle de Scudéry after her death in 1701, and penned a triumph for another bluestocking friend, Mme Des Houlières, describing her apotheosis on Parnassus and the punishment of her detractors: Boileau is condemned to be bitten by Cerberus as many times as he has insulted women, while Mme Des Houlières is counted among the Muses as the tenth.[55] In *Le Misanthrope*, though sympathies are more ambiguously distributed than in Molière's other plays, Alceste is driven to flight and despair by Célimène's verbal brilliance and volubility. But when

Perrault, the champion of women, defender of old wives' wisdom, came to paint his paragon of a wife, he still extolled her *bouche enfantine*, her childlike mouth, her soft-spokenness, her forbearance.

In the seventeenth century, the tongues of women were chiefly associated with curses, with nagging and gossip; there even exist, from the same century that saw the development of Mother Goose Tales, branks or scold's bridles – contraptions like dog muzzles designed to gag women who had been charged and found guilty for something they had said.[56] In England in 1624, a law against cursing was passed, and its targets were not only men who swore, but women who could conjure.[57] Victims identified as witches in league with the devil by inquisitors and prickers were often poor old folk, who might use curses to retaliate against maltreatment or neglect in default of other means of defence, as the research of Christina Larner and Alan Macfarlane has shown.[58]

Gossip was a predominant target in perceptions of women's folly, and the changes in meaning of the word 'gossip' illuminate the participation of women in storytelling; originally a word for a baptismal sponsor, a godmother, it referred almost exclusively to women by the mid-fourteenth century, and by the period 1590–1670 had come to designate in particular women friends invited to be present at the birth of a child. Only after this did a gossip come to mean 'a person, mostly a woman, especially one who delights in idle talk'. A 'gossipping' is an old word for a christening feast.

There are several strands in this web of associations around women as gossips which, pulled together, enhance the portrait of Mother Goose, or the tale-teller. Women dominated the domestic networks of information and power; the neighbourhood, the village and the street, not only the household, were their arena of influence.[59] The gatherings of women together were the focus of much male anxiety about women's tongues: typical women's meeting places, especially the spinning room, were feared to give rise to slander and intrigue and secret liaisons.[60] An early seventeenth-century English broadsheet 'Tittle-Tattle; or the several branches of Gossipping' depicts the places where women are alone: and able to communicate without supervision. The first place is 'At Childbed', appropriately; then come the market, the bakehouse, the alehouse, the baths, church, and the river for the washing of clothes. The preacher concludes:

> Then Gossips all a Warning take,
> Pray cease your Tongue to rattle;

Go knit, and Sew, and Brew, and Bake,
And leave off TITTLE-TATTLE.[61]

In France, the same theme was interpreted in a print called *Le Caquet des femmes*, in which the women are seen in the midst of savage brawls as a consequence of their chatter. The linguistic link between godmothers and gossips is crucial in the world of fairytale; the fairy godmother or magic old woman and the crone storyteller are often made to look alike by illustrators, the doubled subject of the story or rhyme.[62] The gnarled and toothless storyteller (Dame Fidget) who appears on the frontispiece of a chapbook of 1808,[63] Cruikshank's hunched crone on the frontispiece of his Fairy

Frontispiece, *The Grimms' Fairy Tales*, vol. 2, by George Cruikshank (London, 1823)
Source: Victoria and Albert Museum, London.

Library,[64] and various other Mother Geese are the lookalikes of
Cinderella's fairy godmother, both in Cruikshank's own Cinderella
and in Arthur Rackham's later images.[65] To know fairytales well
enough to tell them is to be in some degree fey yourself.

Mother Goose often doubles the part of the fairy in the tale that
she tells: it is she who knows Cinderella's true worth, for instance,
and imparts it to her listeners, it is the story she tells that reveals the
heroine's identity and resolves her triumph in the same way as the
fairy godmother. The overlap of the crone and the witch, of the fairy
and the storyteller has been pointed out many times: the word *fata*,
from which the French *fée* derives, shares the same root as Fate, itself
from the Latin past participle of the verb *fari*, to speak. The Parcae
of the Greeks and the Norns of the Norse pantheon tell the story of
the lives of mortals and determine their adventures and their ends;
they also tell, in the sense of count, the number of their days.

Thomas Didbin caught this exactly in his pantomime, when he
made Mother Goose the engine of the pantomime's happy ending
and when he gave her the role of the fairy godmother. The omni-
science and *parti pris* of the narrator are replicated by the wisdom
and loyalty of the fairy. When moralities are appended in the mock
pedantic manner of Perrault, it is sometimes difficult to know
whether Mother Goose is speaking in her own voice or quoting the
knowing message of the wise old fairy in the tale.

In the light of this identification of the narrator with the magical
figure in the story itself, who sees into the future and can affect it,
possessing both the gift of instruction and occult knowledge, it is
interesting to look at two seventeenth-century fairytales which feature old beldames or grannies: Perrault's 'Red Riding Hood', and
Mlle Lheritier's version of 'Diamonds and Toads'.[66] For fantasy can
work to heal as well as to harm, and the fairytale, mediated through
the courtly writings of the French writers of *contes*, helped to revise
the estimation of women's talk, of old wives' tales; and Mother
Goose, a benevolent witch, a kindly female tale-spinner and gossip,
participated in this benign process of civilization.

Perrault as usual adapted a traditional story, in which a little girl
takes food and drink to her grandmother and meets a wolf.[67] But he
chose to leave out several aspects which must have struck him as
crude: the wolf tricking the granddaughter into eating a piece of her
granny's flesh and drinking some of her blood. He also changed the
ending: in a unique intervention in the usually comic, happy world of
the fairytale, Little Red Riding Hood is eaten by the wolf and that's
that. In the traditional version, the little girl manages to get away by

refusing to get into bed because she has to go to the lavatory. The wolf urges her to do it in the bed, but she won't, and so she slips outside.[68]

From the point of view of Mother Goose's symbolic identity and its connection to women's talk, Perrault's re-telling continues an important aspect: the possibility of confusion between the wolf and the grandmother. They both dwell in the woods, and they both need food urgently, one because she is sick, the other because he hasn't eaten for three days, and as everyone knows, Little Red Riding Hood cannot quite tell them apart. The wolf is kin to the forest-dwelling witch, or crone; he's a male counterpart, a werewolf who swallows up grandmother and then granddaughter. (In the witch-hunting fantasies of early modern Europe they are the kind of beings associated with marginal knowledge, who possess pagan secrets and are in turn possessed by them.) The climactic image of Red Riding Hood, the wolf's mouth, has led many commentators to note the emphasis on orality. This orality has been interpreted, by the Freudian Geza Roheim, as an allegory of a child's aggressive feelings towards the mother's breast.[69] But the orality has not been interpreted as encoding another form of maternal nurturance: language, or oral knowledge. The story is indeed a *conte au vieux loup* as well as a Mother Goose take.

Perrault's tragic change to the original folk tale's *dénouement* becomes very interesting indeed in this light, for his little girl is swallowed up into the body of the wolf along with her granny, and does not emerge again. One possible reading – among many possible readings – of this ending yields another thought: like the children who grow up in traditional lore and language, Little Red Riding Hood is incorporated, the lineal and female descendant of her grandmother who has herself been ingested by the wolf beforehand, and he does not release either of them. The wolf to whom they are thus assimilated could represent the indigenous inhabitants of the countryside, hairy, wild, unkempt, untrammelled by imported acculturation, eating raw foods and meat, a native beast in the native landscape, where a specific age-old corpus of home-grown literature flourishes and is passed on. Such a counterpoint between the woods and the home Red Riding Hood leaves with her basket of prepared food – butter and cake – is suggested in the Perrault, and the theme was made explicit later in the interpretive literature. Certain German patriots, for instance, commenting on the tale in the 1920s, allegorized the grandmother as ancient Aryan mother-right who must be regenerated by the granddaughter.[70] On the other hand, to accept gladly Red Riding Hood's death inside the animal as an allegory of national tradition clearly entails reading against the cautionary message of the story and against the morality Perrault appended to the tale, in which he warns little girls against wolves. However, in these final verses, Perrault alters the identity of the wolf, and comments:

> Now, there are real wolves, with hairy pelts and enormous teeth; but also wolves who seem perfectly charming, sweet-natured and obliging, who pursue young girls in the street and pay them the most flattering attentions.
> Unfortunately, these smooth-tongued, smooth-pelted wolves are the most dangerous beasts of all.[71]

It is this well-spoken seducer, urbane, not rustic, who turns out to be Perrault's wolf, who eats up little girls and grandmothers, and he makes possible yet another twist in the significance of the story. For he overwhelms and absorbs them in the same way, one could say, as classical learning, metropolitan manners and other customs, alien rather than authochtonous, swallow up the home-bred nursery culture of old women and their protégées, of Mother Goose and her young listeners. It is not unusual in Perrault to find his moralities introducing an irony: here the wolf stands no longer for the savage wilderness, but for the deceptions of the city and the men who wield authority in it. He openly turns the usual identity of the wolf on its head and locates him near at hand, rather than far away and Other. It is almost as if Perrault did not want to follow the ending in which the Granny is dead and Little Red Riding Hood escapes, because he wanted them to remain united, in the wolf's belly; nor, apparently, did he want to introduce a huntsman, the figure of masculine civilization who restores them to life, as in the Grimm version. But yet he could not stop at their ultimate and unregenerate incorporation into the wolf either, as he knew, deep down, that this resolution did not represent the true facts of the matter. Tradition cannot be kept sealed off and apart; so at the last minute, in the moral, he switched the emphasis and turned the wolf from a forest creature into a polished and sweet-talking man, and by the way produced an allegory about the impossibility of separate female lore and language.

Perrault was also in two minds about the pristine, aboriginal source that Mlle Lheritier proclaimed, for his jaunty tone consistently belies the earnestness with which he presses the claims of fairytale to wisdom. His stories have been so romanticized in subsequent retellings that it comes as quite a revelation to find him cracking his typical jokes, at the expense of his material. When the Sleeping Beauty's death has been ordered by her cannibal mother-in-law (an episode usually left out these days), Perrault comments: 'She was over twenty years old, not counting the hundred years she had slept: her hide was a little tough, though lovely and white . . .'[72] Though Perrault often asseverated the contrary in the quarrel with Boileau, the style of his Mother Goose tales betrays that he could not take the claims of native literature altogether seriously, that for him Mother Goose would always raise a laugh.

No wolf was really needed to dish up Mother Goose to hungry listeners: in some ways the most successful of accomplished Mlle Lheritier's disguises was her concealment of her true wolf nature. For it was she who came along and gobbled Grandmother, or Mother Goose, by making her polite and sociable and *sortable*.

In her story 'Les Enchantemens de l'éloquence, ou les effets de la douceur', the issue of women's talk is central.[73] One day, when Blanche is drawing water at the well, a prince out hunting – inevitably – wounds her by mistake, but her soft answer enchants him, and he falls in love with her mild and unreproachful speech as much as with her beauty. Later, a fairy appears at the house in disguise as a poor old peasant woman to give Blanche a magic balm for her wound. Her fairy name is Dulcicula – Little Sweet, reminiscent of the *dolce stil novo* of the Italian troubadours. Blanche receives her kindly, even though – Mlle Lheritier is careful to tell us – she does not swallow old wives' tales readily. Alix, the unkind and foul-mouthed stepsister, meanwhile flies off the handle in her fishwife way, and bawls her out in colourful idiom, calling her an old fool, a midwife and a beast in a single tirade.[74] (Mlle Lheritier unconsciously relishes the opportunity to foul her own mouth, it seems, by impersonating the profane Alix.) After this visit the fairy confers the gift of ever-gentle speech on Blanche, and perpetual invective on Alix, thus locking them in their original personalities, rather than working any magical transformation. When another fairy, this time a brilliant court lady, radiant with jewels and silks, later appears by the fountain, she asks to drink. Blanche tilts the vessel to her lips; Alix visiting the fountain refuses with a stream of abuse. In consequence, diamonds and other jewels begin to spill from Blanche's mouth as she speaks, while Alix is condemned to spit toads and snakes and other ingredients of the witches' broth.[75]

The complications and inconsistencies of Mlle Lheritier's tale – Why two fairies? Would Alix really have been so rude to such a grand lady asking for a drink after she knew how Blanche had been rewarded? – can be unravelled if her partisan purposes are kept in mind. The first, seemingly redundant test – the offer of the peasant cure – is much more apt to her argument than the request for water at the well, because it exactly reflects her own belief in taking from the simple folk what is good, with common sense, discrimination and unfailing courtesy. Alix is punished, at this stage, for being *grossère* with the poor. The fairy offering her remedy in the guise of a peasant with a possibly quack medicine is another Mother Goose, the source of pure water that does however need to be filtered. The second, resplendent fairy is called Eloquentia nativa (Native Eloquence) and she meets Mlle Lheritier's need to enter her own text as a new kind of speaking woman. There is no reason for the first fairy not to metamorphose into Eloquentia nativa. But by keeping them distinct, the narrator can occupy the latter's place, and also continue her invitation to Mme de Murat, issued in her preface, to write with native eloquence of native things herself. Eloquentia nativa is an awkward, Spenserian allegorical figure, in the midst of a lively story of virtue rewarded and vice punished, but she represents the issue of language in the present day for the tale's author; she bodies forth the potential gift of female eloquence, of speaking diamonds, not toads, for the modern receivers and disseminators of the tale, among whom Mlle Lheritier counted herself. Mother Goose must learn to speak according to the principles of *civilité*, the aristocratic and *précieux* ideal of proper language, and Mlle Lheritier continues to struggle to align this ideal with feminism. At one moment she pauses to issue another personal challenge, explicitly valuing women's eloquence over classical male oratory: 'I'd just as much like to say that pearl and rubies fell from Blanche's mouth . . . as say that lightning flashes issued from that of Pericles.'[76] As Marc Fumaroli has pointed out, the vindication of the heroine in fairytales often expresses the teller's desire to vindicate the feminine, with which the genre was so closely identified.[77]

Paradoxically, Perrault imitated convincingly the bantering, old-womanly style of tale-telling associated with Mother Goose,[78] while Mlle Lheritier rejected false naïveté in favour of polish. For the feminine in Mlle Lheritier's hands had to conform to certain governing principles of the courtly *douceur* of her title: the toads were black magic, illusion, coarseness, unkindness, colloquial speech or orality and the upstart bourgeoisie; the diamonds were theurgy, or white magic, truth-telling, refinement, kindness and written literature mediating peasant wisdom. The oral character of Mother Goose vanished into the courtly and scripted figure of Eloquentia nativa, who is Mlle

Lheritier's ultimate source figure in a new travesty or disguise, all cleaned up and polished, *poli* – polite.

La Comtesse de Murat did follow her friend Mlle Lheritier's urgings, and wrote several fairytales soon after. She dedicated her *Histoires sublimes et allégoriques* of 1699 to *Les Fées modernes* – modern fairies – and she articulated a subsequent metamorphosis of Mother Goose with great clarity as she addresses them:

> Oldentime fairies . . . no longer appear anything but wags next to you. Their occupations were lowly and childish, and the most significant effects their art brought about was to make people weep pearls and diamonds, blow emeralds out of their noses and spit rubies. Their entertainment was dancing by the light of the moon, turning themselves into Crones, and Cats and Monkeys, and werewolves to terrorize children and weak minds. That's why all that remains today of their Exploits and Deeds are only Mother Goose Tales. They were almost always old, ugly, badly dressed and badly housed; and apart from Mélusine and half a dozen or so like her, all the rest of them were just beggarwomen . . .[79]

Is there any irony in Mme de Murat's *envoi*? or any regret? She certainly puts her finger on the identity of the fairies, the crones, the beggarwomen, the witches and the tale-tellers like Mother Goose. The campaign Mlle Lheritier proclaimed through her tale 'Les Enchantemens de l'éloquence' shows how a woman of independent mind had to manoeuvre between negative and positive images of her sex in order to continue what she was doing and argue for its value and acceptance. She had to sentence the foul-mouthed Alix to failure (she dies abandoned in the woods), eye the peasant's remedy with circumspection, rinse the stories she accepted in the purifying language of the court, disinfect Mother Goose of her associations with babbling and spells, and turn her into Eloquentia nativa, the lifeless but direct predecessor of the Sugar Plum Fairy, or even Tinkerbell. She championed the feminine, but in order to do so successfully, she had to define its virtues very closely, and in some way betray the origins of the very literature she was defending by repudiating the *grossier* in favour of *douceur*, by consuming granny and spitting her out again as diamonds and flowers.

Mlle Lheritier achieved some of the fame and standing she desired. She was the first woman elected to one of the prestigious and exclusive French *académies*, the Académie de Lanternistes of Toulouse, in 1696. She was also admitted, the following year, to the Ricovrati of Padua, who chose nine women for the nine muses to their company.

But she is not read today, paradoxically because the highly refined and embroidered style she chose, the mannered and flowery eloquence she evolved in order to stave off criticisms about unsuitable material in improper hands, have dated and become tedious compared to the flashing and humorous concision of Perrault, who did not have to struggle so hard with the figure of aboriginal female wisdom, Mother Goose, as he could annex her without being confused with her.

It is a shame that Mlle Lheritier is such a prolix and genteel writer, that her flashes of feline wit and her moments of inventive cruelty are few and far between. Her predicament, poised between respectability and exclusion, mirrors that of the contemporary woman writer, which is why I felt I had made a discovery when I first read her and then felt cheated that she lacked the courage to be as robust and earthy and potent as the nurses and old women she invoked, the Mother Geese of tradition. The editor of this volume of essays, Roy Porter, has asked the contributors to reflect upon their own relation to the *lieux de mémoire* they have chosen – otherwise I would continue to hide behind my cerebral quest for Mother Goose. For of course I want Anon. to be a woman, I would like old wives' tales to be just that, for Mother Goose to prove the existence of ancient female narrative, and for the prejudice that clings to old women, to female language and speech, to the very phrase 'old wives' tale' and the folly of Mother Goose to become a matter of history, even though I appreciate, as I hope I have shown, how much power nose-thumbing actually accords to these persistent notions. But the problem of Mother Goose's double tongue remains: is she truly a female storyteller, only now and then in drag, or does the drag constitute a claim on credence, advanced by men invoking something more authentic than themselves? If Mlle Lheritier were as bawdy and comic and knowing as she describes her peasant sources and as the British panto tradition has developed, wouldn't she have fed the prejudices that make old wives' tales suitable fare for none but children? Or would she have been able to overcome that persistent tinge of contempt? I know it to be a mistake to try to occupy some imaginary primordial femaleness, an essentialist *hortus conclusus* where history and law and all the other factors in sexual politics have not gained entry. So Mother Goose is another false trail in the quest for the women's version. Furthermore, there is a distinction between a woman telling a story, and telling a story as a woman, though both run up against the difference femaleness makes. Mother Goose does the latter; she may not have been a woman at all, but only a fantasy of nursery, of nurture, of female magic, of woman at the hearth. She vividly represents in Victorian culture and in our own the continuing mixed feelings both men and women experience about such a voice, such a practice. For a female writer, Mother Goose's presence is a comfort and a source of unease at one and the same time, holding up before us a long history of enchantment on the one hand, of ridicule on the other. Any writer who has identified herself with women's issues knows how she'll trip up over mockery; yet laughter can still be answered in kind, for it has its own retaliatory strength, as a goose knows when she cackles.

NOTES

1 I would like to express my gratitude to the Folklore Society, who did me the honour of inviting me to give the Katherine Briggs Memorial Lecture in 1989. Some of the material in this paper was first presented then, and a version was published: 'Mother Goose Tales: Female Fiction, Female Fact?' in *Folklore*, 1990, vol. 101, no. 1, pp. 3–25.

2 Ryoji Tsurumi, 'The Development of Mother Goose in Britain in the Nineteenth Century', *Folklore*, 1990, vol. 101, no. 1, pp. 28–35; David Mayer III, *Harlequin in his Element: The English Pantomime* (London, 1949), p. 25.

3 *Mother Goose's Melody: Or, Sonnets for the Cradle*, published by John Newbery, ?1780. See article on 'Mother Goose' in Humphrey Carpenter, *Oxford Companion to Children's Literature* (Oxford, 1986), pp. 362ff.

4 'The Comic Adventures of Old Mother Hubbard and her Dog', in Iona and Peter Opie (eds), *A Nursery Companion* (Oxford, 1980), pp. 5–8, 28–31.

5 See E. F. Bleiler's introduction to *Mother Goose's Melodies*, facsimile of the Munroe and Francis copyright 1833 version, for a careful bibliographical account of the different editions published in England and the United States from 1729 to 1845.

6 Attributed to Oliver Goldsmith, in J. Barchilon and H. Pettit, (eds), *The Authentic Mother Goose Tales and Nursery Rhymes* (Denver, 1960).

7 'Advice to her Young Readers', *Tales of Past Times by Old Mother Goose with Morals* (London, York, 1798), pp. 93–4.

8 Charles Perrault, *Contes*, ed. G. Rouger (Paris: Garnier, 1967); the frontispiece was considered 'the soul of a book' in the seventeenth century. See Alastair Fowler, 'The Art of Storing a Mind', review of Mary Carruthers, *The Book of Memory: A Study of Memory in Medieval Culture*, *Times Literary Supplement*, 28 December–3 January 1991, p. 1391.

9 Cyrano de Bergerac, quoted in Mary Elisabeth Storer, *La Mode des contes de fées* (Geneva, 1928), p. 12; Scarron, *Le Virgile travesti, II* (Paris, 1648), quoted in Perrault, *Contes*, p. 53.

10 'The common people give the name tale of old wolf, old wives' tale, Mother Goose tale, tale of the stork, donkeyskin tale, tale to fall asleep on your feet, yellow, blue, violet tale, one-eyed tale, to ridiculous fables such as those with which old people entertain and amuse children.' Quoted by Claire L. Malarte-

Feldman, 'Du Conte de fées littéraire au conte pour enfant', in *Merveilles et Contes*, 1991, vol. 5, no. 2, pp. 235–45.

11 Mme de Sévigné, quoted in Perrault, *Contes*, pp. xxi–xxii.

12 Jean de La Fontaine, *Oeuvres complètes*, ed. Jean-Pierre Collinet (Paris, 1991), vol. 1, pp. 299–300.

13 Compare such Gallic saws on women's chatter as: 'La poule ne doit point chanter devant le coq', from Molière's *Les Femmes savantes*, V, iii; or the earlier lines from Jean de Meung's Roman de la Rose: 'C'est chose qui moult me deplaist,/Quand poule parle et coq se taist.'

14 From Rhodes, by the Pistoxenos Painter, Attic red-figure, *c*.460 BC, on display in the British Museum.

15 La Fontaine, 'L'Oraison de St Julien': 'La petite loie; enfin ce qu'on appelle/En bon français les préludes d'amour' (*Oeuvres complètes*, p. 135).

16 Charles Perrault, *Le Labyrinthe de Versailles* (Paris, 1677).

17 Charles Perrault, *Fables in English and French. Translated from Original Latin of Gabriel Faerno* (London, 1741).

18 Perrault, *Contes*, p. 3.

19 Lucius Apuleius, *The Golden Ass, with English translation by William Aldington*, Loeb edition (London, 1915); also *The Transformations of Lucius, otherwise known as The Golden Ass*, trans. Robert Graves (London, 1952; Harmondsworth, 1970), pp. 95–6.

20 Perrault, *Contes*, pp. 6–7 (my translation).

21 For instance, *Histories of Past Times, Told by Mother Goose with Morals, 'Englished' by G. H. Gent* (Salisbury, 1802); also, *Tales of Past Times from Mother Goose*, Ross's Juvenile Library (Edinburgh, 1805); Julia Corner, *The Little Play of Mother Goose*, illus. Harrison Weir (n.d.); *Familiar Selections from the Rhymes of Mother Goose with New Pictures by Chester Loomis*, (London, 1888); Kate Greenaway, *Mother Goose, or the Old Nursery Rhymes*, printed Edmund Evans (n.d).

22 *Perrault's Popular Tales*, ed. and trans. Andrew Lang (Oxford, 1888), p. vii.

23 *Old Mother Goose*, Routledge 3d. Toy Book; *The History of Old Mother Goose and her Son Jack*.

24 Iona and Peter Opie (eds), *The Oxford Dictionary of Nursery Rhymes* (Oxford, 1977), p. 316.

25 *Pasquil's Jests Mixed with Mother Bunch's Merriments* (1604); *Mother Bunch's Closet Broke Open*; see Carpenter, *Oxford Companion*, p. 364.

26 Wellesley College; Jan Steen, 'David Returning Triumphant', Statens Museum for Kunst, Copenhagen. See Pat Rogers, 'Gulliver's Glasses', in *Eighteenth Century Encounters: Studies in Literature and Society in the Age of Walpole* (Sussex, 1985), pp. 1–10, esp. p. 5; *The Authentic Mother Goose Tales*, p. vii.

27 Cathérine Clément, 'The Guilty One', in Hélène Cixous and Cathérine Clément, *The Newly Born Woman*, trans. Betsy Wing (Manchester, 1975), p. 33.

28 The writer Angela Carter, in one of her last pieces before she died in February 1992, evoked the Pantomime Dame: 'Double-sexed and self-sufficient, the Dame, the sacred transvestite of Pantoland, manifests him/herself in a number of guises . . . He/she bestrides the stage. His/her enormous footsteps resonate with the antique past. She brings with him the sacred terror inherent in those of his/her avatars such as . . . the sacrificial priest who, in the Congo, dressed like a woman and was called: "Grandma"' ('In Pantoland', *Guardian*, 24 December 1991).

29 See E. Tietze-Conrat, *Dwarfs and Jesters in Art* (Oxford, 1957).

30 Carpenter, *Oxford Companion*, pp. 364–5.

31 In *To The Lighthouse* Mrs Ramsay tells the story of The Fisherman's Wife. (I am very grateful to Roy Foster for recalling this to me.)

32 George Eliot, *Felix Holt* (London, 1866), ch. 42. I am grateful to Roy Palmer for citing this to me.

33 See Rudolf M. Dekker, 'Women in Revolt: Popular Protest and its Social Basis in Holland in the Seventeenth and Eighteenth Centuries', *Theory and Society*, 1987, vol. 16, pp. 337–62 at p. 353.

34 See Pierre, Abbé de Villiers, *Entretiens sur les contes de fées et sur quelques autres ouvrages du temps. Pour servir de préservatif contre le mauvais goût* (Paris, 1699); also Paul Bonnefon, 'Les dernières années de Charles Perrault', *Revue d'histoire littéraire de la France*, 1906, vol. 13, pp. 606–57.

35 Louis Marin, 'La Voix d'un conte: entre La Fontaine et Perrault, sa récriture', in *Littératures*, 1980, vol. 36, no. 394, pp. 333–42, and Hélène Cixous, 'Sorties', in *The Newly Born Woman*, inspired the idea of this connection.

36 Mme la Comtesse D'Aulnoy was the first to write down a *conte*, framed by her novel *L'Histoire d'Hippolyte* of 1690, and many others followed suit: Mme la Comtesse de Murat, Mlle de la Force, Mme d'Auneuil, and Mme de Villeneuve, who wrote the first 'Beauty and the Beast'. The material of the tales often reveals a female bias, not just in the gender of famous protagonists, but in the experience they record: 'Tom Thumb' could be read as a story about the hardships of marriage to a blundering ogre who mistakes his own children for his supper.

37 Marie-Jeanne Lheritier de Villandon, *Bigarrures ingénieuses, ou Recueil de diverses pièces galantes en prose et en vers* (Paris, 1696) (also known as *Oeuvres Meslées*); *La Tour ténébreuse et les jours lumineux. Conte Anglois, accompagnés d'Historiettes, et tirez d'une ancienne Chronique composée par Richard, Coeur de Lion* (Paris, 1705). See also Storer, *La Mode des contes de fées*, pp. 44ff; Paul Delarue, 'Les Contes merveilleux de Perrault: Faits et rapprochements nouveaux', *Arts et traditions populaires*, 1954, no. 1 (January–March), pp. 1–22; no. 3 (November), pp. 250–74.

38 Jeanne Roche-Mazon, *Les Fées de Perrault et la véridique Mère l'Oye* (Paris, 1968), p. 158.

39 Lheritier, *La Tour ténébreuse*, pp. 236ff.

40 Lheritier, *Bigarrures*, pp. 169ff. See, for instance, Charles Perrault, *Les Contes de fées*, in the 'Librairie pittoresque de la jeunesse' (Paris, 1847).

41 'Un récit sans façon et comme on parle': Lheritier, *Bigarrures*, p. 169.

42 'Je ne cherche que quelque moralité . . . vous y verrez comment nos Ayeux savoient insinuer qu'on tombe dans mille désordres': ibid., p. 169.

43 See Jack Zipes, 'Introduction', in *Beauties, Beasts and Enchantment: Classic French Fairy Tales*, trans. Jack Zipes (New York, 1989), pp. 1–12.

44 Lheritier, *Bigarrures*, p. 171.

45 Ancient Gaul urges you/Stoop to bring to light these tales,/So ingenuous, though cunningly wrought,/Which the troubadours invented: ibid. p. 171.

46 For a while I hoped that the morphology of *Oie* was related to *Oil*, as in *Langue d'oil* or French as it was spoken in the north, and that *La mère l'oye* was a corruption of *la mère l'oil* – this fancy, it seems, might be all right in a fairytale, but is out of place elsewhere.

47 'Ces Contes se sont remplis d'impuretez en passant dans la bouche du petit

peuple; de même qu'une eau pure se charge toujours d'ordures en passant par un canal sâle. Si les gens du peuple sont simples, ils sont grossiers aussi: ils ne sçavent pas ce que c'est que bien-séance. Passez légèrement sur une action licencieuse et pleine de scandale, le récit qu'ils en feront ensuite se remplit de toutes ces circonstances. On racontoit des actions criminelles pour une bonne fin, qui étoient de montrer qu'elles étoient toujours punies; mais le peuple, de qui nous les tenons, les rapporte sans aucun voile, et il les a même si bien liées au sujet ainsi dévoilées, qu'il n'en coûte pas peu à present pour raconter ce mêmes aventures et les enveloper': Lheritier, *Bigarrures*, p. 241.

48 'Une Dame très instruite des antiquitez Grècques et Romaines, et encore plus savante dans les antiquitez Gauloises, m'a fait ce Conte quand j'etais enfant': ibid., p. 112.

49 'une de ces Fables gauloises qui viennent en droite ligne des Conteurs ou Troubadours de Provence': ibid., p. 112.

50 Ibid., p. 3.

51 See Rudolf Dekker and Lotte van de Pol, 'Republican Heroines: Cross-dressing women in the French Revolutionary Armies', *History of European Ideas*, vol. 10, no. 3, pp. 353–63, n. 23 for full details of the translations of Prechac's tale.

52 Lheritier, *Bigarrures*, p. 221.

53 See Storer, *La Mode des contes de fées*, Lang, *Perrault's Popular Tales* and Delarue, 'Les Contes merveilleux de Perrault' for Perrault's position in the quarrel; also, C. A. Walckenaer, 'Lettres sur les contes de fées attribués à Perrault, et sur l'origine de la féerie', in *Les Contes de Charles Perrault* (Paris, 1826), pp 203–61.

54 Charles Perrault, *Oeuvres Posthumes* (Paris, 1706), pp. 358ff.

55 Lheritier, *Bigarrures*.

56 See Antonia Fraser, *The Weaker Vessel* (London, 1985), illus. f.p. 101.

57 Ibid., p. 114.

58 Christina Larner, *The Enemies of God: The Witchhunt in Scotland* (London, 1981); Alan Macfarlane, 'Witchcraft in Tudor and Stuart Essex', in Mary Douglas (ed.), *Witchcraft: Confessions and Accusations* (London, 1970), pp. 81–99.

59 See Rudolf M. Dekker, 'Women in Revolt: Popular Protest and its Social Basis in Holland in the Seventeenth and Eighteenth Centuries', *Theory and Society* 1987, vol. 16, pp. 337–62 for informal, female lines of communication in Holland.

60 I am grateful to Alison Stewart of the Photograph Archive at the Getty Center for the History of Art and the Humanities for leading me to this imagery.

61 My thanks to Roger Malbert, who showed me this print which is included in the exhibition he organized and selected for the South Bank Centre, London, 'Folly and Vice', 1989–90.

62 See, for instance, *The Cabinet of Amusement and Instruction*, published by J. Harris (London, 1819). The artist is probably Robert Branston. Opie and Opie, *A Nursery Companion*, pp. 40–43, 123–4.

63 Noah Webster, *The Prompter, or Common Sayings, and Subjects, which are full of common sense, the best sense in the world* (London, 1808). See Gumuchian et Cie., *Les Livres de l'enfance. A Catalogue of 15th to 19th Century Books*, 2 vols (Paris, 1930; repr. 1985), vol. 2, pl. 58, fig. 5815.

64 George Cruikshank, *A Fairy Library*, 3 vols (London, 1853–64).

65 *The Arthur Rackham Fairy Book* (London, 1933), illus. f.p. 226.

66 One of more than a thousand variations of Aarne Thompson tale type 480, 'The Kind and Unkind Girls'.

67 See Jack Zipes, *The Trials and Tribulations of Red Riding Hood* (London, 1983) for a full account of the tale's journey and meanings.

68 See also Paul Delarue, 'The Story of Grandmother', in Alan Dundes (ed.), *Little Red Riding Hood: A Casebook* (Madison, 1989), pp. 13–20, and Alan Dundes, 'Interpreting "Little Red Riding Hood" Psychoanalytically', in ibid., pp. 192–236.

69 Geza Roheim, 'Fairy Tale and Dream: "Little Red Riding Hood"', in ibid. pp. 159–67.

70 Werner von Bülow, quoted in Dundes, *Little Red Riding Hood*, p. 239.

71 *The Fairy Tales of Charles Perrault*, trans. Angela Carter (New York, 1977), p. 28.

72 Perrault, *Contes*, ed. Rouger, p. 105.

73 Perrault turned this particular tale more concisely and more memorably in his collection as 'Les Fées', sometimes known as 'The Fairy', and by folklorists as 'Diamonds and Toads'. But specialists – notably Paul Delarue – have examined the manuscript evidence and convincingly shown that Perrault must have had the story from Mlle Lheritier, and adapted it. The Grimm Brothers collected a variation of it in their 'Three Little Men in a Wood' (no. 13). Their plot does not turn as narrowly on the question of proper language as in the earlier French versions, but more on proper conduct. See *The Complete Grimms' Fairy Tales* (London, 1975), pp. 78–83.

74 Ibid., p. 147.

75 Perrault tidied up the plausibility and the dynamics of the story, introducing a single fairy in a single test of the protagonists: both girls meet her disguised as a beggarwoman at the well, and react in their own way. But both narrators coldbloodedly despatch Alix to the same end.

76 'J'aime autant dire qu'il sortait des perles et des rubis de la bouche de Blanche, pour désigner les effets de l'Eloquence, que de dire qu'il sortoit des éclairs de celle de Periclès': Lheritier, *Bigarrures*, pp. 164–5.

77 See Marc Fumaroli, 'Les enchantements de l'éloquence: Les Fées de Charles Perrault, ou de la littérature', in Marc Fumaroli (ed.), *Le Statut de la Littérature: Mélanges offerts à Paul Bénichou* (Geneva, 1982), pp. 153–86.

78 See Sanjay Sircar, 'The Victorian Auntly Narrative Voice and Mrs. Molesworth's Cuckoo Clock', *Children's Literature*, 1989, vol. 17, pp. 1–24, for the continuation of this traditional tone.

79 'Les anciennes Fées . . . ne passent plus que pour des badines auprès de vous. Leurs occupations étoient basses et puériles . . . et les effets les plus considérables de leur Art se terminaient à faire pleurer des perles et des diamants, moucher des émeraudes et cracher des rubis. Leur divertissement étoit de danser au clair de la lune, de se transformer en Vieilles, en Chats, en Singes, et en Moynes-bourus, pour faire peur aux enfans et aux esprits foibles. C'est pourquoy tout ce qui nous reste aujourd'huy de leurs Faits et Gestes ne sont que des Contes de Ma Mère L'Oye. Elles étoient presque toujours vieilles, laides, mal vêtues et mal logées; et hors Mélusine et quelque demy douzaine de ses semblables, tout le reste n'étoient que des gueuses . . .': Mme de Murat, *Histoires Sublimes et allégoriques* (Paris, 1699), preface.

3

THE FIFTH OF NOVEMBER REMEMBERED
David Cressy

Unlike new nations that celebrate their independence, or old nations that commemorate their revolutions, the English observe no national anniversary to focus and express their patriotism. St George's Day is virtually meaningless; the Queen's birthday has limited appeal; and none of the great national victories, from Agincourt to the Armada, from Trafalgar to the Battle of Britain, operates in the calendar or in consciousness like the Fourth of July in America or the Fourteenth of July in France. Much of the festive energy available for such occasions has been devoted, instead, to commemorations of the Fifth of November.

Of all historical providences engrained in the memory of English Protestants, the discovery of the Gunpowder Plot on the eve of 5 November 1605 was the most enduring. Other events of the Tudor and Stuart period may have been more important, but the story of Guy Fawkes's attempt to blow up King and Parliament with gunpowder was most widely and systematically remembered. The annual celebration of its defeat enlivened autumns from the Jacobean period to the Victorian. In an attenuated form we remember it still.

Everyone raised in England knows the rhyme, 'Remember, remember, the fifth of November, Gunpowder, Treason and Plot; I see no reason why Gunpowder Treason should ever be forgot.' And an older generation may recall the more aggressive alternative, 'Penny for the Guy, Hit him in the eye, Stick him up a lamp-post [or chimney] and there let him die.'[1] For almost 400 years the English have commemorated the unsuccessful attempt by Guy Fawkes and his associates to blow up the Houses of Parliament. And on the eve of the twenty-first century we still celebrate Guy Fawkes' Day or

Bonfire Night with fireworks and bonfires, ritualized begging, charitable collecting, costuming, masking, mischief, the burning of effigies and the recitation of doggerel verse. The character of the celebration may have shifted from religious exaltation to rowdy disturbances, from ruffians' activity to quaint English custom, but the commemorative action endures.

A series of questions springs to mind, and this essay begins to explore some of them. Why is the only annual firework celebration in the English popular calendar associated with the collapse of a seventeenth-century Roman Catholic conspiracy? What does the commemoration mean, and what different meanings have attached to it in the past? What kind of memory has been perpetuated, through what processes and for what purposes? What was the role played by Church and state, political parties and radical groups, newspapers and community organizations, in orchestrating and interpreting the celebration? When did the various names for the anniversary – 'Gunpowder Treason Day', 'Guy Fawkes' Day', 'Firework Night', etc. – come into use, and what cultural and political freight did they carry? How was a highly charged national Protestant calendrical memory created in the seventeenth century, and how has it been sustained, manipulated, altered and appropriated, between the Jacobean period and the present? How deeply embedded was the memory of 1605, and to what degree were the commemorations self-consciously 'kept up'? To what extent did the Gunpowder Plot commemoration create a common and cohesive festival that gave unity to English popular culture, and to what degree was it used, by contrast, to express sectional, partisan, political, social and confessional antagonisms? Was it, in its Victorian manifestation, an exclusively local opportunity for a rough plebeian charivari, or was it still influenced by national debates about politics and religion?[2] Whose festival was it, and where is it situated in the interplay between elite and popular cultures?

Much speculative nonsense has been written about the bonfire traditions that developed around the anniversary of the Gunpowder Plot on 5 November. Folklorists, anthropologists and historians have often claimed that Guy Fawkes Day is a secular replacement of the Ancient Celtic and Nordic fire festivals of Samhain or *nod-fyr* (need-fire). The medieval Church absorbed these pagan festivals and transformed them into the Christian holy days of the Eve of All Hallows (Hallowe'en) and All Souls' Day. But much of the pre-Christian meaning is said to have lingered in an attenuated form. Besides its nominal religious content, the occasion stood out as a harvest festival and a marker of the end of summer, when there might be debris or surplus materials to burn. Bonfires were lit, it is believed, to strengthen the power of the waning sun. With the decay of All Hallows in England after the Reformation, the argument continues, the people found it convenient to transfer their festivity (and their fires) to the newly appointed Gunpowder Treason day.

The folkloric theory, set forth under the influence of Sir James Frazer's *Golden Bough*, was that 'Guy Fawkes' Day' exemplified 'the recrudescence of old customs in modern shapes'. It was 'a decadent survival' with 'maimed rites' of an ancient agricultural festival that was taken over for 'ecclesiastico-political' purposes in the seventeenth century. Modern celebrations of the Fifth of November in South Yorkshire, Lancashire and Derbyshire are supposedly linked to 'an old feast held in honour of the Scandinavian god Thor'. Some folk-lorists have even suggested that the burning of Guy Fawkes in effigy was 'the commemoration of a pre-Christian human sacrifice', a rem-nant of an ancient primitive religion.[3]

The first part of the story is doubtless true. Given the propensity in human culture to adapt existing materials, the claim that an ancient autumn festival lies behind the Christian observances of All Hallows has strong plausibility. But there is no historical evidence to support the notion that Guy Fawkes' Day shares these origins. The choice of 5 November for Gunpowder Treason Day comes from the timing of the opening of Parliament and the discovery of the Gunpowder Plot, and had nothing to do with the continuing obser-vance of ancient fire festivals. There is barely a flicker of evidence for autumn fires in England at the beginning of the seventeenth century; and although eighteenth- and nineteenth-century observers could point to rustic practices involving ritual fires at this time of year, the evidence is unclear as to whether these were survival, revival or invention. Further suspicions are aroused by the observation that most of these bonfires were reported from the Celtic fringe or the north and west, whereas the Guy Fawkes–Gunpowder Plot commem-orations took strongest root in the south and east.

It is, of course, possible that the Gunpowder Treason observances triggered a synapse in the English folk memory, and that they may have sounded echoes of a lost or vestigial tradition. But without evi-dence we cannot support this conclusion. It is more likely that the 5 November bonfires involved the application of an established festive form (the celebratory bonfire) to a new festive occasion sponsored by the state. The burning of effigies (of popes and devils, not of Guy Fawkes) was unknown to the first generation of the Stuart era and was rare before the 1670s; it owes nothing to a putative heritage of human sacrifices. The origins of the festival can be found in the 1606 Act of Parliament, and in the Elizabethan and Jacobean tradition of politicized bell-ringing and celebration. European Renaissance societies lit bonfires as *feux de joi*, to celebrate royal births and marriages, victories and homecomings. They lit them too at midsummer, at midwinter and on holy days, as expressions of joy and gratulation. Protestant England adapted this custom to its particular religious and dynastic celebrations.[4]

In 1605 a group of Catholic gentlemen hatched a desperate plot to kill King James and to overthrow the Protestant regime. The government learned of the plot, and found Guy Fawkes – the man with the match – in the cellars at Westminster with thirty-six barrels of gunpowder. The conspirators were rounded up, tortured and executed. All credit for the discovery was given to God. Parliament passed 'An act for a public thanksgiving to Almighty God every year on the fifth day of November . . . to the end this unfained thankfulness may never be forgotten, but be had in perpetual remembrance'.This is one of the earliest examples of legislated memory, and it provided a model for subsequent acts of commemoration.[5]

The preamble to the legislation lays out the official interpretation:

Forasmuch as almighty God hath in all ages showed his power and mercy in the miraculous and gracious deliverance of his church, and in the protection of religious kings and states, and that no nation of the earth hath been blessed with greater benefit than this kingdom now enjoyeth, having the true and free profession of the gospel under our most gracious sovereign lord King James, the most great learned and religious king that ever reigned therein, enriched with a most hopeful and plentiful progeny proceeding out of his royal loins promising continuance of this happiness and profession to all posterity: the which many malignant and devilish papists, Jesuits, and seminary priests much envying and fearing, conspired most horribly, when the king's most excellent majesty, the queen, the prince, and the lords spiritual and temporal, and commons, should have been assembled in the upper house of Parliament upon the fifth day of November in the year of our lord 1605 suddenly to have blown up the said whole house with gunpowder; an invention so inhuman, barbarous and cruel, as the like was never before heard of.

Special prayers were written, appealing to the 'Lord, who didst this day discover the snares of death that were laid for us, and didst

wonderfully deliver us from the same, be thou still our mighty protector, and scatter our enemies that delight in blood. Infatuate and
defeat their counsels, abate their pride, assuage their malice, and
counfound their devices.' Most parishes purchased the *Form of Prayer
with Thanksgiving to be used yearly upon the Fifth day of November:
For the happy Deliuerance of the King, and the Three Estates of the
Realm, from the most Traiterous and bloody intended Massacre by
Gun-powder.* These anti-Catholic sentiments – a curse as much as a
prayer – remained in the Church of England service book until 1859.[6]

To Jacobean divines the discovery of the plot was a wonderful
providence, a confirmation of God's covenant with England and an
endorsement of the Protestant Stuart dynasty. Remembering it helped
to solidify their sense of the English as a chosen people. Bishop
Lancelot Andrewes preached at Court on the first anniversary, 'this
day of ours, this fifth of November, a day of God's making . . . is
the Scripture fulfilled in our ears . . . the destroyer passed over our
dwellings this day. It is our Passover, it is our Purim.'[7] It was also an
occasion for anti-Catholic vindictiveness and patriotic merry-making.
As far as Church and state were concerned, the Gunpowder Plot
should be remembered for ever.

The physician Francis Herring's remarks were typical: 'The
Powder-treason, that monstrous birth of the Romish harlot, cannot
be forgotten without great impiety and injury to ourselves . . . We
shall be guilty of horrible ingratitude, the foulest of all vices, if we
do not embrace all means of perpetuating the memory of so great, so
gracious, and wonderful a preservation.' The plot represented 'the
quintessence of Satan's policy, the furthest reach and stain of human
malice and cruelty, not to be parallelled among the savage Turks, the
barbarous Indians, nor, as I am persuaded, among the more brutish
cannibals.'[8] Latin poets like John Milton punned on the quintessence
of cruelty, 'in quintum Novembris'.[9]

George Carleton, James I's Bishop of Chichester, explained the
diabolical comprehensiveness of the Gunpowder plotters.

Their hellish device was at one blow to root out religion, to destroy
the state, the father of our country, the mother of our country, the
olive branches the hopeful succession of our king, the reverend clergy,
the honorable nobility, the faithful councillors, the grave judges, the
greatest part of our knights and gentry, the choicest burgesses, the
officers of the crown, council, signet, seals, and other seats of judgement, the learned lawyers, with an infinite number of common people,
the hall of justice, the houses of parliament, the church used for the

coronation of our kings, the monuments of our former princes, all records of parliament, and of every particular man's right, with great number of charters, and other things of this nature, all these things had the devil by his agents devised at one secret blow to destroy.[10]

Their failure was a cause for perpetual rejoicing. Almanacs, histories, litanies and sermons, as well as the ritual celebration of bonfires and bells, helped imprint the memory of the Gunpowder Plot on the English popular consciousness. The commemoration was an act of loyalty as well as piety, with national, dynastic and religious connotations. Many parishes heard sermons on 5 November, and many more augmented the commemoration with public drinking or solemn processions. In some towns, such as Canterbury and Norwich, the celebration of 5 November displayed much of the festive energy that before the Reformation had been reserved for saints' days. The anniversary became a day of indulgence, of drinking and festivity as well as worship and meditation, even though it was never an official day of absence from work.

After 1618 renewed concerns about Catholicism, anxieties about James's pro-Spanish foreign policy and alarm that international Protestantism was in retreat led to sermons calling for greater solemnity and more profound thanksgiving each 5 November. Radical Puritans like Thomas Hooker and moderate episcopalians like George Carleton agreed on the significance of 5 November and the duty of holding it in memory.[11] The opening of Charles I's reign and the renewal of hostilities with Spain saw a remarkable unity among English Protestants which became especially manifest on Gunpowder Treason Day. Parish observances, both festive and solemn, united centre and localities, court and country, in a common patriotic occasion.

But the Gunpowder Treason anniversary soon lost its unifying character and took on an increasingly partisan tone. In the 1630s Charles I, married to a Catholic, found the anti-papist bonfires distasteful, and sought to muffle the commemoration. The Arminian ceremonialists who rose in the Church preferred the old calendar of saints' days to the newer cycle of Protestant deliverances. All of this – plus restored altars, slack sabbaths, and rigid discipline – threw Puritan preachers on to the defensive, and some of them retaliated by re-emphasizing and re-interpreting 5 November. Radicals like the London minister Henry Burton used the anniversary to challenge what they saw as creeping popery, and to stress the need for further reformation.

Burton explained, in the printed version of his sermons, 'I deemed that day, the memorial whereof should cause all loyal subjects forever to detest all innovations tending to reduce us to that religion of Rome, which plotted matchless treason, the most seasonable for this text . . . This is a time of sorrow and humiliation, but this day a day of joy and festivity.' It was time, on 5 November 1636, to recall the true meaning of the deliverance from the Gunpowder Plot, 'a deliverance never to be cancelled out of the calendar, but to be written in every man's heart forever.[12] Formidable collisions took place over the interpretation of 5 November, and Burton's sermon brought him before the High Commission and to the pillory, where he lost a portion of his ears.

In the revolutionary decade of the 1640s the Gunpowder commemoration became charged with new significance as fresh conspiracies were feared or uncovered. Parliamentary sermons on 5 November blended historical and biblical reminiscence with calls to action in England's continuing emergency. Preaching before the House of Commons on 5 November 1644, Charles Herle spoke as if he were preparing the members for combat: 'You must expect to stand in need of more deliverances: the same brood of enemies that then durst venture but an undermining, dare now attempt an open battery.' The Philistine pioneers were tunnelling 'from Oxford, Rome, Hell, to Westminster, and there to blow up, if possible, the better foundations of your houses, their liberties and privileges'. Parliamentarians took possession of the November anniversary, though Royalists disputed their interpretation.[13]

Some features of the Gunpowder commemoration were neglected or suppressed in the revolutionary 1650s. There was awkwardness and uncertainty as to whether the republican regime should commemorate a Stuart dynastic deliverance. But most parishes still rang their bells each 5 November, and preachers adapted their anniversary sermons to the changing conditions. Unofficially, the day was marked by the lighting of bonfires and the exploding of squibs and crackers. On the night of 5 November 1657 the Master of Jesus College, Cambridge, was greeted by a gunpowder squib thrown through his window, by no means the last fireworks disturbance in the university town.[14]

Writing during Oliver Cromwell's Protectorate, Samuel Clarke shared the determination that Gunpowder Treason should never be forgotten. He wrote to the end 'that all sorts may be stirred up to real thankfulness and transmit the same to their posterity; that their children may know the reason why the fifth of November is celebrated; that God may have glory, and the papists perpetual infamy'. Clarke rehearsed the narrative of the plot 'least the remembrance of so signal a mercy and deliverance, vouchsafed by God both to our church and state, should be buried in oblivion'.[15]

But any danger that the anniversary might lapse into oblivion was soon overcome by its continuing utility for religious polemic and political mobilization. Formal observance of the Gunpowder Plot was fully reinstated with the Restoration. The annual thanksgiving was still enjoined by statute, and provided a model for the two new statutory anniversaries of 30 January and 29 May – the one for the execution of Charles, King and martyr; the other for the restoration of his son, the May King, on Royal Oak Day.[16] Officially 5 November marked the preservation of King and Church, and was honoured in these terms by courtiers, high Anglicans and Tories. But in Charles II's reign the anniversary took on alternative and oppositional meanings. By this time the memory of 1605 belonged to political culture at large, and could not be controlled by any one interest.

By the 1670s London apprentices were turning 5 November into a dramatic anti-Catholic fire festival, as well as a challenge to sobriety and good order. They stopped coaches and demanded money for alcohol and bonfires. And in 1673 they paraded an effigy of the Whore of Babylon, decked out with 'all the whorish ornaments' of papal crosses, keys, beads and triple crown, and carried it in a torchlight procession to 'a great bonfire' in the Poultry. Before this date we hear little about the burning of effigies on 5 November, but henceforth they would be a standard feature of the commemoration. Anti-Catholic processions and demonstrations featured effigies of the Pope, his minions, and figures from English history.[17]

At the height of the Popish Plot and the Exclusion struggle the Whig opposition orchestrated elaborate pope-burning processions, while the mob engaged in battles over bonfires and drunken attacks on Catholics' houses. The organized pageantry even had its own souvenir programmes, such as *The manner of the Burning of the Pope in Effigies in London On the 5th of November, 1678, With the manner of carrying him through several Streets, in progression to Temple-Bar, where at length he was decently burned.* Publications of this sort commemorated the commemoration, and reconnected the spectacle of the street with the political discourse of print. The anniversary became politicized, a point of division between Whigs and Tories. And at the same time it was acquiring a folk life of its own, with a vocabulary of symbolic action – including burning effigies and breaking windows – that was barely controlled by the Parliamentary elite.

The accession of a Catholic King in 1685 gave an ironic twist to the observance of anti-Catholic anniversaries. James II's government banned fireworks and tried to limit celebrations, but most parishes kept up their traditions of bellringing, sermons, and bonfires. And after 1688 the anniversary of the landing of William of Orange – significantly but fortuitously on 5 November – focused attention on the double deliverance of liberty and religion. Celebrations of William's birthday on 4 November became entwined with commemorations of his landing on the fifth. In a further mutation, the Gunpowder anniversary was harnessed to the struggle against arbitrary government and Jacobite tyranny, as well as popish religion.

By the end of the Stuart period the Gunpowder anniversary had become a polysemous occasion, replete with polyvalent cross-referencing, meaning all things to all men. In the calendar of Court and Parliament it was a day of thanksgiving and prayer, with appropriate appearances and feasting; the legislation of 1605 was still in force, and ministers recited the prayers calling God to scatter England's enemies. High Anglicans used the occasion to recall God's blessings on the established Church and to warn of the danger from dissenters; others warned of the continuing danger from Rome; Jacobites raised glasses to the Stuart dynasty, recalling the deliverances of 1605 and 1660; the Whigs made 5 November a holiday to enjoy the blessings of the revolution. And below the level of the politically and religiously engaged elite, common people in town and country lit bonfires and threw fireworks, drank heavily and settled their own scores under the cover of England's unique anniversary.[18]

During most of the eighteenth century the courtly, parliamentary and civic observances of the Gunpowder Plot were dutiful but muted. Customary routine preserved the Fifth of November as a 'holiday at all the public offices', but much of the fire had gone out of it, as just one among forty-nine official holidays.[19] The new Hanoverian elite had diminishing interest in seventeenth-century religious deliverances, so long as church and state were secure. As far as high society and high politics were concerned in Walpole's time, the Gunpowder anniversary had shed most of its meaning. Whigs might still reflect on the liberties that were secured on 5 November, though they were more inclined to remember 1688 than 1605; Tories might still recall dynastic history and the salvation of the Church of England. But public attention was directed towards formulaic observance, rather than impassioned political or religious memory. Were it not for the service books and the almanac, it is possible that Gunpowder Treason would have been forgot.

Eighteenth-century almanacs continued to mark the day in red letters, but with more respect to antiquarian than to present concerns. (Almanacs were often the most archaic of publications.) Often the Gunpowder anniversary became submerged beneath other, current enthusiasms that adopted a similar vocabulary of celebration. In 1741, for example, *The Gentleman's Magazine* reported no domestic occurrences on 5 November, but the following Thursday, 'being the birthday of Admiral Vernon, was distinguished with ringing of bells, bonfires, and illuminations in the cities of London and Westminster, Liverpool, etc.'[20] The Fifth of November observances in the 1760s were overshadowed by John Wilkes's birthday on 28 October, the Duke of Cumberland's birthday on 7 November, and by the ceremonies for the Lord Mayor's Day or the opening of Parliament. *An Almanac for . . . 1775*, showed thirteen red-letter days in November, including the birthdays of Prince Edward, the Duke of Cumberland, the princess Sophia Augusta and the Duke of Gloucester, as well as the day of the 'Papists Conspiracy'.

In most years under George II and George III the anniversary thanksgiving was observed with no more than 'the usual solemnity'; the Park and Tower guns were fired, and the evening concluded with 'bonfires, illuminations, ringing of bells' and fireworks on the river. Gunpowder Treason had became a state-sponsored spectacle, a polite entertainment rather than an occasion for vitriolic thanksgiving. Only in 1745, with Charles Stuart's rebellion, did 5 November resume its old flavour of mockery, defiance and religious venom.[21]

Below the level of the elite, however, other groups invested the anniversary with social and political meanings of their own. Class hostilities took cultural form, as the Gunpowder commemoration developed into a festival of order against disorder, of respectability against misrule. The Fifth of November provided an annual occasion for the contest between rowdiness and discipline, a ritualized challenge to hierarchical power, in which the events of 1605 were largely forgotten. It barely mattered that Guy Fawkes had been a Catholic, or that the conspirators had tried to blow up Parliament. Now the historical anniversary served as a pretext for violence, a cover for challenges to the established order. Establishment politicians withdrew their sponsorship leaving young working men in temporary possession of the streets.

Newspapers complained of outrages and affronts to civility, though from different perspectives the same behaviour might be seen as cheerful good-fellowship and letting off of steam, or the articulation of class antagonisms. Enthusiasts lit bonfires in defiance of local authorities, and celebrants enlivened firework displays by throwing 'serpents', squibs and crackers among the crowd.[22] Masked revellers ran wild and revenged themselves on unpopular or uncharitable neighbours by breaking windows and burning fences. It was time for settling scores, whether personal or socio-economic.

On 5 November 1766 'a dreadful fire broke out at Kettering in Northamptonshire, occasioned by the boys throwing squibs . . . The common people, instead of joining to extinguish the flames, called out tauntingly to a farmer whose ricks were on fire, "Now, farmer, will you sell your wheat at seven and sixpence a strike?"' Almost a century later the mob at Guildford asserted a different moral economy by making their Guy Fawkes' bonfire from the palings of a sports ground proprietor who charged too much for admission.[23]

On Gunpowder Night in the late eighteenth century 'greasy rogues' intimidated politer Londoners, and bonfire boys dunned passers-by for money. Youths outraged their elders and 'roughs' and 'ruffians' menaced householders in other towns. Respectable tradesmen complained of 'the swarm of boys' who extracted contributions, and solid citizens braced against the depredations of 'blackguards' and pickpockets. Mobs of 'idle fellows' caused 'great annoyance' to 'the public' and to the magistrates who feared their 'depredations and disorders' as artisans and apprentices took temporary possession of the streets.[24] (The middle-class writers who provided these newspaper accounts had no doubts about their own socio-cultural affiliations.)

For both children ard adults the anniversary of the Gunpowder Plot provided a temporary privileged arena in which ordinary standards of lawfulness and civility could be set aside. It was commonly believed that reciting the verses for 5 November – 'Remember, remember' – licensed the bullying of passers-by into giving money. Wood could be stolen, fences broken down, so long as it became fuel for the bonfire. In some country parishes villagers claimed the right to hunt over private ground on 5 November. Magistrates and property-owners disagreed.

In 1785 the traditional bonfire celebration at Lewes in Sussex degenerated into a riot and severely divided the community. 'Wicked, obstinate and malicious persons' alarmed 'the principal inhabitants' of Arlesford on that same 5 November 1785, when 'a lawless mob . . . pelted the Justice and constables with stones, brickbats and sticks'. Only the fortitude of the magistrate, bailiff and principal inhabitants, so it was claimed, prevented 'a dangerous insurrection'.[25]

The social challenge of Guy Fawkes' Day continued into the nine-teenth century. 'Ruffianism, theft, and riotous conduct' were standard features of the Dickensian 5 November. A correspondent from Lewes complained in 1847 of the 'the grossest riots and excess' that took over the town each year. 'Ruffians' intimidated respectable house-holders. 'Bonfire boys' in masks and 'fantastical dress' and armed with bats and bludgeons rolled lighted tar barrels through the streets. Lewes took Guy Fawkes' Night seriously, and its annual bonfires were long believed to have been lit 'from time immemorial'. But other towns, especially in southern England, developed equally vigor-ous traditions. At Guildford gangs of bonfire celebrants calling them-selves 'guys' put the town under siege during their 5 November 'lark'. 'Respectable tradesmen' and 'peaceable inhabitants' barred their doors against 'facetious rustics' and the menacing 'guys' during these annual 'riotous proceedings'. The immediate memory centred on local grudges, excess and damage, rather than historical or ideo-logical recollections.[26]

Guy Fawkes himself had always featured in the narrative of the Gunpowder Plot, but during the seventeenth century when it came to parading and burning effigies the figure of Guy was upstaged by the Pope and the devil. By the end of the eighteenth century, however, Guy Fawkes had emerged as the principal figure to be displayed and burned in effigy; and early in the nineteenth century Gunpowder Treason Day became 'Guy Fawkes' Day', informally renamed in his honour. By the accession of Queen Victoria the autumn fire festival was invariably known as 'Guy Fawkes' Day',[27] and twentieth-century folklorists seem not to know it as anything else.

The Times reported in 1788 that 'Guy Faux in his usual state was carried about the streets in commemoration of the gunpowder plot.' In 1790 the newspaper mentioned boys 'begging for money to burn Guy Faux'. In 1792 'Guy Faux was burned by the populace', and so on. The desperado with the tall hat and dark lantern (both objects now on view at Oxford's Ashmolean museum), became a familiar figure on the autumn streets and in country towns and villages. William Cobbett, on his rural ride through Kent, remarked on the annual burning of 'Guy Fawkes, the pope and the devil'.[28] As anti-Catholic agitation and historical memory subsided, Guy Fawkes took on the roles of all-purpose bogeyman and carnival grotesque. Children made their own versions with rags and paper (as they do today), but early Victorian technology inspired novel representations. In 1839 The Times reported: 'A machine twelve feet in height, constructed with tissue, filled with hydrogen gas, and representing the figure of Guy Fawkes . . . rose in a perpendicular manner' over Pentonville and drifted south over the City. It was last seen heading across the river towards Kent.[29]

A recurrent refrain in the nineteenth century was that the celebration of the Gunpowder Plot had declined. From time to time throughout Victoria's reign the newspapers claimed that the bonfire festivity no longer matched the livelier celebrations of yesteryear. Without ideological passion or organized force to drive it, the annual commemoration was indifferently 'kept up'. In 1834 *The Times* noted that the 'fiery zeal' of the Fifth of November had 'gradually decreased, and neither men nor boys any longer take a part or interest in such observance of the day.' The Gunpowder Plot had lost its religious and patriotic meaning, 'and children carry about their "poor Guy" with no other sentiment or knowledge respecting him than that his exhibition procures them a few pence'. A magistrate who dealt with a Guy Fawkes' Day affray in 1839 'said, he thought the day was almost forgotten'. In 1843 a correspondent wrote that 'the observance of the fifth of November has been considerably on the decline for some time'. Even the association of Guy Fawkes 'with little boys and fireworks . . . has subsided of late'. In 1850 *The Times* described the anniversary as 'of late years almost forgotten'. Again in the 1860s the occasion was 'but indifferently observed'.[30] The anniversary 'passed off very tamely' in 1877, and *The Times* remarked on the tameness of Guy Fawkes' Day in each of the next few years. Activities on 5 November 1882 were lamentably 'of the tamest kind', with 'few grown lads or adults' taking part. By 1884 it appeared that 'the observance of the day' in London was 'gradually dying out'.[31] In fact Gunpowder Treason Day was changing again, not dying, and its apparent subsidence or tameness reflected other Victorian trends.

Revived religious antagonisms lent new power to the Gunpowder anniversary as Irish Catholics settled among Protestant Londoners. Guy Fawkes provided a mask for ethnic, social and religious confrontations. In 1838,

> the effigy of Guy Fawkes was carried by some boys followed by a crowd of others into a court inhabited chiefly by Irish coal-whippers and ballast-getters; who taking umbrage at the appearance of the effigy, and the shouts of the children calling out 'No popes' and 'Pray remember the fifth of November', were attacked by a number of Irish boys, who captured poor Guy and carried him off in triumph. The

protestant boys obtained a reinforcement and made an attack on the
'Popes', as they called the catholic boys, and succeeded in regaining
the effigy. The two parties commenced flinging stones at each other.

And later in the Victorian era there would again be affrays involving
Irish labourers and a belligerent 'party with Guys'.[32] Whether these
collisions were more acute in areas like Liverpool has yet to be
examined.

Catholic emancipation in 1829 and the advance of 'the Popish
interest' in early Victorian politics also redirected attention to older
religious issues. Conservative ministers took to their pulpits and
made sure that the anti-Catholic service for the Fifth of November
was vigorously observed. Popular histories revived the story of Guy
Fawkes and the Gunpowder Treason. The call in the 1830s to 'Prefer
the religion of the Bible to the blasphemies of the Vatican' echoed
confessional tensions of the seventeenth century.[33] But it is a mark of
the diminution of religious conflict that when in 1833 the Houses of
Parliament actually burned down, by accident, there was no rush to
blame the Catholics, and no explicit association of the disaster with
the Gunpowder Plot.

The re-establishment of a Catholic hierarchy and the revival of
papal dignities in England in 1850 triggered a fresh round of protestant sermons on the 'errors of popery' and the 'aggressions of Rome'.
Conservative Anglicans lent support to popular radical opinion, as
local and national issues intertwined. Anti-Catholic demonstrators
took to the streets on 5 November with placards proclaiming 'no
wafer gods' and 'no catholic humbug'. The 'Papal Aggression' of
1850 sparked firework disturbances at Towcester, Kettering, and
Northampton. Opposition to the Roman revival produced an elaborate anti-Catholic pageant and bonfire in the cathedral yard at
Exeter, where figures of the Pope and his officers were consigned to
the flames. Elsewhere in England 'the bonfires were double in number
and more than double in size those of former years'. Old men
remarked that they had never seen such a 5 November as that of
1850. Not surprisingly, more Guys were reported in London on Guy
Fawkes' Day 1850 than in recent memory.[34]

In this new climate a movement grew to remove rather than to
revive the service for 5 November, and with it the obsolete services
for 30 January and 29 May. Some liberals found the seventeenth-century language 'offensive to the feelings of our catholic fellow subjects', or 'utterly repugnant to the religious feeling of the present
day'. The institutionalized memory, they argued, was divisive and

anachronistic. Hard-line conservatives, of course, disagreed. In Dublin one zealous Protestant even tried to bring an action under the Act of Uniformity against a minister who omitted the special service for 5 November, but neither local magistrates nor the Queen's Bench in London would take up the case. As the Archbishop of Canterbury observed in 1858, the service was 'irregularly disregarded' and had 'fallen into desuetude'.[35]

During 1858 and 1859 the matter was before Parliament, and Lords and Commons debated the removal of the 'political' services that were still enshrined in statute. The speeches reported in *Hansard* reveal divided opinion on the value of remembering the Fifth of November, but general agreement that the time had come for change. George Hadfield, the Liberal member for Sheffield, found the ancient services 'offensive to every Christian', and was astonished that the statutes requiring them 'should have remained in existence for so many years'. Even the Bishop of London acknowledged that the wording of the special prayers was 'likely to call up feelings of indignation in the breasts of their fellow countrymen.'[36]

Leading the campaign for repeal, Lord Stanhope

> did not for an instant deny that the deliverance of the sovereign and both houses of parliament from a sudden and cruel attack of conspirators was an act of providential mercy deserving to be held in grateful remembrance, and for which thanks were due to almighty God; nor was he inclined to speak in other terms than those of gratitude for the political and religious benefits which this country derived from the landing of King William III; but he submitted to their lordships that in all questions of this kind the lapse of time was a most important element. No man would think, for example, of celebrating by special thanks the expulsion of the Danes by King Alfred, or the return of Coeur de Lion from captivity.[37]

The Duke of Marlborough was reluctant to see change, and suggested that 'even if the services themselves were expunged, some memorial ought to be retained in the liturgy of the church of the events therein commemorated.' These events, he insisted,

> were great events, calling for some solemn acknowledgement of gratitude, and [he told the Lords] he should be sorry to see the recollection of those events done away with in the future, and the matter passed over in silence. The particular mode of commemoration enjoined by the acts of parliament might possibly not be suited to the present day,

but a mode might have been adopted which would have answered all the required purpose in duly testifying the national gratitude for these great events.[38]

Finally, the Anniversary Days Observance Act became law in March 1859, and a tradition of two and a half centuries' duration came to a close. Observance of the Fifth of November was removed from the calendar of the established Church of England, to continue henceforth as an unofficial and secular tradition.[39]

Much of the vitality of Gunpowder Treason Day from year to year came from its utility as a vehicle for dramatizing current political concerns. The street theatre of placards and processions, crowds and disguises, effigies and bonfires lent itself to the derisive depiction of political figures who had played no part in the original drama of the seventeenth century.

In 1745, after the Stuart rebellion, the fading anniversary of 5 November was revived by burning effigies of the Pope and the Pretender. In 1785 'the greasy rogues' of London 'dressed up a tall thin figure and . . . instead of "pray remember the fifth of November," the cry was "pray remember Pitt and the shop tax."' In 1788, it was reported, 'some arch dogs carried a Charles Fox' in the same manner as effigies of Guy Fawkes, 'and exalted him at the bonfire'. In 1792 it was the turn of the Duke of Brunswick.[40] The Revolution Society held its annual dinner on 5 November, with toasts to the French Revolution. The date was a popular dining night for Orange lodges. The anti-Catholic agitations of 1850 produced effigies of Pope Pius IX and the new Cardinal Archbishop of Westminster, along with 'St Guy the martyr'. The Crimean War years saw burning effigies of Tsar Nicholas on 5 November. Interest in Italian affairs in 1867 produced a pageant of the Pope about to be struck down by Garibaldi on Guy Fawkes' Day. *The Times* reported: 'In many districts the ritualists shared with the pope the honour of being represented as "guys".'[41]

Foreign and imperial affairs brought new figures into the Guy Fawkes pageant. Effigies of the 1870s included Pope Leo XIII, the Tsar of Russia, the Sultan of Turkey, the Amir of Afghanistan, Araby Pasha and the king of the Zulus. The Irish leader Parnell appeared on the bonfires in 1879. As *The Times* wryly noted in 1880, many of the 'guys . . . had nothing to do with the hero of the Gunpowder Plot, but rather burlesqued the incidents of the present time'. Historical memory gave way to current affairs.[42]

The beginning of the twentieth century saw burning effigies of militant suffragists; and in 1909 the Hampstead bonfire featured a placard representing Lloyd George's Budget. Later it was the turn of the Kaiser and Adolf Hitler, among other celebrities, to go up in flames.[43] And in the England of the 1980s, Mrs Thatcher and some of her ministers have been similarly honoured, alongside diabolized third-world bogey men like Saddam Hussein.

From the eighteenth century to the present, local animosities often substituted an unpopular neighbour for the figure of the Guy. The Somerset diarist James Woodforde recorded on 5 November 1768 that 'the effigy of Justice Creed was had through the streets of Castle Cary this evening upon the [fire] engine, and then had into the park and burnt in a bonfire immediately before the Justice's house . . . the whole parish are against the Justice'. Victorian worthies who were similarly burned in effigy included local Members of Parliament, an enemy of the Kettering shoemakers, four 'persons prominent in the Plumstead common agitation', and the disgraced borough councillors of St Albans who had illegally enclosed land in Sandpit Lane.[44]

The riotousness of Guy Fawkes' Night, especially notorious in the late eighteenth and early nineteenth centuries, diminished from the mid-Victorian period as public officials determined to bring the festivities under control. The sale of fireworks was regulated and in some places prohibited. Police and magistrates planned strategies to avoid the worst excesses, contesting with revellers for control of the streets. In 1847 the authorities at Lewes determined to restrain the annual disorder, and brought in extra detachments of police and troops. The result was a series of skirmishes between 'bonfire boys' and the constabulary, with some of the tradesmen taking the revellers' side and others barricading their doors. The authorities at Guildford similarly reinforceed themselves in 1863 with 160 special constables, fifty dragoons, 150 soldiers and two local corps of rifle volunteers in reserve. 'Several bands of roughs' disputed this show of force, but the mayor read the Riot Act (although there was no riot), and constables with drawn truncheons attempted to clear the streets.[45]

Within a few years this policy of intervention paid off; respectability and decorum began to prevail in this area of Victorian life as in so many others. At Godalming in 1870, *The Times* reported, 'the preparations made for the preservation of order were enough to overawe the most determined peace-breakers'. Guildford and Lewes, formerly famous for their extravagance on Guy Fawkes' Night, saw the anniversary pass without incident. At Oxford and Cambridge, where Gunpowder Night violence once pitted town against gown, the proctors and constables worked to prevent serious disturbances. By 1876 it could be claimed that 'the utmost decorum prevailed' at Oxford, and the following year 'the anniversary of the Gunpowder Plot passed off very tamely in the metropolis'. Guy Fawkes' Night had been tamed.[46]

Further changes took place in the late nineteenth century, as the anarchic elements of Guy Fawkes' Night gave way to organized entertainment. The middle class returned to the ceremony, and took over. Bonfires and street activities which had once been the work of 'roughs' and 'idle mobs' now became the planned projects of societies and clubs. Special committees sprang up throughout southern England to mount and to manage the Guy Fawkes celebrations. The 'principal inhabitants' who had earlier withdrawn behind their shutters on 5 November now came forth as proud sponsors. Landowners provided special fields for the bonfires, thereby diverting the most dangerous festivity from the centres of towns. The more menacing aspects of the Guy Fawkes tradition were eliminated, and a spectacle that had once been divisive and dangerous was remade in wholesome and benevolent garb. In several towns the aggressive masking and disguising of an earlier generation was channelled into jolly costume parades.

The Hitchin Bonfire Club organized torchlit parades in which over 400 masqueraders took part. Dorchester enjoyed a procession of costumed 'guys', with music from the town band and a display of fireworks costing fifty pounds – in 1879 the subscribers included Lord Alington and the local MP. At Horsham in 1880 the festivities took place 'with the sanction of the Local Board authorities, and under the patronage of most of the chief families of the town and district'. Bridgwater adopted 5 November for an elaborate, annual carnival. Patriotic processions featured imperial themes. At Winchester the parade was headed by the city fire brigade, while at Salisbury the bonfire was lit by the mayor.[47]

The famous festivity at Lewes became the work of 'four recognised bonfire societies', each with its 'bishop' and commander-in-chief (the Cliffe, Borough, Grand Square and Waterloo societies). Although the local Baptist minister protested against 'heathen mummery' on the Fifth of November, and although there were still risks of the festivity getting out of hand, the overall tenor of the day was one of 'good order and temper' in pursuit of 'pleasure and amusement'. The Lewes carnival became a celebration of the Lewes community, with a ritual parading of territory and a final coming together, rather than a violent commemoration of events in the distant Stuart past.[48]

Previously scattered activities in London coalesced around the organized parades of the Lewisham Bonfire Society in the south and the Hampstead Bonfire Club in the north. Like their counterparts at Hitchin and Lewes, these were social and philanthropic associations, reminiscent of medieval confraternities. A 'novelty' in 1880, the 'annual carnival' at Lewisham quickly became an established tradition. The procession featured bands, fancy dress, the banners of friendly societies and a smiling police escort, but it no longer concluded with a bonfire. On the other side of London the 'cavalcade' of the Hampstead Bonfire Society drew some 50,000 spectators to see costumed equestrians, musicians, a representation of Britannia, and a grand bonfire on the heath. But the bonfire did not necessarily burn a Guy. By the Edwardian era this carnival had become a fund-raising event with 'Ye Olde Hampstead Bonfire Club' (the self-conscious archaism a sure sign of an invented tradition) collecting money for local hospitals.[49]

The anniversary changed again in the twentieth century, with the triumph of the consumer society. Guy Fawkes' Day became 'Firework Night' as commercial manufacturers like Messrs Brock and Paine stepped up production. The Brock company sold 30 million fireworks in 1908: Paine unloaded almost 500 tons. In 1909 a special set piece was available featuring *Dreadnought*, a model of the great battleship which 'explodes with a fiery display'. *The Times* observed that year that 'firework parties are becoming quite an institution in the suburban districts'. In 1910 the demand for fireworks was said to be up 25–30 per cent from the previous year. Firework enthusiasm was set aside during the Great War, 'but resumed in the 1920s, when much of the money-raising activity of children – 'a penny for the Guy' – was intended to purchase fireworks. The festivity became increasingly the concern of children – more an amusement than a commemoration – so that a correspondent in 1930 suggested turning 5 November into 'Children's play day'.[50] Children's firework parties, with adult supervision, became a common feature of childhood memories of the 1950s and 1960s. The instruction 'light the blue touch paper and retire immediately' still evokes a kaleidoscope of sounds, lights and smells.

The late twentieth century has seen further modifications to the tradition, mostly in the direction of safety and control. Fewer children handle fireworks or build bonfires; more attend spectacles put on by charitable or service organizations. With paid admission, spectator areas and a narrated programme, the fireworks 'show' has increasingly replaced the bonfire party. The rockets go higher and burst with more colour, but they have less and less to do with memories of the Fifth of November. The story of Gunpowder Treason, once taught from the pulpit and revenged in the streets, is now a history lesson in schools. Furthermore, the expensive displays of fireworks put on to celebrate royal and patriotic occasions have in recent years stolen the thunder of the Fifth of November. It might be observed that Guy Fawkes' Day is finally declining, having lost its connection with politics and religion. But we have heard that many times before.

From being a matter of life and death that threatened 'the martyrdom of the kingdom' the Gunpowder Plot had been transformed into (*The Times*'s phrase) 'an annual jest'. Over almost 400 years it has been associated with a creative festive tradition, with shifting sponsorship, varying intensity and periodic reinfusions of meaning. As a late Stuart Almanac put it, 'what ere's forgot, the memory of the Powder Plot will hardly die'.[51] Shaped and re-shaped by social, religious and political currents, the anniversary of 5 November has proved remarkably hardy and remarkably versatile. It has endured as a cultural phenomenon because of its mutability, because English society has repeatedly reinfused it with fresh meanings.

It appears, then, that the long history of the fifth of November is not one of simple survival or customary continuity, but rather one of recurrent reconstruction, re-making and adaptation to changing concerns. The calendar provided the grid, the anniversary supplied the occasion, but its meaning, its social location, and its religious, political and cultural implications have repeatedly been subject to change. Even now, we remember, remember. But part of the task of history is to keep memory honest.

One final custom deserves mention. The practice of searching the cellars at Westminster, re-enacting the vigilance that discovered Guy Fawkes in 1605, is believed to date from the 1690s when a second Gunpowder Plot was feared. This custom has continued into the twentieth century as a quaint anachronism, a parliamentary folly, involving lamplit searches (ignoring the electricity), and concluding with cakes and wine for the Beefeaters. In 1812 *The Times* reported the ritual searching of the cellars at Westminster before the opening of Parliament. The Lord High Chamberlain, the Usher of the Black Rod, a yeoman usher and a dozen yeomen of the guard conducted their search, 'according to custom, since the days of Guy Faux'. The last cellar they came to was occupied by a wine-merchant, so 'some of the inspectors tasted the contents of the pipes, to ascertain that they did not contain gunpowder'.[52]

NOTES

1 A. R. Wright and T. E. Lones, *British Calendar Customs: England*, vol. 3: *Fixed Festivals, June–December, Inclusive* (London, 1940), pp. 145–56; Charlotte S. Burne, 'Guy Fawkes' Day,' *Folk-Lore*, 1912, vol. 23, pp. 409–26; Ervin Beck, 'Children's Guy Fawkes Customs in Sheffield', *Folklore*, 1984, vol. 95, pp. 191–203.

2 Compare Robert D. Storch, '"Please to Remember the Fifth of November": Conflict, Solidarity and Public Order in Southern England, 1815–1900', in Robert D. Storch (ed.), *Popular Culture and Custom in Nineteenth-Century England* (London, 1982), pp. 71–99, and D. G. Paz, 'Bonfire Night in Mid Victorian Northants: The Politics of a Popular Revel', *Historical Research*, 1990, vol. 63, pp. 316–28.

3 Mabel Peacock, Charlotte S. Burne and W. Henry Jewitt, 'Correspondence', *Folk-Lore* 1903, vol. 14, pp. 89–91, 185–6; 1907, vol. 18, p. 450; 1912, vol. 23, pp. 406–26; *The Times*, 5 November 1923, 5 November 1926; Jeffrey Burton Russell, *Witchcraft in the Middle Ages* (Ithaca, NY, 1972), p. 51; Christina Hole, *British Folk Customs* (London, 1976), p. 85.

4 David Cressy, *Bonfires and Bells: National Memory and the Protestant Calendar in Elizabethan and Stuart England* (London, 1989), esp. chs 5, 9.

5 The early history is best told in S. R. Gardiner, *What Gunpowder Plot Was* (London, 1897) and Joel Hurstfield, 'A Retrospect: Gunpowder Plot and the Politics of Dissent', in *Freedom, Corruption and Government in Elizabethan England* (Cambridge, Mass., 1973), pp. 327–51. *Statutes of the Realm*, 3 Jac. I. c.1. Comparable commemorations were enacted after the 1622 massacre in Virginia, the 1641 rebellion in Ireland and the Restoration of 1660.

6 Pollard and Redgrave, *Short Title Catalogue of English Books*, 1475–1640, 16494 (London, 1606).

7 Lancelot Andrewes, *XCVI Sermons*, 3rd edn (London, 1635), pp. 889, 890, 900.

8 Francis Herring, *Popish Pietie. Or the First Part of the Historie of that Horrible and Barbarous Conspiracie, Commonly Called the Powder Treason* (London, 1610), sigs. A3v–A4.

9 Samuel Garey, *Great Brittans Little Calendar: Or, Triple Diarie, in Remembrance of Three Daies* (London, 1618), pp. 184–5; Stella P. Revard, 'Milton's Gunpowder Poems and Satan's Conspiracy,' *Milton Studies*, 1972, vol. 4, pp. 63–77.

10 George Carleton, *A Thankfull Remembrance of Gods Mercy* (London, 1624), p. 217.

11 Thomas Hooker, 'The Church's Deliverances', in George H. Williams et al. (eds), *Thomas Hooker, Writings in England and Holland, 1626–1633* (Cambridge, Mass., 1975), pp. 68–9. For more examples see Cressy, *Bonfires and Bells*, pp. 148–55.

12 Henry Burton, *For God and the King. The Summe of Two Sermons Preached on the Fifth of November Last* (London, 1636), pp. 1, 54, 100–2, 130–2.

13 Charles Herle, *Davids Reserve, and Rescue* (London, 1645), pp. 11, 12, 13, 16; Cressy, *Bonfires and Bells*, pp. 156–70.

14 James Crossley (ed.), *The Diary and Correspondence of Dr John Worthington* (Manchester, 1847), p. 90.

15 Samuel Clarke, *Englands Remembrancer, Containing a True and Full Narrative of those Two Never to be Forgotten Deliverances: The One from the Spanish Invasion in Eighty Eight: the Other from the Hellish Powder Plot November 5, 1605* (London, 1657).

16 *Statutes of the Realm*, 12. Car. II. c.14. See also *A Form of Common Prayer to be Used Upon the Thirtieth of January* (London, 1661) and *A Form of Prayer With Thanksgiving, to be Used . . . the 29th of May Yearly* (London, 1661).

17 *The Burning of the Whore of Babylon, As it was Acted, with Great Applause, in the Poultrey, London, on Wednesday Night, being the Fifth of November Last* (London, 1673).

18 Cressy, *Bonfires and Bells*, ch. 11; George Parker, *Parkers Ephemeris for the Year of Our Lord 1712* (London, 1712).

19 John Goldsmith, *An Almanack for . . . 1735* (London, 1735); similarly 1769, 1771, 1776, 1779.

20 *Gentleman's Magazine*, 1741, vol. 11, p. 607; Kathleen Wilson, 'Empire, Trade and Popular Politics in Mid-Hanoverian Britain: The Case of Admiral Vernon', *Past and Present*, 1988, no. 121, pp. 74–109.

21 *The Monthly Intelligencer*, November 1731; *Gentleman's Magazine*, 1744, vol. 14, pp. 616–17; *Daily Universal Register*, 5 November, 1785, 6 November, 1786; *The Times*, 5 November 1788, 5 November 1790; *An Essay Towards a New History of the Gunpowder Treason* (London, 1765), preface. See also Francis Griffin Stokes (ed.), *The Blecheley Diary of the Rev. William Cole 1765–67* (London, 1931), pp. 146, 284, and David Vaisey (ed.), *The Diary of Thomas Turner 1754–1765* (Oxford, 1985), pp. 16, 71, 121, 237, 281.

22 *Gentleman's Magazine*, 1751, vol. 21, p. 520.

23 *Gentleman's Magazine*, 1766, vol. 36, p. 546; *The Times*, 2 October 1863. Cf. Storch, '"Please to Remember the Fifth of November"'.

24 *The Times*. 5 November 1790, 4 November 1802.

25 *Daily Universal Register*, 12, 14 November 1785.

26 *Daily Universal Register*, 12 November 1785; *The Times*, 10 November 1847; 7 November 1853; 2 October, 6, 7 November 1863.

27 *The Times*, 4 November 1837.

28 *The Times*, 6 November 1788; 5 November 1790; 6 November 1792; 17 November 1825 (report from Gateshead); William Cobbett, *Rural Rides*, ed. George Woodcock (Harmondsworth, 1983), vol. 2, pp. 458, 387.

29 *The Times*, 12 November 1839.

30 *The Times*, 6 November 1834, 6 November 1838, 5 November 1843, 6 November 1850, 7 November 1867.

31 *The Times*, 6 November 1877, 6 November 1878, 6 November 1879, 6 November 1880, 7 November 1882, 6 November 1884.

32 *The Times*, 6 November 1838, 6 November 1880.

33 *The Times*, 7 November 1838, 6 November 1839, 5 November 1841.

34 *The Times*, 6, 7, 9 November 1850; Paz, 'Bonfire Night in Mid Victorian Northants'; Roger Swift, 'Guy Fawkes Celebrations in Victorian Exeter', *History Today*, 1981, vol. 31, pp. 5–9.

35 *Hansard's Parliamentary Debates* (hereafter *Hansard*), ser. 3, vol. CLI (1858),

pp. 483, 487; *The Times*, 11, 14 December 1854, 29 November 1855, 20 November 1857.

36 *Hansard*, 3, CLII (1859), p. 148; CLI (1858), p. 491.

37 *Hansard*, 3, CLI (1858), pp. 475–86, esp. p. 478.

38 *Hansard*, 3, CLI (1858), pp. 492–4, 660–1; CLII (1859), p. 852.

39 *Hansard*, 3, CLI (1858), pp. 475, 477–503, 1660–5; CLII (1859), pp. 117–18, 148–50, 850–2; CLIII (1859), p. 792.

40 *Gentleman's Magazine*, 1745, vol. 15, p. 609; *Daily Universal Register*, 7 November 1785; *The Times*, 6 November 1788, 6 November 1792.

41 *The Times*, 6, 7 November 1850, 7 November 1867, Paz, 'Bonfire Night in Victorian Northants', p. 325.

42 *The Times*, 6 November 1877, 6 November 1878, 6 November 1879, 6 November 1880, 9 November 1882, 6 November 1884, 6 November 1880.

43 *The Times*, 6. November 1909; Hole, *British Folk Customs*, p. 85.

44 John Beresford (ed.), *The Diary of a Country Parson: The Reverend James Woodforde. 1758–1802*, vol. 1 (Oxford, 1926), p. 81; Paz, 'Bonfire Night in Mid Victorian Northants', p. 328; *The Times*, 6 November, 1877, 6 November 1879, 6 November 1880, 7 November 1882, 6 November 1884.

45 *The Times*, 10, 27 November 1847, 2 October, 6, 7, 23, 28 November 1863.

46 *The Times*, 6 November 1876, 6 November 1877, 7 November 1870, 7 November 1872, 6 November 1873.

47 *The Times*, 6 November 1877, 6 November 1878, 6 November 1879, 6 November 1880, 6 November 1884, 7 November 1887, 6 November 1888.

48 *The Times*, 6 November 1877, 7, 9, 11, 15 October 1884, 6 November 1886, 7 November 1887.

49 *The Times*, 6 November 1880, 7 November 1882, 6 November 1880, 7 November 1882, 6 November 1883, 6 November 1886, 6 November 1908.

50 *The Times*, 1, 3, 6 November 1909, 5 November 1910, 6 November 1926, 31 October, 6 November 1930.

51 Samuel Garey, *Amphitheatrum Scelerum: Or, the Transcendent of Treason: For the Fifth of November* (London, 1618); *Poor Robin: An Almanack After the Old and New Fashion* (London, 1695).

52 *The Times*, 26 November 1812; also 5 November 1841, 6 November 1884, 5 November 1920, 5 November 1923.

4

THE TRAMP
M. A. *Crowther*

Wandering is such a potent symbol of the human condition that its literary roots are both ancient and international. The homeless beggar has a place in many religions, but in the Christian tradition, following a Master with no fixed abode, he offers his perennial challenge to property and complacency. The rich man can reach heaven only through his charity to Lazarus, most abject of mankind. To enter the condition of Lazarus, as did the mendicant friars, was to offer the final proof of humility. The theme is repeated in the secular literary tradition, and its most famous English expression is this:

> Poor naked wretches, wheresoe'er you are,
> That bide the pelting of this pitiless storm,
> How shall your houseless heads and unfed sides,
> Your looped and window'd raggedness, defend you
> From seasons such as these? O! I have ta'en
> Too little care of this. Take physic, pomp;
> Expose thyself to feel what wretches feel,
> That thou mayst shake the superflux to them,
> And show the heavens more just.
> 　　　　　　　　　　　(*King Lear*, III, iv)

In reality, of course, the tramp, the beggar, the busker, the gypsy, the tinker, the inhabitant of Cardboard City, provoke a mixed reaction in the settled population. Vagrants have long attracted not only charity, but the harsher actions of the law. The myths concerning them are potent, but are not like the manufactured patriotic symbols described in *The Invention of Tradition*.[1] Patriotic traditions are essentially single-minded, fostered in an effort to promote national unity. The vagrant population inherits a many-sided and contradictory mythical tradition which partly accounts for the continuing confusion of social attitudes and official policies towards them.

Although the tramp myth belongs to many nations, local conditions give it a particular flavour in each. In a relatively well-policed country like later nineteenth-century Britain, tramps were not seen as a serious menace, and the way was open to romanticize their condition. Also, the British policy of dealing with tramps through the Poor Law was unique; most Continental countries and the United States dealt with them either through charity or through the criminal law, and (in spite of a few experiments) British policy towards the tramp never achieved the regulatory approach of German labour colonies. It may be that the British, knowing that there was some kind of safety net for tramps, however inadequate, regarded them with less fear and more sentimentality.

'The Tramp Life, the underside of the world, generally appears in writing in exaggerated sunshine or gloom,' wrote C. F. G. Masterman in 1909.[2] The vagrant, like the monarch, is a creature of myth, but the essence of this myth is the mysterious nature of vagrancy. The gulf between the wanderer and the settled man may be wider than that between citizen and king. Judith Okely's study of modern gypsies notes how society, ignorant of gypsy customs, projects its own fantasies on to them.[3] Vague memories, once fostered by *The Gypsy Baron* and *The Raggle-Taggle-Gypsies-O*, and still encouraged by *Carmen*, equate the wandering life with freedom of choice, especially in sexual matters. Such fantasies have also attached to other kinds of wanderers. Because of his abnormal condition, homeless and masterless, the vagrant aroused three powerful emotions: fear, pity and envy. These are not mutually exclusive, and each age constructs its own version. The sturdy beggar of Tudor times, the intimidating Victorian 'moucher' and the twentieth-century alcoholic provoked different kinds of fear, reflected in official policies. Pity took both religious and humanitarian forms in the past: the later twentieth century has tended to institutionalize it through hostels, psychiatrists and social workers, though still relying heavily on charitable agencies. Envy, the most complex emotion, arises from the suspicion that the vagrant, in spite of his wretchedness, is a free spirit. This essay will examine the myths of vagrancy in a transitional stage, from the mid-nineteenth century to the First World War, and particularly the romantic and sentimental tramp of the Edwardians.

Although the homeless were a common sight before the Second

World War, and have become so again, their lives and motives are always mysterious. Since they rarely spoke for themselves, others tried to interpret their behaviour to the public. When the interpreters were police, prison or Poor Law officers, the interpretation was likely to be hostile; charitable reactions varied from the severity of the Society for the Suppression of Mendicity in the early nineteenth century to the missionary efforts of the Salvation Army at its end. Yet official and charitable bodies could provide only limited and self-interested information about the motives of vagrants, and so there remained an unsatisfied public curiosity to be exploited by creative writers and journalists claiming intimate knowledge of tramp life. This was nothing new. Beier argues that Tudor policies towards vagrants were influenced by highly coloured literary accounts of their habits,[4] and later policy-makers had little more to rely on. In the public perception, the tramp was a kind of Frankenstein's monster, constructed indiscriminately from journalism, police reports and poetry.

Tramps were not, of course, a homogeneous group, and this partly accounted for the confused reaction to them. In the writings of Dickens, for example, fear, pity and intolerance all have a place. Tramps as fearsome predators appear in *David Copperfield* (1849), when the child David is forced to join them on the highroad in Kent:

> The trampers were worse than ever that day, and inspired a dread that is yet quite fresh in my mind. Some of them were most ferocious-looking ruffians, who stared at me as I went by; and stopped, perhaps, and called after me to come back and speak to them, and when I took to my heels, stoned me. I recollect one young fellow – a tinker, I suppose, from his wallet and brazier – who had a woman with him, and who faced about and stared at me thus; and then roared at me in such a tremendous voice to come back, that I halted and looked round.
>
> 'Come here, when you're called' said the tinker, 'or I'll rip your young body open.'[5]

The tramp then steals David's neckerchief, and, when the woman intervenes, punches her in the face.

Dickens gives an alternative account in his journal *All the Year Round*, describing his midnight walks in London:

> Once – it was after leaving the Abbey and turning my face north – I came to the great steps of St. Martin's church as the clock was striking Three. Suddenly, a thing that in a moment more I should have

*"This is a sweet place, ain't it? a lovely spot? and I wonder
if they'd give two poor, foot-sore travellers, like me and you, a drop
of fresh water out of such a pretty, genteel crib? We'd take it wery
kind on 'em, wouldn't us? wery kind, upon my word, us would."*

"Tramps."—CHARLES DICKENS.

FROM "THE UNCOMMERCIAL TRAVELLER."

BY G. J. PINWELL, R.W.S.

By permission of Messrs. Chapman & Hall.

A mid-Victorian illustration of Dickens shows both the author's and the artist's
indecision as to whether tramps were pathetic outcasts or social nuisances.

trodden upon without seeing, rose up at my feet with a cry of loneliness and houselessness, struck out of it by the bell, the like of which I
never heard. We then stood face to face looking at one another, frightened by one another. The creature was like a beetle-browed hare-
lipped youth of twenty, and it had a loose bundle of rags on, which it
held together with one of its hands. It shivered from head to foot, and
its teeth chattered, and as it stared at me – persecutor, devil, ghost,
whatever it thought me – it made with its whining mouth as if it were
snapping at me, like a worried dog.[6]

Dickens's response here was to feel in his pocket for a coin; but he
also wrote in a more conventional way of comic tramps and cunning
beggars who preyed on the credulous.[7]

Dickens did not romanticize the homeless poor, but in the later
decades of the century other writers sounded another note later
repeated in innumerable school anthologies:

> Give to me the life I love,
> Let the lave go by me,
> Give the jolly heaven above
> And the by-way nigh me.
> Bed in the bush with stars to see,
> Bread I dip in the river –
> There's the life for a man like me
> There's the life for ever.[8]
> (R. L. Stevenson, *The Vagabond*)

Stevenson's 'The Vagabond', with its refrain 'Give the face of
earth around,/and the road before me', is an expression of psychological longing, since, as Chesterton remarked, Stevenson's poor
health precluded such behaviour in reality: 'His picture of himself as
a vagabond with blue fingers on the winter road is avowedly an ideal
picture; it was exactly that sort of freedom that he could never
have.'[9] But it helped to foster a whole genre of suburban wanderlust,
well parodied in a spectacularly successful novel published in 1908.
The anti-hero, overcome by the lure of the open road, shows his latest purchase to a friend:

> He led the way to the stable yard accordingly, the Rat following with
> a most mistrustful expression; and there, drawn out of the coach-
> house into the open they saw a Gypsy caravan, shining with newness,
> painted a canary yellow picked out with green and red wheels.

'There you are!' cried the Toad, straddling and expanding himself. 'There's real life for you, embodied in that little cart. The open road, the dusty highway, the heath, the common, the hedgerows, the rolling downs! Camps, villages, towns, cities! Here to-day, up and off to somewhere else to-morrow! Travel, change, interest, excitement! The whole world before you, and a horizon that's always changing!'[10]

The fictional accounts give some clues to the wide variety of real vagabonds.[11] The tinker who threatened David Copperfield had an occupation, since he was carrying his brazier; he belonged to the disreputable section of the itinerants making a living by selling small goods or doing repairs in a society where retailing was not yet highly developed. If well established, he might have a horse and cart, and was unlikely to be staying in workhouse casual wards unless times were very hard: if he did not have his own covered cart or tent, he would use a common lodging house or inn. He was travelling with a woman: tinkers and gypsies usually travelled in family groups, unlike the majority of residents in common lodgings or casual wards, who were lone males.

The tinker was only one of the types of working man likely to be found on the mid-Victorian road: there would be others whose tramping was intended to be strictly temporary, such as navvies walking from one job to another, sailors moving from port to port, or, at the most respectable level, the tramping artisans, who flourished before the 1870s: 'compositors, lithographers, tailors, coachmakers, bookbinders, smiths, engineers, steam-engine makers, stonemasons, carpenters, ironfounders, coopers, shoemakers, boilermakers, plumbers, bricklayers and various other crafts'.[12] All of these were mobile and fluctuating trades; their members had to move in search of new employment, supported on the way by their unions and brother craftsmen. In 1841–2, as Hobsbawm records, the journeymen steam-engine makers alone relieved 2,226 wandering men, a figure swollen by hard times. Added to this was the regular seasonal migration of workers, often whole families, to bring in the harvest, whether they were the Irish who migrated annually to Scotland, or the London poor who went south every summer for the fruit and hop picking.[13] Dickens, in a more friendly vein, described them returning from the harvest:

there is a vast exodus of tramps out of the country; and if you ride or drive round any turn of any road . . . you will be bewildered to find that you have charged into the bosom of fifty families, and that there are splashing up all around you, in the utmost prodigality of confusion, bundles of bedding, babies, iron pots, and a good-humoured multitude of both sexes and all ages, equally divided between perspiration and intoxication.'[14]

Dickens uses the word 'vagabond' interchangeably with 'tramp' or 'tramper' for his wandering folk, but this modern usage obscures the older difference between the words, which reflects a real difference in economic status. The old words 'vagrant' or 'vagabond', with their Latin roots, signify the aimless wandering of the dispossessed: 'tramp' did not enter the language until the later seventeenth century, when it was applied to men moving purposefully in search of work; the artisan went 'on the tramp' between jobs.[15] The two terms were synonymous by the nineteenth century, but policy-makers believed that it was possible, and necessary, to distinguish between the two types of wanderer.

The pitiable figure Dickens found outside St Martin's church is another type of vagrant, presented here as deformed and possibly insane. Given his mental state, he was not likely to be looking for work, but would scratch a living between begging, charity and the Poor Law. He was probably a vagabond only in a limited sense, not much interested in the open road, but sticking to the city, where there was more shelter and organized charity. He would find plenty of company among the abandoned children, Irish immigrants deposited penniless from the cattle-boats, and other social refuse which many charitable institutions, from the Society for the Suppression of Mendicity to the Strangers' Friend societies, attempted to clear from the streets in their different ways.

Then there was the group envied by Mr Toad and many other romantics: the gypsies, professional beggars and tramps, travelling showmen, gamblers, fairground people and other exotic wanderers who served many a useful turn in the plots of drama, novel or opera.[16] These groups had a particular piquancy, the gypsies because of their supposed racial separateness, and both gypsies and professional vagabonds because of their secret languages. The gypsy caravan, however, was a development of the late nineteenth century: in earlier decades most gypsies had nothing more weathertight than a tent.[17] These were both the most interesting and the most alarming sections of the vagrant population: the gypsies were suspected of poisoning farm animals and stealing washing, if not children; the professional tramps of terrorizing unprotected housewives, thieving, burning ricks and, by long association back to the days of plague, being the carriers of cholera and smallpox.[18]

The wanderers on the roads, the sleepers in the crannies of cities, therefore presented an extremely varied appearance, and, as an importunate and obvious part of everyday life, were a difficult problem for policy-makers. The general objective of social policy in the nineteenth century was to quantify, define and regulate each type of social problem. Vagrants were not amenable to counting or classification; nor was it certain what kind of problem they were. This uncertainty, so obvious in the imaginative literature of vagrancy, expresses itself also in the writings of would-be policy-makers. Was the vagrant a threat to social order, a figure of pity or merely a necessary feature of the labour market? Should he be disposed of by the police, charity, the Poor Law or a better system of labour regulation? Before these questions could be answered, it was necessary to find out who he was.

Nineteenth-century statistics are open to many criticisms, but they do offer a rough guide to population, pauperism, certified lunacy, convicted criminals, and so forth. Vagrants, however, did not wait to be counted. The police were sent out every ten years in the interests of the census to count all those sleeping rough – an impossible task. The figures for admission to workhouse casual wards represent only those desperate enough to seek this kind of accommodation, and are affected over time by the opening and closing of common lodging-houses as alternative and more attractive places to stay. The Scottish police, unlike the English, conducted their own census of vagrants every year from 1888, including not only those sleeping rough, but everyone in lodging-houses charging fourpence or less per night. This produced some very odd statistics, showing Glasgow, by then a much larger city, to have fewer vagrants than Edinburgh.[19] The police themselves did not believe this. The problem lay in accounting for all the different types of cheap lodgings, even in a city like Glasgow with a relatively large force of police and sanitary inspectors to do the counting. The only other statistical information on vagrants was collected whenever they were caught breaking the law. The Vagrancy Act of 1824 (in England) was capacious enough to include almost any kind of action which might be committed by a vagrant – begging, sleeping out in the open, gambling, exhibiting wounds in order to excite compassion, and many other offences of this type.[20] Its enforcement depended entirely on the zeal of the local police. A Departmental Committee on Vagrancy reported in 1906 that there were likely to be 30,000–40,000 vagrants in England and Wales when trade was good, and 70,000–80,000 when it was bad.[21] Vagrancy figures were also subject to sudden and alarming surges, such as the

Arrest of a tramp in Dundee, early twentieth century
Source: Dundee District Libraries Photographic Collection.

influx of ex-servicemen at the end of wars, or of Irish during the famine.

Local information on vagrancy was furnished by police and Poor Law officers, but their main aim was to identify habitual or 'professional' tramps, the main threat to public order. The police were interested in potentially criminal vagrants; workhouse masters were anxious to preserve the often fragile order of the casual wards, and so watched out for known troublemakers. This obsession was reinforced by legislation in the 1870s which made it an offence for a tramp to apply to the same casual ward twice within a specified period – the aim being to hound the professionals and keep them moving on.[22]

Absence of reliable information about vagrants therefore left the field open to the private investigator and to the creation of myth. Mayhew included vagrants and beggars in his study of London labour (1861–2), classifying them under the dual heading of 'those who cannot work' and 'those who will not work', while his collaborator Andrew Halliday paid particular attention to the more colourful

professional beggars and impostors, their tricks and secret language.[23] James Greenwood's *Seven Curses of London* (1869) followed
in a similar vein, with bloodcurdling accounts of begging impostors.
Such stories, bolstered by tales from selected workhouse masters and
the Society for the Suppression of Mendicity, formed the basis for a
massive and purportedly scholarly work, C. J. Ribton Turner's
History of Vagrants and Vagrancy and Beggars and Begging (1887),
and have influenced more recent histories such as Kellow Chesney's
Victorian Underworld (1970).[24]

Mayhew was the precursor of all the fearless investigative journalists who were to venture into the vagrant underworld, their note-
books giving way in time to the tape-recorder and the video camera.
Their informants provided colourful and highly articulate stories.
Doubts about the veracity of such evidence led others to seek more
spontaneous information by disguising themselves as tramps.
Journalists, clergymen (and a clergyman's wife, the redoubtable Mary
Higgs), would-be reformers and novelists all donned suitable rags
and set off to discover the vagrant population.[25] By the time Jack
London arrived in England to gather material for *People of the Abyss*
(1903), his actions were part of a well-established formula. Leaping
into a cab, the novelist ordered the startled driver to 'drive me down
to the East End', and immediately purchased 'a pair of stout though
well-worn trousers, a frayed jacket with one remaining button, a pair
of brogans which had plainly seen service where coal was shovelled,
a thin leather belt, and a very dirty cloth cap'.[26] For evidence of the
public's continuing reliance on these ambassadors, one can only compare Jack London with Jeremy Sandford, author of the influential
television dramas on homelessness, *Cathy Come Home* and *Edna, the
Inebriate Woman*. In 1972, Sandford descended into the 'bilges of
society' after similar attention to his toilette.

> A friend working in a Mission to down and outs gave me suitable
> clothes.
> He gave me heavy and filthy boots, tied with string.
> He gave me shapeless hideous trousers, and the sort of shirt that has
> no collar.
> He gave me a succession of other tattered shirts to wear under this,
> and string to go round my trousers below the knee to keep out the cold
> . . .[27]

Most of the make-believe Victorian vagrants spent a very short
time observing the problem, and they naturally headed for the places

where vagrants could most easily be found: the workhouse casual ward or 'spike'. Nearly all their accounts tended to concentrate less on the vagrants themselves than on the physical conditions in the casual ward – the dirt, lack of medical attention, and (depending on the point of view of the observer and which ward had been visited), either the cruel regimentation or the total lack of discipline within the Poor Law system. Although there are some memorable accounts of meetings with particular tramps, the nature of vagrancy is not usually the main issue: Jack London's, in spite of its melodramatic presentation, comes the nearest to offering an explanation in terms of the economic vulnerability of the working class. His vagrants are presented as victims of fate, men in later life struck down by illness or an accident at work, widowed, unemployed, childless. Unlike the British pseudo-tramps, Jack London saw vagrancy as a product of the social system rather than a problem of administration.

Vagrancy, therefore, was more elusive than most social problems, and so literary accounts had a stronger influence on social attitudes towards it. During the Victorian and Edwardian periods, official attitudes towards vagrancy concentrated on policing and regulation. Any suggestion that the numbers of vagrants was increasing was usually followed by repressive legislation. The Vagrancy Act of 1824, though mild in comparison with the old statutes with their whippings and brandings, threatened beggars and vagabonds with cumulative prison sentences. Nor was the hostile attitude of the Poor Law towards wanderers much diminished. Although political economists attacked the Laws of Settlement for obstructing labour mobility,[28] these laws were not repealed, since they defended Poor Law unions against the cost of destitute strangers, especially the Irish.

The Society for the Suppression of Mendicity, begun in London in 1818, anticipated the Charity Organization Society by attempting to investigate the circumstances of beggars. Subscribers gave beggars tickets rather than money, and the applicant could then claim help from the society if his story was verified. Although the society spent over £3,000 in 1827 for the relief of beggars, and in paying constables to arrest vagrants, it obviously had little effect.[29] The development of the workhouse system transferred the deterrent policy to the Poor Law, particularly in the 1870s, when vagrants could be detained for two nights in the casual ward. The aim was always to distinguish the 'genuine work seeker' from the professional tramp: harsh policies were justified because the work seeker was assumed to be on the road for only a short time. The culmination of this process came in the years after the Boer War, during a further panic about increasing

Casual ward cells from the outside, Paddington, 1938; an example of the type of cells favoured in the late nineteenth century. Each casual slept in a separate cell adjoining the small work cell, where stones were broken and put through the chutes into the courtyard.
Source: Greater London Photograph Library.

vagrancy, with the recommendations of the Departmental Committee, and the Royal Commission on the Poor Laws, that habitual vagrants be incarcerated in labour colonies on the German model.[30] This was being considered as a serious policy option when the First World War intervened.

Severe policies had little practical effect. The public continued to give coins to beggars, and also to support a large number of night asylums, houseless poor asylums, soup kitchens, the Salvation Army and many local charities offering shelter to the homeless poor. At one level, the campaign against beggars and vagrants offended specific teachings of Christianity: at another, it upset sensibilities cultivated within the literary tradition. By the end of the century, literary convention was reshaping the vagrant myth, further undermining the campaign against the wanderers.

The three emotions of fear, pity and envy aroused by the vagrant are subject to sudden shifts in emphasis. This may be caused by obvious changes in the vagrant population, or by a readjustment of public attitudes. Vagrancy, in spite of nineteenth-century efforts to link it to fecklessness and twentieth-century interpretations in term of 'social inadequacy', appears to be closely related to the state of the labour market.[31] Hence public attitudes may be suddenly challenged at times of high unemployment, when vagrancy invariably increases. In the inter-war period, Orwell described tramps as economic as well as social casualties, noting that many of them were the young unemployed.[32] After the Second World War, in conditions of virtually full employment, vagrancy was reinterpreted as a problem of ageing single men, alcoholics and social misfits. A collection of essays by sociologists, social workers and voluntary activists, published in 1979 under the title *Vagrancy: Some New Perspectives*, presented vagrancy almost entirely in these terms. Within a few years the entire perspective was once again altered by mass unemployment among the young and a visible increase in sleeping out and begging in London. Reinterpretation had to begin afresh, taking into account family breakdown, refusal of benefit to school-leavers and the closure of large institutions for the mentally ill.[33]

During the nineteenth century, fear of the vagrant gradually diminished. In a society with more effective policing, the 'sturdy vagabond' appeared as a petty criminal rather than a major threat to public order. The Elizabethans had feared menacing gangs of sturdy beggars: the Victorians feared no more than isolated individual acts of extortion or pilfering. With the fragmentation of cities between class boundaries, common lodging-houses and places of resort were confined to working-class areas, where they posed less threat to the propertied classes, and could be monitored by the police. Pity, too, remained a constant stimulus to charitable efforts for the homeless poor, reinforced by attempts at social realism in the arts, whether the literary and journalistic efforts quoted above or the graphic representations of artists like Fildes, Doré and Herkomer.

The most characteristic nineteenth-century contribution to the literature of vagrancy, however, lay in the transformation of the emotion of envy. Previously, the envy aroused by the vagrant population was of a particular kind. Its origins lay at least as far back as the Tudors, preoccupied with the growth of vagrancy as both a threat to public order and a corrupter of morals.[34] Many old ballads and plays emphasize that the vagrant enjoys life more than the settled man. The vagrant is free of master and priest, and can ignore social conventions. The ballads of the jolly beggar nearly all stress his lack of responsibility, and some go further in arguing that, without doing any work, he can live better than the labouring man:

> Within a hollow Tree
> I live and pay no Rent;
> Providence provides for me,
> And I am well content,
>   And a Begging we will go, we'll go, we'll go,
> And Begging we will go.
>
> Of all Occupations,
> A Beggar lives the best,
> For when he is a weary,
> He'll lie him down and rest:
>
> I fear no Plots against me,
> But live in open cell;
> Why who wou'd be a King,
> When a Beggar lives so well?
>   And a Begging we will go, we'll go, we'll go,
> And Begging we will go.[35]

In the old plays and ballads, the tinkers and beggars are not only well provided with money, but have the best of food and drink, and live riotously with their doxies (sometimes more than one at a time) without benefit of wedlock. Although centuries apart, the carousing beggars framing the action in *The Taming of the Shrew* and the *Beggars' Opera*, and those appearing in Robert Burns's poem *The Jolly Beggars*, are merely high-class representations of this type: powerful fantasy figures, offering escape from work, social convention and, ironically, poverty.

The jolly beggar of Tudor myth, his pockets filled by begging and pretty crime, lived on in the minds of the Poor Law Commissioners after 1834.[36] Chadwick himself gathered information in 1836 for his work for the Royal Commission on rural police, and one of the local constables gave him an archetypal account of vagrants: their clothes were outwardly tattered, but warm in reality; they begged considerable sums of money, and also quantities of food, which they sold to the innkeeper. They spent their evenings at the inn, with the best of food and drink, and slept there stark naked, several men and women in one bed. The local youth, not surprisingly, were reported to be envious.[37] These 'official' accounts echoed the old ballads: they would not confess to personal envy of the beggarly vagrant, but

Burns's *Jolly Beggars* attracted many nineteenth-century illustrators: Cruikshank best reflects the long-held view that beggars had a good time. Later Victorians invariably bowdlerized the scene.

feared his corrupting effect on impressionable members of the labouring class.

By the end of the nineteenth century, envy was no longer confined to the labourer who saw the vagrant as materially better off than himself, but had been transformed into middle-class envy of vagabond freedom. The Romantic movement was clearly the turning-point, though the high point of sentimentality was not reached until the Edwardian period. The Lake poets applauded the simplicity of the labouring poor and their closeness to the elemental world of nature, but did not make many specific connections with vagrancy, apart from encouraging the cult of walking for self-improvement.

The book chiefly responsible for romanticizing the vagrant life, George Borrow's *Lavengro*, appeared in 1851, and its sequel *The Romany Rye* in 1857. It has never been resolved whether Borrow's strange and shapeless works, with their accounts of his life as a tinker and intimate of the gypsies and travelling folk, are intended as a factual autobiography, or, as their author called them 'a dream'.[38] Since there was little serious information on gypsies at that time, scholarly works like Ribton Turner's accepted Borrow's account of gypsy life as genuine. Borrow's reception by the reading public was curious: neither of his gypsy books sold well at the time of publication, but by the late nineteenth century they were esteemed by literary men, and were being produced in numerous cheap reprints, recommended especially to the adventurous young. The words given to the gypsy, Jasper Petulengro, in response to Borrow's own sense of despair, appeared in many anthologies of English prose: 'There's night and day, brother, both sweet things; sun, moon, and stars, brother, all sweet things; there's likewise a wind on the heath. Life is very sweet, brother; who would wish to die?'[39]

Borrow's reputation reached its zenith in the Edwardian period, and in 1913 an enthusiastic biographer was writing 'May we not say that an enthusiasm for Borrow's *Lavengro* is now a touchstone of taste in English prose literature?'[40] *Lavengro* appeared two years before Matthew Arnold's 'The Scholar Gypsy', with its perception of the wandering life as the antidote to religious doubt. Robert Louis Stevenson then fed the desire for accounts of exotic wanderings, followed by the much-anthologized John Drinkwater. Even Thomas Hardy, who usually knew better than to sentimentalize the poor, produced an unconvincing hymn to vagrant life.[41] Contemporaries knew why they found the vagrant life attractive: Lionel Johnson in 1899 explained his passion for Borrow in these terms:

> [these books] take you far afield from weary cares and business; into the enamouring airs of the open world, and into days when the countryside was uncontaminated by the vulgar conventions which form the worst side of 'civilised' life in cities. They give you the sense of emancipation, of manumission into the liberty of the winding road and fragrant forest, into the freshness of an ancient country-life, into a *milieu* where men are not copies of each other.[42]

By the Edwardian period, the tramp was not only his traditional self, but had taken on a new form as the guardian of primeval instincts against the encroachments of business and city life. Being

close to nature, he understood elemental values. The practical corol-
lary of this, for the newly leisured classes, was Mr Toad's comfortable gypsy cart, or the new craze for camping, hiking and sleeping
out – even though the latter contravened the Vagrancy Act and
caused problems with the rural police. One of the first ventures of
this kind was made by a retired naval surgeon and prolific author of
stirring yarns, Gordon Stables, in the early 1870s. Stables, who
started the Caravan Club, designed a 'gypsy' caravan, complete with
all possible comforts. Assiduously writing his nature notes, he made
his way from London to Inverness, accompanied by his coachman
and valet. At one point he met a genuine procession of gypsy carts,
and was thankful they were going in the opposite direction.[43] In
terms of popular appeal, however, the most influential must have
been the minor literary figure E. V. Lucas, who in 1899 produced an
anthology of poetry entitled *The Open Road*, 'a garland of good or
enkindling poetry and prose fitted to urge folk into the open air', and
handily sized for slipping into the pocket on country rambles. Jasper
Petulengro's words were on the title-page; Arnold and Stevenson had
pride of place. By 1922 the book was in its thirty-first edition.

Romanticization of vagrancy produced blurred vision about the
realities of tramp life, as seen in the enthusiastic reception accorded
to two genuine doss-house poets, W. H. Davies and Francis
Thompson. Davies was the perfect figure of romance – with his wild
youth spent tramping and begging in America, the loss of his leg
while jumping a ride on a train, his return to England to life on an
eight-shilling weekly inheritance, the painful writing of poetry in
London doss-houses and the struggle to publish it.[44] Davies wrote
several poems of tramp life, with a genuine ambivalence: the selection of his poems in *Georgian Poetry* (1912) included both the raptur-
ous:

> Yes, I will spend the livelong day
> With Nature in this month of May;
> (*In May*)

and

> one night when I went down
> Thames' side, in London Town,
> A heap of rags saw I,
> And sat me down close by.

That thing could shout and bawl,
But showed no face at all.
                        (*The Heap of Rags*)

To most of the poetry-reading public, however, it was the nature
worship, the 'What is this life if, full of care/We have no time to
stand and stare' part of Davies which appealed, rather than the social
realism. Davies's magnificent, if bowdlerized, *Autobiography of a
Supertramp* appeared in 1908, with a preface by Bernard Shaw.
Davies did not minimize the hardships of his career, but its romance
and adventure charmed the public. At exactly the same time that his
fellow Fabians on the Poor Law Commission were recommending the
incarceration of tramps, Shaw was deserting the standard in his preface to Davies's book: 'When I think of the way I worked tamely for
my living during all those years when Mr. Davies, a free knight of
the highway, lived like a pet bird on titbits, I feel that I have been
duped out of my natural liberty.'
    Romanticization of vagrant life was taken to even wilder extremes
in the reception of the first collection of Francis Thompson's poetry
in 1893. Thompson, an opium addict, had cut himself off from his
middle-class family and taken to the streets in London. Like Davies,
he wrote poetry in common lodging-houses until he was adopted by
literary patrons. Unlike Davies, however, Thompson's poetry bears
almost no direct reference to his experience of living rough. His
urban muse received the divine vision at Charing Cross, and his
abstract and symbolic language shows as little interest in bucolic
detail as is possible for a poet.[45] Nevertheless, the public was
delighted not only with poems such as *The Hound of Heaven*, but
with the book's publicity, which emphasized Thompson's irregular
life. A literary review included the following passage:

Day after day Thompson wandered around the streets of London,
barely earning enough to even pay for the poorest accommodations in
the cheapest lodging houses . . . This life he continued for four whole
years, and during that entire time he never ate a full meal, nor did he
sleep in a comfortable bed. His meals consisted chiefly of an apple, a
fish caught by him in a rural brook, and fried over a few pieces of
wood on the shore.[46]

Since Thompson's wanderings had been entirely confined to the
streets of central London, the rural brook was an invention, in keep-

ing with the perceived status of the vagrant as repository of natural lore.

Meanwhile, the Departmental Committee on Vagrancy was interrogating witnesses, mainly Poor Law officials, on the remedies for vagrancy. It was plain that, in spite of all attempts to control him, the public allowed the tramp too many escape routes. The chairman of the Gloucestershire Vagrancy Committee, dedicated to the regulation of vagrants, also gave the game away by admitting the appeal of the vagrant life:

[Q] The pleasure of the tramp is his absolute freedom to go where he pleases; do you not think the discipline of the prison . . . acts as a deterrent? . . .

[A] In the summer they lie under the hedges; in the winter, as long as they are not at work, they do not care where they are; if they have sore feet . . . they would prefer being detained . . .

[Q] Then there is no such thing as deterring people from being tramps?

[A] If you could get the public not to encourage them.[47]

There is no evidence that the official suggestions for the suppression of vagrancy ever achieved any popularity, and certainly not the popularity of Borrow or Stevenson. Stern advice from the Social Darwinists, that the tramp was a physical and mental degenerate best treated by incarceration, was largely ignored.[48] As long as the public supported the tramp, he could avoid the casual ward and the prison. Even the Vagrancy Committee made his life seem attractive. Hence policy towards vagrancy was subverted: this became even clearer after the First World War, when attempts by the Ministry of Health to revive the pre-war disciplines of the casual ward caused a public outcry.[49] The mystery of the travelling life fostered myths which became so much part of the literary tradition that they were accepted as reality, in spite of their contradictory messages. The vagrant was simultaneously poor and a hoarder of ill-gotten wealth; a criminal, and yet spiritually richer than the householder.

In a sense, our knowledge of tramps hardly exists outside literary and other creative sources. The pamphleteers and ballad mongers of Tudor times were followed by Victorian novelists, poets and journalists, who interpreted the underworld according to their own conventions. In the case of vagrancy, the tradition prevented any single-minded interpretation: vagrancy remained an issue where the creative writer offered as much guidance as a blue book, especially as the basic tools of the reformer – plausible statistics – were lacking.

The final apotheosis of the Edwardian tramp was his movement into a new medium, an unmistakable figure of myth with baggy trousers, tight jacket and splay feet. As Charlie Chaplin explained his creation to Mack Sennett: 'You know this fellow is many-sided, a tramp, a gentleman, a poet, a dreamer, a lonely fellow, always hopeful of romance and adventure. He would have you believe he is a scientist, a musician, a duke, a polo-player. However, he is not above picking up cigarette-butts or robbing a baby of its candy.'[50] This was the most enduring image of the nineteenth-century romantic tramp, though he had now crossed the Atlantic. Indeed, in lands where the frontier myth was strong, he appeared to have a special attraction. In Australia, the swagman became deeply embedded in national tradition. In the USA the hobo, sometimes motorized, continued to influence a whole genre of picaresque movies, appealing particularly to the restless imagination of the 1960s in films like *Easy Rider*. In literature, his progeny still changed with the economic climate: the tragic wanderers of *The Grapes of Wrath* were supplanted by more affluent post-war fantasies in Kerouac's 'drop-out' novels.

Meanwhile, real-life vagrants were coming under the scrutiny of the doctor and the sociologist. Disguised journalists continued to descend into Skid Row;[51] television producers examined the homeless in 'gritty' drama documentaries. Governments went on trying to quantify vagrants and their accommodation,[52] but at the time of writing the duty of counting vagrants for the census of 1991 had fallen largely on voluntary organizations, and considerable doubts were being expressed about the possibility of ever reaching an accurate figure. Vagrants still baffle the census and defeat classification; and even in Cardboard City their mystery remains, awaiting whatever fantasy settled society will ascribe to them.

NOTES

1 Eric Hobsbawm, 'Introduction: Inventing Traditions', in Eric Hobsbawm and Terence Ranger (eds), *The Invention of Tradition* (Cambridge, 1983). See particularly David Cannadine's essay on the monarchy in this collection, as an example of the self-conscious construction of a national symbol.

2 C. F. G. Masterman, *The Condition of England* (London, 1960 [1909], p. 139.

3 Judith Okely, *The Traveller-Gypsies* (Oxford, 1983).

4 The pervasiveness of this literary theme is explored in A. L. Beier, *Masterless*

Men: The Vagrancy Problem in England 1560–1640 (London, 1985), pp. 7–8. Beier also includes a bibliography of the early literature on vagrancy, which depended heavily on literary sources, e.g. F. Aydelotte, *Elizabethan Rogues and Vagabonds* (Oxford, 1913).

5 Charles Dickens, *David Copperfield*, ch. 13.

6 Charles Dickens, 'Night Walks', repr. in *The Uncommercial Traveller* (London, 1861).

7 See 'Tramps,' repr. in *The Uncommercial Traveller*.

8 R. L. Stevenson, 'The Vagabond'. 'The lave', which was never explained to us at school, is Scots for 'the rest'.

9 G. K. Chesterton, *Robert Louis Stevenson* (n.d.), p. 18.

10 Kenneth Grahame, *The Wind in the Willows*, ch. 2. In a later chapter, of course, the Rat himself becomes infected with the urge to wander as a ship's rat, but is restrained by the incurably domesticated Mole.

11 For an account of the different types of wandering people, see R. Samuel, 'Comers and Goers', in H. J. Dyos and M. Wolff (eds), *The Victorian City: Images and Realities* (London, 1973), vol. 1, pp. 123–60.

12 E. J. Hobsbawm, 'The Tramping Artisan', in *Labouring Men*, 3rd edn (London, 1968), p. 40. For a summary of the literature, and an account of the highly elaborate arrangements of the tramping artisan, see Humphrey R. Southall, 'The Tramping Artisan Revisits: Labour Mobility and Economic Distress in Early Victorian England', *Economic History Review*, 1991, vol. 44, no. 2, pp. 272–96.

13 The seminal work on labour migration was Arthur Redford, *Labour Migration in England 1800–1850*, 3rd edn (Manchester, 1976), first published in 1926. For a more recent account, see D. Baines, *Migration in a Mature Economy: Emigration and Internal Migration in England and Wales, 1861–1900* (Cambridge, 1985).

14 Charles Dickens, 'Tramps', in *The Uncommercial Traveller*.

15 Cf. *Oxford English Dictionary*.

16 It seems hardly necessary to give examples. Travelling showmen are essential to the plots of *The Old Curiosity Shop* and *Hard Times*. Gypsy curses, warnings, child-stealing, etc., were favourites of the Gothic novel, but reached their apotheosis in popular foreign imports like *Il Trovatore* and *The Hunchback of Notre Dame*.

17 C. J. Ribton Turner, *A History of Vagrants and Vagrancy and Beggars and Begging* (London, 1887), p. 499.

18 David Jones, *Crime, Protest, Community and Police in Nineteenth-Century Britain* (London, 1982), ch. 7, includes a perceptive discussion of the vagrant as a problem of social control, but the other views of tramps as helpless and pitiable, or as a problem of the labour market, should also be stressed.

19 Scottish Record Office HH 55/149, 17 January 1889.

20 For the wide-ranging nature of this Act, see M. J. D. Roberts, 'Public and Private in Early Nineteenth-century London: The Vagrant Act of 1822 and its Enforcement', *Social History*, 1988, vol. 13, no. 3, pp. 289ff.

21 For discussions on vagrancy statistics, see Jones, *Crime, Protest*, pp. 181ff and M. A. Crowther, *The Workhouse System 1834–1929* (London, 1981), pp. 252ff.

22 34 and 35 Vict. c.108 (1871); 39 and 40 Vict. c.79 (1876); 45 and 46 Vict. c.36 (1882).

23 H. Mayhew, *London Labour and the London Poor* (London, 1968 [1861–2]) vol. 4, pp. 23–4, 393ff. The section on beggars was written not by Mayhew himself, but by Andrew Halliday.

24 Ribton Turner, *A History of Vagrants*, ch. 31, shows the kind of literary and anecdotal eridence he used. See also Kellow Chesney, *The Victorian Underworld* (London, 1970), chs 3, 7. Lionel Rose, *'Rogues and Vagabonds': Vagrant Underworld in Britain 1815–1985* (London, 1988), pays attention to large-scale economic migration, but also repeats the colourful 'underworld' stories; see chs 6, 7.

25 E.g. J. Greenwood, *The Amateur Casual, or a Night in the Workhouse* (London, 1877); C. W. Craven, *A Night in the Workhouse* (London, 1887); J. Flynt, *Tramping with Tramps* (London, 1900); M. Higgs, *Five Days and Five Nights as a Tramp among Tramps: Social Investigations by a Lady* (Manchester, 1904) and *Glimpses into the Abyss* (London, 1906); E. Wyrall, *The Spike* (London, 1909). See also R. Vorspan, 'Vagrancy and the New Poor Law in late-Victorian and Edwardian England', *English Historical Review*, 1977, vol. 92, pp. 67–8.

26 Jack London, *People of the Abyss* (London, 1903), ch. 1.

27 J. Sandford, *Down and Out in Britain* (London, 1972), p. 24. See also Robin Page, *Down among the Dossers* (London, 1973), for further accounts of disguised wanderings, this time by a civil servant. For a perceptive critique of such behaviour, and its influence on modern policy, see Peter Beresford, 'The Public Presentation of Vagrancy', in Tim Cook (ed.), *Vagrancy: Some New Perspectives* (London, 1979), pp. 144ff.

28 Led by Adam Smith; see *An Inquiry into the Nature and Causes of the Wealth of Nations* (London, 1776), book 1, ch. 10, part 2.

29 *Ninth Report of the Society for the Suppression of Mendicity* (London, 1827), p. 29.

30 *Report of the Departmental Committee on Vagrancy*, 1906, Cd. 2852, vol. 1, ciii, pp. 91, 120–1; *Report on the Royal Commission on the Poor Laws and Relief of Distress* (HMSO, 1909), vol. 2, p. 270; and the *Separate Report*, p. 588. The majority and minority reports were agreed on this solution for vagrancy. See also Jose Harris, *Unemployment and Politics* (Oxford, 1972), p. 187.

31 More detailed evidence is offered in Crowther, *Workhouse System*, pp. 252–4.

32 George Orwell, *Down and Out in Paris and London* (London, 1933), chs 27, 34. See also F. Gray, *The Tramp, his Meaning and Being* (London, 1932).

33 For contemporary popular arguments, see e.g. 'More than 1,000 Homeless Bed Down in the Snow', *Observer*, 10 February 1991, p. 1; 'Street Act Leaves Homeless Pair Cold', *Guardian*, 5 June 1991, p. 4.

34 Beier, *Masterless Men*, pp. 7–8.

35 Quoted in Ribton Turner, *A History of Vagrants*, p. 617, from a ballad collection of 1744.

36 E.g. *Report from his Majesty's Commissioners for Inquiring into the Administration and Practical Operation of the Poor Laws* (Cmd. 44), appendix E, Parliamentary Papers 1834, p. 37.

37 Chadwick MSS. no. 4, University College, London.

38 One of the most recent biographies, David Williams, *A World of his Own: the Double Life of George Borrow* (Oxford, 1982), accepts the account of Borrow's tramping as factually correct. Michael Collie, *George Borrow,*

Eccentric (Cambridge, 1982), a more scholarly account, reads *Lavengro* as a psychological study, although rooted in personal experience.

39 G. Borrow, *Lavengro* (London, 1851), ch. 25.

40 C. K. Shorter, *George Borrow and his Circle* (Boston, New York, 1913), p. 278. For an account of Borrow's reception, and biographies, see Michael Collie and Angus Fraser, *George Borrow: a Bibliographical Study* (London, 1984).

41 Thomas Hardy, 'Vagrant's Song', in *Human Shows* (London, 1925).

42 Quoted in Shorter, *George Borrow and His Circle*, pp. 435–6n.

43 Gordon Stables, *The Gentleman Gipsy* (London, 1886; Kylin Press repr. 1984), p. 96.

44 A full account of Davies's life is given in Richard J. Stonesifer, *W. H. Davies: A Critical Biography* (London, 1963). Pp. 96–9 deal with *Georgian Poetry*.

45 According to one biographer, Thompson was no believer in the redeeming power of nature, his inspiration being more directly religious. Brigid M. Boardman, *Between Heaven and Charing Cross: The Life of Francis Thompson* (New Haven, 1988), pp. 141–2.

46 Quoted in John Walsh, *Strange Harp, Strange Symphony: The Life of Francis Thompson* (London, 1968), p. 139.

47 *Minutes of Evidence given to the Departmental Committee on Vagrancy* (Cd. 2891), vol. 2, Parliamentary Papers 1906, qs 1624–7.

48 Eugenist theories about vagrants as a branch of the criminal class were discussed by Havelock Ellis, *The Criminal*, 2nd edn. (London, 1895), pp. 222–3.

49 Crowther, *Workhouse System*, pp. 261–3.

50 Charles Chaplin, *My Autobiography* (1974 edn; first publ. 1964), p. 146.

51 Beresford, 'The Public Presentation of Vagrancy', p. 150.

52 E.g. National Assistance Board, *Homeless Single Persons*, (London, 1966). For a bibliography see Rose, *Rogues and Vagabonds*, pp. 217–12.

5

THE ENGLISH BOBBY: AN
INDULGENT TRADITION
Clive Emsley

Every police constable in the force may hope to rise by intelligence and
good conduct to the superior stations . . .
He will be civil and obliging to all people of every rank and class, and
ready to give information and assistance when required . . .
He must be particularly cautious not to interfere idly or unnecessarily,
in order to make display of his authority; when required to act, he will
do so with decision and boldness . . . He must remember that there is
no qualification so indispensable to a police-officer as a perfect command of temper, never suffering himself to be moved in the slightest
degree by any language or threats that may be used.

Metropolitan Police Instructions, September 1829

Superintendent Hammond: What's an old fashioned PC, Ron?
Superintendent Cherry: A man of experience, unswerving in his desire
to serve the public, polite yet chirpy, conciliatory but always ethical, a
bastion of moral fibre and a power of example. And then we joined the
Filth.

Arthur Ellis, *The Black and Blue Lamp*, BBC2, 7 September 1988

Reviewing the classic British police film *The Blue Lamp* in 1950, the
critic of *The Times* suggested that the two central characters, PCs
George Dixon and Andy Mitchell, were not 'policemen as they really
are but policemen as an indulgent tradition has chosen to think they
are'.[1] PC Dixon was shot dead in the film; however, after a gap of
five years he was resurrected for a television series, *Dixon of Dock
Green*, which ran for 434 episodes over twenty-one years. Dixon,
described by one commentator as 'a classic boy scout, living up to
Baden Powell's standards of civilised behaviour at all times',[2] was
rapidly acknowledged as the personification of the ideal English
Bobby. Such an image of the policeman, as *The Times*'s critic suggested, was not new, but Dixon gave it a comforting and corporeal
existence. The 'tough' styles of policing which appeared to character-
ize the 1980s, with the inner-city riots and the miners' strike of
1984–5, were commonly contrasted with Dixon's style, that of a man
who knew everyone on his 'manor' and who never had recourse to a

The archetypal English Bobby, PC George Dixon (Jack Warner), gently questions a jeweller attacked and robbed of his shop keys in *The Blue Lamp* (1950).
Photo: The British Film Institute. Reproduced by kind permission of Weintraub.

violent response whatever the problem, the dangers or the provoca-
tion.[3] This essay will address itself to three questions: Where did the
image of the English Bobby originate? How was it maintained and
developed? When, and why, did it begin to disintegrate?

As is apparent from the extracts from the Metropolitan Police
Instructions quoted above, the image of the polite, self-controlled
constable was projected by the founders of the force in 1829.
Recognizing the long-standing antipathy of the 'free-born
Englishman' to standing armies and spies – things which appeared
peculiarly European, and particularly French – the Home Secretary,
Robert Peel, and his first two Metropolitan Police Commissioners,
Colonel Charles Rowan and Richard Mayne, put their police into
uniform, so that they could not be branded as spies, and made the
uniform blue and closer to civilian rather than army style, so as to
undermine the charge that the new force was military. The pay was

kept low, only twenty-one shillings a week for a constable (less two shillings towards the cost of the uniform), so as to dissuade gentlemen and commissioned officers from joining and again limit the taint of militarism. Peel probably also recognized that a uniformed gentleman ordering a costermonger to move his barrow from a street would look like a particularly aggressive form of class control. The upper ranks of the police were to be filled from below; conscientious hard work and self-improvement, it was maintained, would enable a man to rise from constable to superintendent.[4]

A few men of the hoped-for calibre were recruited, but the turnover of recruits in the early years of the Metropolitan Police was enormous. Many men left of their own volition; they had joined, not for a career, but to tide themselves over a period of temporary unemployment or to see what the new life was like. It was hard and harshly disciplined. Within two months of the force's foundation one ex-constable was lamenting

> Cursed was I the day I left a comfortable situation to be drilled and dragged thro Regulations . . . what man of sober industrious habits would or could consent to take up his abode in a Barrack for the pay of a bricklayer's laborer [sic] and work or watch 7 days and nights in the week, it is absurd to expect it.[5]

Many other men were dismissed for disciplinary offences, often relating to drink.[6] The force met much criticism and hostility; no matter that its founders had wanted it to appear non-military, that was precisely how many thousands of Londoners perceived it. A contributor to the *Monthly Magazine* spoke for these when he asked 'Might not the pocket-handkerchiefs of the Strand-going population have been better protected by a less onerous expedient than that of raising a regular battalion officered [by Colonel Rowan] from the military depot?'[7]

But there was an increasing feeling among persons of property that some change was needed in the system of policing. An influential body, including Utilitarian reformers like Edwin Chadwick, continuously sang the praises of the new institution and no government ever seriously contemplated an alternative 'expedient'. On the contrary, the Municipal Corporations Act of 1835 required borough authorities to establish police forces, while the rural constabulary legislation of 1839 and 1840 authorized county benches to establish their own police forces if they so wished. Some counties acted on this legisla-

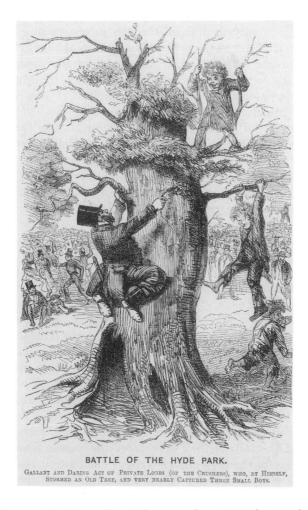

BATTLE OF THE HYDE PARK.

GALLANT AND DARING ACT OF PRIVATE LOBBS (OF THE CRUSHERS), WHO, BY HIMSELF,
STORMED AN OLD TREE, AND VERY NEARLY CAPTURED THREE SMALL BOYS.

In its early years the Metropolitan Police was often criticized as a military body
(hence 'Private' Lobbs) and for spending more time pursuing petty offenders
than serious criminals. 'Crusher' was a slang term, popular with costermongers,
for policemen.
Source: *Punch*, 21 July 1855.

tion, while others tried different experiments to improve the existing
system. The County and Borough Police Act of 1856 required those
boroughs which had been lax in implementing the police clauses of
the 1835 Act and those counties which had not taken advantage of
the 1839–40 legislation to establish police forces forthwith. The

legislation relating to policing was part of the Utilitarian infection which spread, in varying degrees, through successive British governments during the nineteenth century. But also, by the mid-1850s, with a rationalized and, in some small measure, centrally supervised system of policing established throughout the country, the Metropolitan Police had acquired an impressive reputation and its critics were increasingly drowned by the choruses of approval.

The reputation of the Metropolitan Police had been enhanced by the policing of both Chartism and the Great Exhibition of 1851. Some heads may have been broken by police batons at Chartist meetings, and constables may have strapped on cutlasses rather than simply wielding their truncheons when faced with potential disorder, but the English middle classes could look with smug satisfaction at the contrast between the policing of the last great Chartist demonstration in London in May 1848 and events in Paris during February and June, as well as in Berlin and in other major towns and cities of continental Europe in the 'Year of Revolutions'. The Great Exhibition celebrated Britain's industrial predominance in the world as well as the Victorian 'Gospel of Work'. There was concern about the vast number of visitors who would be drawn to London for the Exhibition, but no trouble materialized, and again the Metropolitan Police were given much of the credit.[8] Here was an institution which Englishmen could boast of as being peculiarly English in that, in contrast to European police organizations, it was generally unarmed, non-military, and non-political; it suited well the liberal Englishman's notion that his country's success derived from institutions, ideas and practices which provided models for the world. The police constable, to many middle-class Victorians, became the personification of an idealized image of the English legal system – impartial, and functioning with solemnity and a clockwork regularity: 'Amid the bustle of Piccadilly or the roar of Oxford Street, PC X.59 stalks along, an institution rather than a man. We seem to have no more hold of his personality than we could possibly get of his coat buttoned up to the throttling point.'[9] This kind of policeman was unlikely to be found in the provincial towns of Victorian England, since here the constables were often regarded as, first and foremost, servants of the municipality,[10] while the uniforms worn by men in the same force were not always of the same pattern.[11] He might be found in the countryside, though county policemen must have appeared much thinner on the ground and it was difficult to plod a large, sometimes muddy, country beat with the same regularity and authority as one in central London.

There could be caustic criticism of policemen, especially following police action which involved the use of truncheons. Following a baton charge during a miners' strike in Durham in 1891, for example, a local poetaster penned the following pastiche of Tennyson for the *Sunderland Daily Echo*:

Down the hill, down the hill
  Fifty yards onward,
All among the flying folk
  Ran the half hundred.
'Forward the 'Cop's' Brigade!
Charge for the lot!' he said;
    Into the scatt'ring crowd
    Ran the half hundred.

Old men to the right of them,
Women to the left of them,
Bairns right in front of them,
  Bolted and wonder'd;
Left free to have their way,
Nimbly their staves did play,
Into the fleeing crowd,
Into the roaring fun
    Plunged the half hundred.

Flashed all their batons bare,
Flashed as they turned in air,
Thumping at back-skulls there,
Mauling away because
  Someone had blunder'd.
Pounding at ev'ry head,
Quiet folks' blood was shed;
Women and children
Reeled from the blows that sped,
  Moaning and sunder'd.
Then they marched back again
    Gallant half hundred!

When can their glory fade?
O the grand charge they made!
  All people wonder'd.
Honour the charge they made!
Honour the 'Cop's Brigade,'
    Noble half hundred![12]

Such incidents could lead to the reputation of the police reaching a
very low ebb, at least among some sections of the community where
they occurred. Occasionally they prompted fierce questions in
Parliament, especially when the London police were involved. But
Victorian politicians were rarely prepared to maintain any lengthy
and sustained criticism of any one of the pillars of the English constitutional and legal system; and it is at least arguable that the comic
portrayal of the police in *The Pirates of Penzance* in 1880 was in itself
an indication that they had, by that date, achieved such an elevated
status.

Of course, not every comic or musical portrayal of policemen was
as affectionate as that of Gilbert and Sullivan. Policemen in ballad
literature, and later in the working-class music-hall songs and rou-
tines of the second half of tha century, were often possessed of more
vices than virtues.[13] Policemen were also commonly portrayed as
spending an inordinate amount of time with cooks and servant girls;
this kind of humour spread into magazines like *Punch* where jokes
such as 'What article of dress are Cooks most attached to? The
Pelisse' were typical.[14] Yet increasingly the humour about the police
appears to have softened.

Soft or not, however, such humour could upset some members of
the police and their supporters. The first edition of *Police Review and
Parade Gossip* lamented the 'tendency, all too prevalent, as evidenced
on the stage and in the comic Press, as well as on the public foot-
path, to treat a policeman with less regard for his own self respect
than should prevail amongst men towards their fellow-men in all
ranks of life'.[15] In its second edition the journal published an extract
from the *National Observer* expressing concern at the way some
newspapers often sensationalized any confrontation between a police
constable and a member of the public: 'Yet it must be obvious to any
one not under the necessity of providing exciting copy that the public
and the police are on capital terms.'[16] Confining the *National
Observer*'s definition of 'the public' to the articulate and the
respectable, its assertion was probably correct. In spite of its joking
and jibes, as early as 1851 *Punch* was suggesting that the police were
'beginning to take that place in the affections of the people' which
during the Napoleonic wars was occupied by the army and the navy;
they were becoming 'the national favorites'.[17] Indeed, comments such
as this were far more common in the Conservative and Liberal press
than criticism of the police during the second half of the nineteenth
century. When, for example, following a series of armed robberies in
London during the 1880s there was a press debate on arming the

police, *The Times* vigorously opposed the idea on the grounds that this would alter the 'excellent' relations existing between police and people.

> The policeman, who is in foreign cities regarded as an enemy, not only by the criminal classes but by the working classes generally, and who in times of social disturbance is made the first victim of popular hatred, is in England rather the friend of the people than otherwise. It is not only the black-coated respectability that feels at home with him, but the workman and the woman of the people – every one, in fact, but the criminal and the street Arab – look upon him as an excellent fellow, who performs a necessary duty with as little roughness as possible. It is obvious that such a relation between the police and the people is the best of all guarantees of social order, and that to jeopardize it would be a most serious blunder. Would it survive two or three cases of shooting? Even now, when, as occasionally happens, a group of constables lose their temper in a scuffle and treat some unoffending person with harshness, the outcry is loud, and the force for the time becomes unpopular. It would be in danger of becoming not only unpopular but hated, if a few of its members, in moments of error or panic were to fire upon some innocent individuals.[18]

The Bobby, as described in this passage, has all the virtues of the 'indulgent tradition' identified by the same newspaper's film critic over half a century later. It is easy to knock holes in the image: as a result of the scare about armed burglars some uniformed police constables did start patrolling with revolvers, and many senior provincial policemen were keen to train their men in the use of firearms;[19] even towards the end of the century it is unlikely that street traders and the casual poor regarded the policeman as a 'friend' and probably there was little difference in the policing strategies employed on the streets of London and Paris.[20] However, the political stability and political structure of Victorian Britain did enable the Bobby to maintain an image different from that of his continental counterparts. At least one of the functions of the paramilitary *gendarmerie*, *guardia civil* and *carabinieri* was to show the flag of the national government in remote areas where peasants were still in the process of being transformed into Frenchmen, Spaniards or Italians; such a function was irrelevant in Victorian England. Governments in continental Europe feared conspirators lurking at home or waiting in exile with alternative constitutional structures either to unify or to restore a nation state (as in the case of some Germans, Italians and Poles), to

re-establish an old form of government (as in France with
Bonapartists, Royalists and Jacobins) or to create something new.
For this reason, while continental Liberals might admire the English
Bobby and contemplate something similar, they never felt safe
enough, when in power, to dispose of their paramilitary police;[21] and
European governments of every hue considered it essential to have
large departments of political police and to deploy individual agents
and sometimes whole squads of men whose only task was to visit
pubs and cafés to listen to the conversations and songs of the
patrons.[22] Political policing always gave the articulate opposition
(often a victim of such policing) a stick with which to beat the system; in June 1882, for example, Le Figaro protested: 'Aujourd'hui,
comme sous l'Empire, comme sous la Restauration comme toujours,
la police réelle, la police utile cede la place, est subordonnée, est
sacrifiée à la police politique et c'est pour cela qu'au lieu d'un préfet,
connaissant son métier, on veut un homme devoué – un homme politique.'[23] The British constitutional system did not face any similar
threats during the nineteenth century, and therefore, not only could
Victorians smugly criticize the political police of other countries, they
could also avoid creating their own political police – until the end of
the century, when they found themselves confronted by a terrorist
threat from Ireland and also under pressure from European governments to make common cause against anarchists, nihilists and social-
ists.[24]

The devolved nature of policing in England also contributed to the
claim that the Bobby was non-political, in the sense of not being an
overt agent of central government. While the Metropolitan Police
was responsible to the Home Secretary, and while, following the
1856 County and Borough Police Act, all forces were subject to
annual inspections by Her Majesty's Inspectors of Constabulary, the
provincial police forces were primarily supervised by, and responsible
to, local authorities – the watch committees of the boroughs, magistrates and then, after 1888, magistrates and county councillors meeting as Standing Joint Committees in the counties. In the aftermath of
the Cleator Moor riot of July 1884, when an Orange Order parade in
Cumberland had resulted in one Catholic Irish heckler being shot
dead and several wounded by the Orangemen, Irish MPs complained
at the march ever having been permitted and protested at the small
number of police deployed in case of trouble. They wanted to know
what orders the Home Secretary had given, and what steps he had
taken to prevent any disorder. Sir William Harcourt, the Home
Secretary, was able to respond that, although he had received a

report on the incident from the Chief Constable of Cumberland, the preparations for the Orange march had nothing to do with him since police and public order in England were the responsibility not of central government but of the local authorities.[25] In Ireland, by contrast, as in other parts of the British Empire, there were centralized, armed policemen whose tasks, like those of *gendarmes, guardias* and *carabinieri*, involved showing the flag.

If, in contrast to European policemen, the nineteenth-century Bobby appeared neither a military man nor a political spy, he also appeared non-political in contrast to the American cop. The democratic structure of American cities, whereby some police chiefs could themselves be elected as a result of a political campaign, or else appointed by the victors of a local election, made the municipal police forces overtly political institutions. Policemen were known to participate in the electoral process on the side of their political patrons; their involvement in industrial disorders might also be dictated, first and foremost, by political affiliations and considerations.[26] But, at the same time, the openness of democratic government in the United States meant that police behaviour could be under constant public scrutiny. In the first decade of the twentieth century the Home Office and the Commissioner were determined to keep secret the number of discipline cases within the Metropolitan Police and London magistrates were advised not to give public replies to questions which might be detrimental to the police.[27] While he was almost certainly ignorant of these policy decisions, William McAdoo, a former police commissioner of New York City, noted their results. In 1909, after a four-week visit to London, he could write:

The [London] press has no means of knowing of the daily volume of crime except through the courts or the reports of persons made directly to the newspapers, so the police are not held to the same direct accounting as in New York, where the criminal statistics are inspected every hour, or at least were under my administration.

He was astonished that the press praised the police 'on every possible occasion', but that they were not allowed into Scotland Yard; on the other hand, he thought it a good thing that there was less clerical machinery and red tape: 'A New York captain now makes more reports than the commander of a battle-ship.' The lack of continual press investigation and criticism probably contributed to the 'indulgent tradition', though McAdoo noted other things working in the favour of the London policeman – a tradition of integrity among public servants, and no immigration problems comparable with those of New York, to name but two.[28]

It is, of course, possible to find examples which run counter to the non-political image of the English Bobby as compared with the American cop, especially in the case of provincial policemen. As long as a borough constable was considered a servant of the local watch committee he could, for example, be drawn into the conflict between Tory brewers and Temperance Liberals; while orders to the police during industrial disorders to protect blacklegs or bailiffs did not appear neutral to strikers and their families. There was an accidental sleight of hand by which politicians, jurists and journalists in England emphasized the excellence of a theoretical constitutional position in contrast to those occasional actual incidents which contradicted it. However, they chose always to compare the English constitutional position, not with the constitutional position of other countries, but only with events on foreign ground; moreover, their knowledge of the police systems of foreign countries was probably based rather more on prejudice than on actual experience. In July 1900 the Independent Radical MP John Burns told the Commons:

> Notwithstanding the fact that they do not always do everything they should, I believe that the Metropolitan Police, after the City [of London] Police, are the best police force in the world. I ought to know that as I have come into closer contact with them than with any other Member of the House.[29]

Burns had indeed come into close contact with the London police when, as a trade union activist and member of the Social Democratic Federation, he had played an important role in open-air agitation and in the Great Dock Strike of 1889; he had even been arrested. He had visited Austria, France and Germany briefly during the 1870s, but whether this can be said to have made him an authority on their police systems is a moot point.

There is an old adage that if a thing is repeated often enough and with sufficient conviction, then it will acquire the status of truth. Burns was not the first to suggest that the London police were the best in the world, and he was by no means the last; and it needs to be stressed again that the Metropolitan Police of London were commonly taken as typical of, indeed the model for, the different police forces of the whole of England and Wales. In December 1906, for example, *The Times* boasted: 'Our police force is a credit to the men who are responsible for it, and a source of pride to every Englishman who is acquainted with police administration in other countries.'[30] Twenty years later, *The Justice of the Peace* was arguing that it was 'Robert's . . . wonderful faculty for combining official integrity and detachment with the part of a man and a brother that has made the English policeman the envy of the civilised world'.[31] In 1935 Major M. J. Egan, the Chief Constable of Southport, told his colleagues that they were all members of a police service which, in comparison with its foreign counterparts, was 'superior on points of general efficiency, good conduct and character'.[32] The following year, with just a little more reserve, Rhys Davies, the Labour MP for Westhoughton, informed the Commons 'that our police force is probably the best in the world'.[33] Of course, for refugees and even some visitors from central and eastern Europe the Bobby was markedly less menacing than his counterpart in, for example, Berlin or Moscow.

My heart is too full when I think of the sweetest, nicest, most loveable policeman in the world. I can stand on the pavement in London and admire him, I can watch him with pleasure at his various tasks. I can sing his praise in different languages and tunes, and I often do. And I am much pleased whenever I observe that our own Polish policemen, after being schooled by an Englishman, try their best to follow the example of the English bobby.[34]

He may have been sweet, nice and lovable; he may also have been the model which every young Englishman should have sought to emulate;[35] but quite how that made the Bobby the best policeman in the world was never adequately explained. As far as efficiency in both detection and traffic control were concerned, it was manifestly the case, at least by the 1930s, that there was much to be learned from police forces overseas.[36]

For McAdoo the London Bobby was a 'St. Bernard'.[37] The term encapsulates the solidity and dependability of the ideal type of English policeman as envisaged at the beginning of the twentieth century; it also suggests a certain lack of intellectual capacity which was a continuing feature both of humour about the police and of the 'indulgent tradition'. Well might 'An Ex-Detective Inspector' protest, in 1926, 'England has the finest detective and police force in the world . . . Corruption in America is an epidemic. In this country, it is conspicuous – by its absence. An official once said to me, "In

America they look for an arrest. In England they make it!"'[38] But in the representation in popular literature in the late nineteenth and early twentieth centuries, the uniformed policeman and the police detective were generally foils to the astute thinker from a superior social class (Sherlock Holmes, Miss Marple, Lord Peter Wimsey) or from abroad (Hercule Poirot). As one inter-war critic commented: 'On the whole, policemen are portrayed in a favourable light by novelists, except perhaps as regards their intelligence.'[39] Semi-official legal literature might comment on the improving educational quality of police recruits, but it also criticized the pompous Latinate language in which policemen gave their evidence in court, often apparently ignorant of the real meaning of some of the words they were using; an especial favourite was the police constable who used the malapropism 'intellectual course' in place of 'sexual intercourse'.[40] The radio talks given by Police Constable Harry Daley, and reproduced in *The Listener*, were vetted by his superiors at Scotland Yard and gave impression of a solid, working-class chap, contented with his lot; the warts discussed in Daley's subsequent autobiography were not apparent.[41] The Bobby was not a central character in the early British cinema, but when he did appear it was in his stereotyped role. Even in newsreels which showed scenes of the violence of street disorders in the inter-war years, the English policeman was portrayed as moderate and sensible: the epitome of English level-headedness. According to *British Movietone News*, for example, the Battle of Cable Street occurred

> because one man in whom a lot of people placed faith said 'we'll take a walk through the East End of London'. Then several other men, in whom a lot of people placed faith, said 'Not on your .... life you don't.' Then the police said 'Now, now, you children, you can't do that there 'ere,' and started sorting them out. It wasn't easy, but they did it because if you want to place faith anywhere safe, put your money on the police.

Of course, the 'sorting out' was done in the unique English manner, and as truncheons were wielded the cinema audience was invited to 'Watch how this baton doesn't hit!'[42]

In Parliament, during the inter-war years, there was something of a consensus on the excellence of the English police. There were concerns about police arbitrariness in the late 1920s, and a few scandals, notably the case of Sergeant Goddard, who was found to have been in receipt of considerable sums from individuals involved in vice rackets, but nothing was thought to be wrong with the basics of the English 'Police Idea'.[43] The Royal Commission on Police Powers and Procedure, set up in the aftermath of the allegations of arbitrary behaviour, explained:

> [The police] are men like the rest of us, prone on occasion to human infirmities, and more beset than most of us by problems and temptations. That they sometimes make mistakes is of course inevitable and, as has been shrewdly said, people who never make mistakes seldom make anything. But the testimony which has reached us from responsible and judicial authorities has led us to form a very favourable opinion of the conduct, tone, and efficiency of the Police Service as a whole.[44]

Evidence from sections of the working class and from some labour activists night have produced a different picture, but the Labour Party as a body accepted the 'indulgent tradition'. It did nothing for the men dismissed for their part in the police strikes of 1919; and even when it formed a government, the Labour Party was not prepared to rock any of the pillars of the constitution or the legal system. In July 1928 Ramsay Macdonald explained to the Commons that he had no desire ever to see the Metropolitan Police resemble the police of Paris or Berlin; and five years later, addresssing the same house, George Lansbury declared:

> Until the last three weeks if any hon. Member had dared to stand up in this House and cast any reflections on an individual constable in the Metropolitan Police Force, he would have been shouted down by hon. Members opposite. We have been told that it is the most perfect police force in the world; that it is the admiration of the world; that foreigners come here and almost kneel down to worship the man on point duty . . .[45]

Lansbury himself did not deny the supremacy of the English police model; rather, he went on to challenge the need for a Police College and expressed traditional English concerns about a creeping militarization of the police. Governments refused inquiries into the alleged incidents of violence by police acting as a body, most notably in Liverpool in 1921 and Birkenhead in 1932; and where local left-wing politicians faced serious confrontations with their local Chief

Constable, it was the latter who could generally be sure of Home Office backing.[46]

When the police were first established the street had been a place of leisure for large numbers of the urban working classes. From early on the police had been deployed to control the streets and to impose at least a degree of Victorian decorum in them.[47] The inter-war period saw an acceleration of the process by which leisure shifted from public to private or better-controlled space.[48] But while this meant that the police had less to do with sections of the working class, other changes in leisure, particularly the development of the motor car, were bringing police constables into direct confrontation with members of the middle classes in ways and in numbers that were completely unknown during the nineteenth century.[49] At the same time, the use of police against street demonstrations, and the behaviour of some of the police in these instances, created disquiet among many individuals of liberal and left-wing sympathies, and led directly to the creation of the National Council for Civil Liberties in 1934. However, it was not until the late 1950s and the 1960s that there was any serious recognition within English society, and especially among those involved in shaping or broadcasting opinion, that all was not well in relations between police and people and that not every English Bobby was cast in the avuncular George Dixon mould.

During the 1950s several scandals came to light involving police officers, and in 1960 a Royal Commission was established to enquire into a variety of issues including the relations between police and public. The Royal Commission found 'an overwhelming vote of confidence in the police . . . and such change as there has been in public opinion in recent years has mainly been in favour of the police'.[50] This assessment was rather too optimistic, given the data that the Commission had itself collected.[51] But by the end of the decade, clashes in CND and anti-Vietnam rallies together with confrontations over the use of, and searches for, drugs such as LSD and marijuana, were poisoning relations between the police and sections of educated youth.

There was a sharp upward trend in crime beginning towards the end of the 1950s. In their attempts to combat this the police developed new, more technologically developed tactics with the Unit Beat System, known popularly as 'fire-brigade policing'. The constable patrolling a beat was increasingly replaced by constables in cars 'responding' to crime rather than just seeking to 'prevent' it. The police were further distanced from the community by the massive consolidations of the late 1960s which swept away the small local

The Road Traffic Act of 1903 was to bring the Bobby into confrontation with members of the middle class on a scale hitherto unknown. But the patronizing image of the constable as a simple Dogberry remained popular.
Source: *Illustrated London News*, 10 October 1903.

forces with their watch committees and standing joint committees; the large forces created during the 1960s sometimes covered more than one county, and this could leave the county councillors on the supervisory police committees with little common ground and little common interest other than their periodic committee meetings with senior police officers and magistrates.

As the policeman became ever more distanced from the community so his media representation changed. In television police series he remained incorruptible, but he became much tougher and tended to have a less settled home life than Dixon. There was considerable stir when, in the first episode of Z Cars, a police constable was seen arguing furiously with his wife. Ten years later Detective Inspector Jack Regan, the tough rule-breaking hero of The Sweeney, was accepted with little comment as a divorcee, drinking heavily and moving from girlfriend to girlfriend. In the greater freedom of the novel, the cinema and the single play for television, policemen could be portrayed as brutal and corrupt. Colin MacInnes led the way with City of Spades in 1957 and Mr Love and Mr Justice three years later. G. F. Newman clinched the image with his bleak picture of police-men seemingly more corrupt than the offenders they were 'fitting up' in the television plays Law and Order transmitted in 1978. In his black comedy, The Black and Blue Lamp, Arthur Ellis catapulted George Dixon's bewildered murderer forty years into the future into a police station at the end of the 1980s where violence and threats of violence towards suspects were commonplace. Of course, this media representation probably owed much to other influences, not the least of which were American police series transmitted on British television and the tough cops and detectives portrayed in American films and novels. Yet English policemen had apparently survived such a copy-cat image, and the whiff of corruption present in the earlier influx of American culture between the wars; the point is that from the 1950s onwards the police presence on the streets was changing, their con-frontations with the educated and articulate middle classes were increasing, and their tenuous local links with such groups through watch committees and standing joint committees were severed.

Equally important to the changing image of the police was the way in which, during the 1970s, both senior police officers and the Police Federation began campaigning publicly for 'law and order'. They continued to protest that the police were non-partisan, but their plat-form was now uncomfortably close to the 'law and order' arguments espoused by the Conservative Party.[52] By the mid-1980s, following both pay rises far above those of other public sector workers and their deployment against inner-city rioters and striking coal-miners and print-workers, many policemen were expressing concerns about their apparent association with the Conservative Party under Margaret Thatcher:

> The Tories have a reputation for being extremely pro-police . . . Tories tend to be verbally supportive but I think we are in serious danger of being used as a tool. Like we were during the miners' strike. No question, we were 'Maggie's boys'. I hated that. I hated the feeling we were being used . . . We're supposed to be fucking impartial. I don't think we are. Not now. That's the unpleasant truth.[53]

Traditional historians of, and commentators on, the English police have confidently asserted that, after an initial period of uncertainty, the English Bobby was generally popular with the overwhelming majority of the 'law-abiding' population in the country. The truth of such assertions would be difficult to prove. It is clear that such was the general image portrayed in most forms of literature and other representations of the police up until the end of the Second World

A new police image? Members of the Thames Valley Police in riot equipment during disturbances in Oxford, September 1991
Source: Press Association. Photograph: David Jones.

War. But it is also probably true that large sections of the working class continued to eye the police warily even if they did, from time to time, themselves have recourse to their services. Public opinion surveys of the English police taken shortly after the Second World War reveal a very positive attitude towards the Bobby which seems to have been rather different from that in other countries.[54] Perhaps since they were continually being told that they were different from other policemen, gentler, calmer, more polite and restrained, most English Bobbies had sought to act out on the street the role sketched for them, at least with those whom they considered respectable. The 'indulgent tradition' thus did have a meaning as a code of behaviour between policemen and some social groups from the Victorian period to the 1960s and, indeed, beyond. But by the end of the 1980s public opinion polls were expressing considerable reservations about the police; and quality newspapers on both ends of the political spectrum accepted such findings.[55] Perhaps some of this change in attitude was the result of a more realistic attitude to policemen and policing, some to an apparent new partisanship on the part of the police and their involvement as the enforcers of the Thatcher government's policies of confrontation. Some may also have been the result of the new kind of police role model; the image of Dixon of Dock Green was not the one to be relished by the young policeman in a fast white car with 'go faster stripes' on the side and flashing lights on top.

Notes

1 *The Times*, 20 January 1950, p. 8.
2 Alan Clarke, '"This is not the Boy Scouts": Television Police Series and Definitions of Law and Order', in Tony Bennett, Colin Mercer and Janet Woollacott (eds), *Popular Culture and Social Relations* (Milton Keynes, 1986), p. 225.
3 See, *inter alia*, 'We can't leave it to old George any more', *Financial Times*, 28 July 1981; 'The Policing Style has Changed from Dixon to Darth Vader', *The Times*, 10 November 1986.
4 There are many surveys of the origins of the Metropolitan Police of London; see, for example, David Ascoli, *The Queen's Peace: The Origins and Development of the Metroplitan Police 1829–1979* (London, 1979), ch. 3, and Stanley H. Palmer, *Police and Protest in England and Ireland 1780–1850* (Cambridge, 1988), ch. 8.
5 *Weekly Dispatch*, 8 November 1829.
6 In 1834 Rowan and Mayne informed a parliamentary select committee that of the 2,800 constables serving in May 1830 only 562 remained with the force; they also estimated that four out of five dimissals were for drunkenness.

Parliamentary Papers 1834 (600), XVI, *Select Committee on the Police of the Metropolis*, qq. 107–8.

7 'The State of the Empire: Police, Press, Popery and Foreign Relations', *Monthly Magazine*, 1829, new series, vol. 8 (October), p. 363.

8 'The Police System of London', *Edinburgh Review*, 1852, vol. 96, July, p. 21.

9 'The Police and the Thieves', *Quarterly Review*, 1856, vol. 99, June, p. 171.

10 Carolyn Steedman, *Policing the Victorian Community: The Formation of English Provincial Police Forces 1856–1880* (London, 1984), pp. 31, 37, 130.

11 Roger Swift, *Police Reform in Early Victorian York, 1835–1856* (University of York, Borthwick Paper No. 73, 1988), p. 13.

12 *Sunderland Daily Echo*, 28 February 1891, p. 4. For criticism of the Metropolitan Police in crowd actions see Victor Bailey, 'The Metropolitan Police, the Home Office and the Threat of Outcast London', in Victor Bailey (ed.), *Policing and Punishment in Nineteenth-Century Britain* (London, 1981); David Goodway, *London Chartism 1838–1848* (Cambridge, 1982), part 3; Phillip Thurmond Smith, *Policing Victorian London: Political Policing, Public Order, and the London Metropolitan Police* (Westport, 1985), pp. 136–7, 171.

13 See for example, 'I Should Like to be a Policeman' on *Waterloo–Peterloo (English Folk Songs and Broadsides 1780-1830)* recorded by The Critics Group (Argo Record Company, 1968); Wilbur R. Miller, *Cops and Bobbies: Police Authority in New York and London, 1830–1870* (Chicago, 1977), pp. 126–8.

14 *Punch*, January–June 1853, p. 181; see also January–June 1843, p. 105; July–December 1851, p. 173; July–December 1856, p. 10.

15 *Police Review and Parade Gossip*, 2 January 1893, p. 1.

16 Ibid., 9 January 1893, p. 15.

17 *Punch*, July–December 1851, p. 173.

18 *The Times*, 14 September 1883.

19 Clive Emsley, '"The Thump of Wood on a Swede Turnip": Police Violence in Nineteenth-Century England', *Criminal Justice History*, 1985, vol. 6, pp. 125–49.

20 Jennifer Davis, 'Urban Policing and its Objects: Comparative Themes in England and France in the Second Half of the Nineteenth Century', in Clive Emsley and Barbara Weinberger (eds), *Policing Western Europe: Politics, Professionalization and Public Order 1850–1940* (Westport, 1991).

21 Steven C. Hughes, 'Gendarmes and Bobbies: Italy's Search for the Appropriate Police', paper read to the Southern Historical Association, New Orleans, November 1987. My thanks to Professor Hughes for a copy of this paper.

22 Edgar L. Newman, 'Quand les mouchards ne riaient pas: les ouvriers chansonniers, la justice et la liberté pendant la monarchie de juillet', in Philippe Vigier, Alain Faure *et al.*, *Répression et prison politiques en France et en Europe au XIXe siècle* (Paris, 1990), pp. 297–303; Richard J. Evans (ed.), *Kneipengespräche im Kaiserreich: Stimmungsberichte der Hamburger Politischen Polizei 1892–1914* (Reinbek bei Hamburg, 1989).

23 'Today, as under the Empire, as under the Restoration, as always, the real police, the useful police gives way before, is sacrificed and subordinated to, political police, and it is for this reason that, in place of a prefect who knows the job, there is a loyal man – a political man.' *Le Figaro*, 21 June 1882; see also ibid., 9 August 1882. See also Jean Marc Berlière, 'La Professionalisation: Revendication des policiers et objectif des pouvoirs au début de la IIIe

république', *Revue d'histoire moderne et contemporaine*, 1990, vol. 36, pp. 398–428.

24 Bernard Porter, *The Origins of the Vigilant State: The London Metropolitan Police Special Branch before the First World War* (London, 1987).

25 *Hansard*, 291, 15 July 1884, cols 1119–20.

26 For examples of political policemen in big American cities see, *inter alia*, Roger Lane, *Policing the City: Boston 1822–1885* (Cambridge, Mass., 1967), and James F. Richardson, *The New York Police: Colonial Times to 1901* (New York, 1970); and for partiality in industrial disputes see, *inter alia*, Sidney L. Harring and Lorraine M. McMullen, 'The Buffalo Police 1872–1900: Labor Unrest, Political Power and the Creation of the Police Institution', *Crime and Social Justice*, 1975, pp. 5–14.

27 V. A. C. Gatrell, 'Crime, Authority and the Policeman State', in F. M. L. Thompson, *The Cambridge Social History of Britain 1750–1950* (Cambridge, 1990), p. 275.

28 William McAdoo, 'The London Police from a New York Point of View', *The Century Magazine*, 1909, vol. 78, September, pp. 649–70; quotations at pp. 658, 659.

29 *Hansard*, 85, 13 July 1900, col. 1559.

30 *The Times*, 24 December 1906, p. 6.

31 *Justice of the Peace*, 1926, vol. 90, 13 February, p. 112.

32 *Chief Constables' Association: Reports of the General Conference, 12 June 1935, and Special General Conference, 13 June 1935*, p. 16.

33 *Hansard*, 309, 5 March 1936, col. 1661.

34 An unnamed Polish lady quoted by 'An American', *On and Off Duty*, June 1926, p. 88.

35 Rt Rev. R. G. Eden, Bishop of Wakefield, 'The Police in Relation to English Life', *Chief Constables' Association: Annual Report of the General Meeting, 9 May 1913*, pp. 32–41 at pp. 39–41.

36 Metropolitan Police Archives, MS Book 554.85, Report by H. Alker Tripp, Assistant Commissioner on Visit to America, 1934, especially part 1; Home Office, *Report of the Departmental Committee on Detective Work and Procedure*, 4 vols (London, 1939).

37 McAdoo, 'The London Police', p. 661.

38 'An Ex-Detective Inspector', 'Sherlocks of Real Life', *On and Off Duty*, March 1926, p. 35.

39 S. O'M., 'The Policeman in Modern Fiction', *Police Journal*, 1930, vol. 3, pp. 134–45: at p. 144.

40 This incident is reported in *Justice of the Peace*, 1917, vol. 81, 10 February, p. 64, and *Solicitors' Journal*, 1932, vol. 76, 5 November, p. 767.

41 Peter Parker, *Ackerley: A Life of J. R. Ackerley* (London, 1989), p. 126; Harry Daley, *This Small Cloud: A Personal Memoir* (London, 1987); '"Not a Happy One"? My Day's Work by Harry Daley, Metropolitan Policeman', *The Listener*, 27 March 1929; 'While London Sleeps: The Policeman on his Beat', ibid., 13 November 1929.

While Daley's broadcasts, and much of his autobiography, reflect the 'indulgent tradition', he was hardly a typical policeman. Openly homosexual, he became a close friend of the group around Ackerley and E. M. Forster. It was through his links with the former that he was invited to make his broadcasts.

42 Quoted in Tony Aldgate, 'The Newsreels, Public Order and the Projection of

Britain', in James Curran, Anthony Smith and Pauline Wingate (eds), *Impacts and Influences: Essays on Media Power in the 20th Century* (London, 1987), p. 148.

43 'The Police Idea' was the title chosen by Charles Reith for first of his histories chronicling the development of the police in England – an institution which he considered crucial to the march of progress. Charles Reith, *The Police Idea* (Oxford, 1938), pp. v–vi.

44 *Report of the Royal Commission on Police Powers and Procedure*, Cmd. 3297 (London, 1929), p. 111.

45 *Hansard*, 220, 20 July 1928, col. 882; ibid., 278, 23 May 1933, cols 956–57.

46 Barbara Weinberger, 'Police Perceptions of Labour in the Inter-war Period: The Case of the Unemployed and of Miners on Strike', in Douglas Hay and Francis Snyder (eds), *Labour, Law and Crime: An Historical Perspective* (London, 1987); Clive Emsley, 'Police Forces and Public Order in England and France during the Inter-war Years', in Emsley and Weinberger, *Policing Western Europe*.

47 Clive Emsley, *Policing and its Context, 1750–1870* (London, 1983), p. 66; Robert D. Storch, '"The Plague of Blue Locusts": Police Reform and Popular Resistance in Northern England 1840–1857', *International Review of Social History*, 1975, vol. 20, pp. 61–90, and 'The Policeman as Domestic Missionary: Urban Discipline and Popular Culture in Northern England 1850–1880', *Journal of Social History*, 1976, vol. 9, pp. 481–509.

48 Eric Dunning, Patrick Murphy, Tim Newburn and Ivan Waddington, 'Violent Disorders in Twentieth-century Britain', in George Gaskell and Robert Benewick (eds), *The Crowd in Contemporary Britain* (London, 1987), pp. 28–34, 66–71; James Cronin, *Labour and Society in Britain, 1918–1979* (London, 1984, p. 86.

49 Clive Emsley, '"Mother, what did policemen do when there weren't any motors?" The Law and the Regulation of Motor Traffic in England, 1900–1939', paper presented to the fourth Conference of the International Association for the History of Crime and Criminal Justice, Paris, October 1987, forthcoming in *Historical Journal*.

50 *Royal Commission on the Police 1962: Final Report*, Cmd. 1728 (London, 1962), pp. 102–3.

51 See the discussion in Ben Whitaker, *The Police* (Harmondsworth, 1964), pp. 15–17.

52 Robert Reiner, *The Politics of the Police* (Brighton, 1985), pp. 73–6.

53 Unnamed PC quoted in Roger Graef, *Talking Blues: The Police in their Own Words* (London, 1989), p. 74. See also Terence Morris, *Crime and Justice since 1945* (Oxford, 1989), p. 160.

54 Geoffrey Gorer, *Exploring English Character* (London, 1955), ch. 13; Gabriel A. Almond and Sidney Verba, *The Civic Culture: Political Attitudes and Democracy in Five Nations* (Princeton, 1963), pp. 106–12.

55 See, for example, the comments on a MORI poll for BBC TV's *Newsnight* in the *Guardian*, 18 November 1989, p. 22 ('Compared to even a decade ago, public faith in the police has plummeted') and the *Sunday Times*, 19 November 1989, p. B3 ('. . . as the 1980s draw to an end, the police stand lower in public esteem than at any time in their history'). The poll found that 63 per cent of the population believed that the police 'bend the rules' to obtain convictions.

6

NAME UPON NAME: THE GREAT WAR AND REMEMBRANCE

Bob Bushaway

It is not necessary to have a military background to recognize the sombre funereal resonances which begin to sound during the early days of November throughout Britain.[1] A climax is reached with the rituals of Remembrance Sunday at the Cenotaph in Whitehall and the previous night at the Royal Albert Hall and the Festival of Remembrance, with its powerful central image of a million poppy petals falling on the heads of young servicemen and women. None of these rituals existed in any form prior to 1919.

Other national days – Empire Day, Trafalgar Day, Battle of Britain Day – have enjoyed periods of popular and state support. Yet although the national days of Scotland, Ireland and Wales retain their importance for those nationalities subsumed under the hegemony of 'British' identity, St George's Day has never received the same support from the English. Armistice Day alone has taken on the status of a ceremonial occasion in which the nation as a whole is able to redefine its identity and in which rituals of social cohesion are the main constituent. Only in Northern Ireland has remembrance assumed an overtly patriotic character. The reasons for this lie with the history of the formation of the Irish Republic. The significance and complexity of the relationship between the Protestant community of Ulster and remembrance was illustrated in a powerful way by the IRA attack at Enniskillen on Remembrance Sunday, 8 November 1987. Remembrance has also proved a difficult issue for Eire, given the ambivalance of successive Irish governments to the proposal for an Irish national memorial to the dead of the Great War.[2] In most other parts of Britain remembrance rituals are generally free of overtly patriotic trappings, unlike similar occasions elsewhere in

Europe or the equivalent festival in Australia. Anzac Day has become the celebration of the perceived achievement of nationhood and commemorates the landing of British, Australian, New Zealand and French troops on the Gallipoli Peninsula in 1915.[3]

The Tomb of the Unknown Warrior, the Padre's flag, the Flanders Poppy, the Field of Remembrance, the Cenotaph, and the host of town, parish and village war memorials, together with the language, liturgy, hymnody and ceremony used throughout Britain, came into being during or shortly after the end of the First World War and were unprecedented. This is notwithstanding that these constructs now appear to have a timeless quality and are taken for granted or regarded indifferently by the mass of contemporary British society. I will argue in this essay that the theme of remembrance permeated British society during the period between the First and Second World Wars and resulted in the denial of any political critique of the Great War or of post-war society from the perspective of popular expectation or aspiration which, elsewhere, took the form of revolution or nationalism. It is possible to construct a chronology for remembrance: a sequence of events, rituals and other manifestations which formed the background for political and social debate during the 1920s and 1930s. In the absence of models from the past, Church and state drew upon certain themes which had been enunciated during the First World War and which became axiomatic of remembrance itself. I aim to consider those rituals and to locate them in their contemporary context in an attempt to comprehend their social and cultural meaning and origins.

At the heart of British rituals of remembrance lie British First World War casualties. British losses were far in excess of those suffered in any previous war.[4] The British public had not been prepared for either the scale of loss or the nature of warfare on the Western Front. All of the subsequent ceremonial events were developed around the central statistic of British and Empire losses, referred to throughout the 1920s as the 'Million Dead'. This focus on those lost in the fighting was established early in the war with the decision to attempt to record the names of all those killed. By 1928, the Imperial War Graves Commission was able to report that the total number of names registered was 1,081,952, of whom 582,783 had been identified and buried in known graves. Of 499,169 names recorded as 'missing', 173,213 had been found but not identified and were buried as 'unknown'.[5] The reason why Britain's war losses were recorded in this way lies in the expansion of Britain's forces from its small regular army sent to France in 1914. Kitchener's volunteers were regarded differently. 'These new British soldiers', it was later stressed, 'were men whose parents or wives had not accepted as one of the conditions of a professional soldier's career the possibility of an unknown grave in a foreign country; their relatives poignantly and insistently demanded . . . the fullest information as to the location of the graves of those who fell'.[6] From the formation of the Graves Registration Commission, through the establishment of the Directorate of Graves Registration and Enquiries up to the foundation of the Imperial War Graves Commission in 1917, the process of registering the names of the dead, of burying them in cemeteries and of ensuring that the locations of the graves of all British war dead were identified, became a larger and larger task as Britain's war losses mounted. This was particularly the case after 1915 as the British Army began to take on the main strategic role on the Western Front.[7]

For the bereaved, the dead took on a sacred character, and the preservation of their memory, beyond the personal circle of family and friends, began to be seen as a national obligation. One commentator summed up the responsibility of the living for the memory of the dead: 'Those pathetic longings of our dear ones to be remembered must not and shall not be disappointed by us. We, who have learned to see through the shallow deception of death have no need to seek forgetfulness. We delight, on the contrary, to remember those, who, though they are no longer visibly at our side, are still in indissoluble fellowship with us.'[8] This was the aim of post-war official publications, based upon War Office casualty lists, such as *Soldiers Died in the Great War*, which appeared in eighty separate parts in 1920–21, and the War Cemetery Registers, the first of which was published in 1920. Another publishing venture sought to record the names and brief details of all who had died in the National Roll of the Great War, 1914–18, begun in 1920.[9] The families of the dead received individual bronze National Memorial plaques, popularly called the 'Dead Man's Penny', whose design resulted from a national competition authorized by the War Office in 1918. Each memorial plaque was accompanied by a commemorative scroll from the King which recorded that these individuals had 'left all that was dear to them, endured hardness, faced danger, and finally passed out of the sight of men by the path of duty and self-sacrifice, giving up their own lives that others might live in freedom. Let those who come after see to it that his name be not forgotten.'[10]

National registers and records were reinforced by a multitude of rolls of honour in which names of individuals were grouped according to particular allegiances, affinities or associations – workplace, profession, school, university, community, club, church, organization or institution with which they were connected in life.[11] Part of the function of the obsession with lists and rolls was the concern of the bereaved to see proper recognition accorded to the individuality of their loss. Rolls of honour were developed from the original rolls of service which were popular in 1914 and 1915 during the rush of volunteers. The transition of a roll of service into a roll of honour simply required the passage of time and the process of war.

The many service battalions created and attached to existing regiments of the line in the wake of Kitchener's call for men were anxious to record their histories, in particular as a chronicle of the special comradeship which was the particular mark of these so-called 'Pals' units. The 7th (Service) Battalion, the Northamptonshire Regiment, is typical. A short history of its formation was written and published as early as 1915.[12] It is not a record of deeds of valour, or any warlike acts at all, for it is concluded before the battalion was sent on active service. It is a record of comradeship which comes from the nature of its recruitment. Most of its members had volunteered in September 1914, including E. F. Mobbs, the rugby international, who raised a company of 250 among his friends in forty-eight hours. The battalion was sent to Southwick in Sussex for training and formed particular links with that community. The only deeds of valour the *History* records are the results of athletics matches, shooting contests and rugby fixtures. The copy I consulted was owned by one Mrs Elphick of the Green, Southwick, and the list of officers and men which is given at the end of the short account is pockmarked with small black crosses, probably added by Mrs Elphick herself. Their meaning can only be presumed but it is difficult not to conclude that these crosses recorded the battalion's casualties during its subsequent actions, particularly following their rushed introduction to warfare at Loos in September 1915 when the battalion suffered considerable losses. A published roll of service was transformed by this private act into a roll of honour.[13]

Rolls of service were set up early in the war in public places as affirmation of the magnitude of response to the call for volunteers from a particular locality. These could also be reinforced by small notices placed in the windows of individual houses indicating that a man from the household was on active service.[14]

The origin, therefore, of the desire to list the names of the fallen arose with the concept of the volunteer army. In previous wars, Britain's regular forces had not enjoyed such public interest. Only acts of individual valour had been celebrated and commemorated;

regular soldiers had not previously been recorded by name on rolls of honour. Volunteers were different. Their families expected them to be treated differently. As Lloyd George reminded the Cabinet in January 1915:

> In intelligence, education and character it [the New Army] is vastly superior to any army ever raised in this country, and as it is not drawn from the ranks of those who generally cut themselves off from home ties and about whose fate there is therefore not the same anxiety at home, the people of this country will take an intimate personal interest in its fate of a kind which they have never displayed before in our military expeditions.[15]

Rolls of service also took on a sacred as well as a public character. Street shrines which included a list of those serving and those who had been killed from the vicinity began to appear early in 1916. In August 1916, these informal shrines received Royal approval in the form of a symbolic visit to South Hackney by Queen Mary 'to inspect these homely records'.[16] Shrines were also popular in central London. One description records that a shrine consisted of '. . . a decorated wooden tablet surmounted by a cross, put up at a street corner, and containing the names of those from the street who are serving in the Army or Navy, or have been killed. There is a ledge for a vase of flowers.' He also noted that shrines were most popular in 'localities where neighbourliness prevailed'. Correspondingly, they were rarely seen in suburban areas of London. Neighbourliness was engendered in part by the shared experience of bereavement. War shrines were reflective of another feature of change in British society. 'They indicate', continued the same commentator, 'the waning of that social individualism which has hitherto prevailed in the community, splitting it into classes; and the rise in its place of a more natural and neighbourly recognition of a common interdependence and the need of mutual aid and comfort in a national emergency.'[17] Whether this was true or not, street shrines represented a growing disaffection with the usual forms of spiritual comfort and solace provided by the Church in the case of bereavement.

Whether in the official casualty list, National Register, registers of the Imperial War Graves Commission, street shrines or local rolls of honour, the compulsion to record the names of those who had been killed is a remarkable departure from the British experience of earlier wars and was a powerful impulse towards the development of remembrance. In the South African war, rolls of honour had also appeared, but to a limited extent, both because of the relatively small scale of loss and also because the men who died were, for the most part, from the regular army. Only with the City Imperial Volunteers did the experience of the South African war parallel that of the First World War. Those men, volunteers from the London Yeomanry and Territorial Units, had offered themselves for service to a reluctant War Office. The cities, towns and villages of Britain, whose inhabitants in 1914 responded to Kitchener's call for volunteers, would require that each of their casualties received due recognition.

War memorials – registers in stone and bronze – were to become the most familiar and universal indications of the unprecedented British casualty rate. There had been war memorials in previous wars, notably the South African war, but not on the scale that was to be seen after 1918. Their purpose was different, too, many earlier memorials being characterized by patriotic sentiment and allegory, both in form and in content. A typical example of a South African war memorial is the Cheltenham College Memorial. This consists of a memorial cross and reredos in the College chapel. Unveiled in 1903, the memorial was dedicated to the honour of the fifty-four Old Cheltonians who had died in the service of King and Country. In 1904, the reredos was dedicated in a ceremony in which the dead were referred to as 'that living wall which stood between ourselves and our enemies'. The reredos itself was an allegory of service. Among many figures were depicted 'the champions of Christianity', including St Alban, Arthur and St Edmund; other figures included Alfred, Livingstone and Gordon. Indeed, the entire reredos is a hagiography of Victorian values. The memorial desk included the figures of Sir Galahad and Sir Philip Sidney. The reredos is a guide for the living, providing moral examples and role models, rather than a memorial for the remembrance of the dead.[18]

Other examples of South African war memorial allegorical figures demonstrate the patriotic purpose of these erections. At Darwen, Lancashire, a large bronze lion is depicted with one foot standing upon a globe. At Leicester, a group of figures depict Peace, War and Grief. Only one memorial was erected in London by public subscription, in Islington: this includes a figure of Glory holding a victory in her right hand and in her left a wreath of laurels. The inscription on the memorial to the Lancashire Fusiliers at Bury calls to memory those 'who gave their lives for their sovereign and country'. At Birmingham (Cannon Hill Park), a complex group includes soldiers symbolizing Courage and Endurance, a gun carriage, a figure of Peace holding a wreath of glory and a shield. Other figures depict

Sympathy and Grief. At Dudley, a figure of a soldier with a rifle and fixed bayonet defends a wounded comrade; unusually, the memorial bears as an inscription Christ's words, 'Greater love hath no man than this, that a man lay down his life for his friends.' (This particular text was to gain much wider celebrity in Great War memorial architecture.[19]) A particularly fine example of the use of allegory in South African war memorials can be seen in the Royal Artillery memorial in the Mall unveiled in 1910. A winged figure depicting Peace controls a horse which represents the Spirit of War.[20] This can be contrasted with the Royal Artillery Memorial on Constitution Hill, designed by Charles Sargeant Jagger and unveiled in 1925, depicting a 9.2 Howitzer in stone. Fifteen years and 50,000 Great War dead separate these two monuments to the Royal Artillery.[21]

The prevailing language of the Great War memorial is supranational and spiritual rather than conventionially patriotic. The patriotism which is recorded is that of the *patria*, the local sense of place and identity. One contemporary noted that 'the idea of commemorating with a work of monumental art the death, even the death in battle, of hundreds of ordinary men, often united by no stronger bond than a common place of residence, would have been inconceivable before the birth of a modern democracy'.[22] At least at the outset of war, the pattern of recruitment had emphasized the sense that Britain's total military effort was the sum of the contributions of local communities. Whether these communities had much overriding sense of democracy is doubtful, particularly where rural recruitment is concerned, but this pattern did mean that there was a powerful link between British military fortune and the local community. What was true for British elite groups such as the professions, the public schools, the universities and commercial interests was just as true for the lowliest volunteers from the countryside. This link became weaker after conscription was introduced in 1916.

From the beginning of 1916, an interest in war memorials grew through the work of groups such as the Civic Arts Association. Support was given by the Lord Mayor of London and a conference on the subject, widely reported in the press, was held at the Mansion House on 28 January 1916. The Association was partly concerned with aesthetic questions and partly concerned to ensure that the proliferation of war memorials which would occur after the war were based upon professional resources so that proper recognition would be given to the dead in a dignified and permanent way. A competition was held in 1916, under the auspices of the Civic Arts Association, for war memorial designs. The results were widely published.[23]

The British offensive on the Somme in July 1916 and the much increased casualty figures which stemmed from the ensuing series of British attacks provided an urgent stimulation to public interest in the way the British dead were to be remembered. Although the British press wrote of the Somme in terms of victory, British losses appeared to belie these accounts. Simple contexts of victory and defeat no longer provided a sustaining ideology for British society. The belief that the efforts of their dead had contributed to some higher purpose was to offer more consolation.

John Masefield visited the Somme after the battle and wrote a description. His main aim was to picture the battle area for home consumption, to provide a memorial for the dead and *memoria technia* for the bereaved. He foresaw their need to visualize the battlefield site and he made a conscious attempt to use the language of pastoral description – facilitated by the familiarity of the chalk downland Somme landscape to English readers. 'All wars end,' he wrote;

> even this war will someday end, and the ruins will be rebuilt and the fields full of death will grow food and all this frontier of trouble will be forgotten. When the trenches are filled in, when the plough has gone over them, the ground will not long keep the look of war . . . In a few years' time . . . the soldier looking for his battlefield will find his marks gone. Centre Way, Peel Trench, Munster Alley and those other paths to glory will be deep under corn, and gleaners will sing at Dead Mule Corner.[24]

Remembrance was an act rather than an object, although war memorials would dot the battlefield described by Masefield. What form these war memorials took and what words were inscribed upon them derived from the act of remembrance. The form of the continued debate on war memorial architecture from 1916 onwards demonstrates that a language of remembrance was emerging. Long before the outcome of the war was certain, this language had been fixed; and the rituals of remembrance that followed the Armistice in November 1918 and the Peace in 1919 had already been defined by this language.

In February 1916, Professor S. D. Adshead had described the function of the war memorial as neither the celebration of victory, nor the commemoration of peace, but to be 'prophetic and inspiring, as well as retrospective; if it is both it will be sublime'. He was critical of South African war memorials as not embodying 'great national ideals'. On the other hand, the inspiration of patriotism was not, in itself, a sufficient function as it risks 'frightfulness, arrogance and brutality . . . a war cry, rather than a message of peace'.[25] Past memorials were cited as inspirations for appropriate war memorial architecture, but it was thought some expert guidance should be on hand for those considering form and content.[26] The Royal Academy formed a committee in 1917 consisting of leading architects, sculptors and artists to provide such expert advice. In March 1918 the committee issued a short memorandum which suggested points of guidance with respect to the need for professional designs, emphasized the need for care in the choice of site and materials, and advocated simplicity of style, clear lettering and attention to scale and proportion.[27] In June 1918 a meeting of various representatives of the arts and interested public bodies was held at the Royal Academy on war memorials. Its main object 'to secure combined instead of isolated efforts in erecting memorials and to protect churches and public buildings from unsuitable treatments in setting up monuments of the war'.[28] Arbiters of taste and advisers on aesthetic concerns, rather than conduits for popular sentiment or official directive, the committee provided a resource which, it seems, was not often drawn upon by those groups who attempted to make tangible the public desire that the names of the dead should not go unrecorded and uncommemorated. That this was so is illustrated by the formation in 1924 of a Royal Fine Arts Commission 'without powers of statute or compulsion – which might be approached for guidance and counsel by national or municipal bodies'.[29] Sir Aston Webb was appointed to this new advisory body, as he had been in 1917 to the Royal Academy's Committee. Reginald Blomfield, who had also served on both bodies and had drafted the 1918 advisory memorandum on war memorials, recalled in 1932 that altbough 'it was a praiseworthy object . . . little came of it: a few people consulted us but the greater majority of War Memorial Committees preferred to keep matters in their own hands'.[30]

At the same time, the work of another national body had far greater impact in shaping the principal features of remembrance. The Imperial War Graves Commission had begun to consider the form and style of the commemoration of individual soldiers' graves and of cemeteries in specific battle areas. Architects were appointed – Edwin Lutyens, Herbert Baker and Reginald Blomfield – who, together with Rudyard Kipling and Adrian Hill, established the architecture, language and landscape of remembrance which were to become ubiquitous symbols for post-war British society: the headstones, the Cross of Sacrifice and the Stone of Remembrance within a landscaped garden.[31]

The intended effect of the cemeteries was both a physical and a psychological one: 'As the names of the dead and missing gathered throughout the war,' wrote one commentator, 'it was as if a cloud of darkness was spreading over the land.' The work of the Imperial War Graves Commission did much to dispel that cloud and the decision that the graves of Britain's war dead should be maintained in perpetuity as 'an inviolable record for the generations to come of the cost of modern warfare to civilization' was a remarkable one when the scale of that operation is considered, not least because those graves were to be maintained *in situ* and 'in equal honour irrespective of rank or creed'.[32]

Public opposition to the symbols, forms and texts chosen by the Commission was not immediately forthcoming but the determination of the Commission to embody its key concepts did not lessen even when public disquiet culminated in a debate in the House of Commons.[33] Kipling's chosen words, 'lest we forget', taken from his much earlier poem 'Recessional' were transformed by him into a emblematic phrase for remembrance. 'Recessional', intended as a corrective to public rejoicing in Imperial power at the time of Queen Victoria's Diamond Jubilee, had already been set to music as a national hymn; its performance at the burial of the Unknown Warrior in Westminster Abbey in 1920 gave it a new significance.[34] Kipling also selected the text from the Book of Ecclesiasticus which was to become the most famous emblematic text for remembrance: 'Their name liveth for evermore.'[35] This particular text from the Apocrypha had been suggested as an appropriate inscription for memorials as early as March 1917, when it was cited in an address delivered to the Royal Society of Arts by Lawrence Weaver. As well as the Book of Ecclesiasticus, Weaver also made reference to a seventeenth-century definition of the purpose of a memorial as 'a thing erected, made, or written for a memorial of some remarkable action yet to be transferred to future posterities'.[36] This was precisely how the Commissioners of the Imperial War Graves Commission regarded their work. Individual headstones for the graves of the unknown dead carried another of Kipling's phrases: 'A soldier of the Great War known unto God.'[37]

Inscriptions for local memorials were a source of much debate and, in an attempt to provide suitable examples, a selection was published under the auspices of the Victoria and Albert Museum following the exhibition of war memorials held there in 1919. Ranging from such diverse literary sources as Virgil and Lincoln, the collection also included inscriptions already in use with war memorial architecture and a few drawn from memorials of the South African war.[38] Lawrence Binyon found a place with his poem, 'For the Fallen', first published in September 1914, which had already taken hold of the popular imagination.[39] It was published in *The Times* on the first anniversary of the Armistice.[40] In particular, Binyon's famous third verse was to become the standard form of words for remembrance ceremonies. So commonplace did the words become in the next decade that the British Legion sought the author's permission to reprint the verses in 1928, as 'at many branch meetings, verses number 3 and 4 of Lawrence Binyon's poem . . . are quoted. It has been noticed that in some instances these verses were not quoted correctly . . .'.[41] It became part of the ritual of remembrance for the participants in local ceremonies to repeat the phrase 'We will remember them' after the verse had been recited. No other form of words – and there were many suggestions – gained such a hold on the popular imagination.

Few memorials of the Great War were modernist in style, but, as A. C. Benson made clear in 1916, allegory was largely rejected. 'We ought', he wrote, 'to fight shy of elaborate designs, because the pantomime of allegory at once begins. What we rather need is simplicity of statement, with perhaps a touch of emblem, no more, of characteristic materials, of perfect gravity, so that the gazer can see at once that the matter recorded is great and significant, and desires to know more.'[42] He also expressed the hope that 'We should not accumulate resources on one national monument, to astonish tourists and to feed our vanity: but that as many places as possible should have a record of a great fact which has punctuated our national life more deeply than any historical event in the whole of our annals.'[43]

Others favoured utility. Memorials should be of practical use. Why waste money, it was argued, on expensive and inappropriate memorial tributes? Professor W. R. Leatherby posed the question towards the end of the war: 'Must a sort of murder be followed by a sort of suicide?'[44] He was concerned that 'millions of pounds are again to be wasted'. He proposed ten practical suggestions as alternatives to the construction of war memorials which included town and village rebuilding, the foundation of new universities and old-age hospitals, rationalization of the railway system, an Irish 'Channel Tunnel', a Ministry of Civilization and the rebuilding of London.[45] This ambitious programme was, in his view, preferable to memorial architecture. 'We are not ready', he concluded, 'to produce works of art consciously poetic – wherefore again let us do things obviously useful for life's sake . . . would not a pleasant, tidy, little house in every village having on a panel, MEMORIAL COTTAGE and other words and names be the most touching, significant and beautiful of all possible monuments?'[46]

The debate among those who supported utility, those who favoured aesthetically satisfying constructions and those who wished only to produce a memorial to commemorate the dead without reference to other than local considerations, continued from 1916 onwards. What resulted was a multitude of mostly local schemes, some of which were sponsored by notable individuals and some of which were organized by local committees or other bodies. Events in Colchester furnish an example of the operation of the process at local level.[47] Colchester had lost 1,248 men from a population of 43,377 but prided itself on having made a greater sacrifice than many towns of its size. A letter in the local press on Christmas Day 1918 initiated the movement to erect a memorial by public subscription to the town's war dead. 'It should be so distinctive as to have no doubt as to what it is, so situated as to attract attention, so intrinsically beautiful as to command admiration.'[48] A public meeting was held at the Town Hall in June 1919 and several committees were formed to oversee the project. It was decided that both a memorial, costing no more than £3,000 and including sculpture, and a memorial block at the hospital were to be constructed. A plan was agreed to erect a memorial, designate a town space and inter a casket of contemporary materials as Colchester's act of remembrance. Achievement of these aims was substantially helped by gifts from the Cowdray family who provided the site. This form of local government effort can be seen as an extension of local community voluntary work undertaken during the war years. Local public servants and the representatives of leading families, commerce and industry took the most prominent part in the deliberations of the memorial committees whose work was guided by the writings of such as Professor Adshead.[49] In Colchester, the end result was a sculpture by Mr H. C. Fehr which had been submitted as a design to the Royal Academy's 1919 exhibition.[50]

Town memorials were only one form of commemoration of the dead. Local organizations and associations also sought to preserve the memory of the war's dead in the form of specific memorials in workplace, school, place of worship, association and, in some cases, street. Regiments also set up memorials to their dead comrades. Usually erected at regimental headquarters, local drill halls, garrison churches or other public places within the locality, these memorials added to the chronology of remembrance in individual towns and cities. For example, the borough war memorial at Kensington was unveiled on 1 July 1922 while a memorial tablet to the 1st Battalion 13th London Regiment (The Kensingtons) was dedicated in the Church at Abbots Langley, where training had taken place, in November 1922, and a regimental war memorial was set up at the Drill Hall in May 1921.[51] The Kensingtons were a Territorial Unit. Service battalions were also quick to remember their fallen comrades. The 11th Battalion, the Queen's Royal West Surrey Regiment, was raised in Lambeth in 1915 by the Mayor, Sir Charles H. Gibbs. A Roll of Honour was preserved in a Book of Remembrance in Lambeth Town Hall, containing the names of 557 men who died on active service, and a memorial window was unveiled there in 1922. Brixton parish church also contains a memorial plaque which was dedicated on 18 September 1927 to commemorate the 11th Battalion's dead.[52]

The interweaving of these various strands of remembrance in a locality after the war was to produce the backdrop against which post-war lives were lived. Town memorials, works memorials, regimental memorials, school memorials – all were emblems of remembrance for the post-war world, in which the dominant theme was that of sacrifice for the greater good. This interpretation of Britain's war losses constrained the development of popular socio-political criticisms of post-war conditions.[53]

The language of remembrance was based on the notion of sacrifice rather than the patriotic virtues of duty and service. One former soldier wrote:

> There has been too little sense of gratitude to the man who has laid down his life on the altar. Because it was his duty he was doing, because we knew him disciplined to go to it unflinchingly, we have involuntarily discounted his sacrifice . . . The idea of duty rather than of sacrifice has prevailed – something due paid rather than something sacred made. But yet every man who died on those fields was offered up on the altar for Europe's sins.[54]

Rituals of remembrance ensured that local rolls of honour and war memorials were 'sacred made'. John Arkwright's 'O Valiant Hearts', the most enduring remembrance hymn produced by the war, makes the comparison with Christ's Passion evident:

> Still stands His Cross from that dread hour to this
> Like some bright star above the dark abyss;

Still, through the veil, the Victor's pitying eyes
Look down to bless our lesser Calvaries.[55]

The key syntax of sacrifice can be sensed in much Great War litera-
ture and art, from Sassoon's 'The Redeemer' and Owen's 'At a
Calvary near the Ancre' to Kipling's 'Gethsemane' and Hodgson's
'Before Action'.[56] Charles Simms's painting *Greater Love Hath No
Man* exhibited in 1917, was considered blasphemous in depicting a
soldier 'crucified' between his parents and family.[57] A central pivot
for this notion can be found in Kipling's talk to the Household
Brigade Officers Cadet Corps in 1917, 'The Magic Square'.
Ostensibly about the origins of drill, his concluding words point to a
higher purpose:

> Before we dismiss, let's just run over its outlines again on the black-
> board, and make them clearer. Here, as I said, is the Line, here is the
> step and the wheel; and here, at the bottom, the foundation of all, is
> Forming Fours. You see? Do you notice any other change? There isn't
> one, really, because, as I have said, man changes little, yet it seems to
> me that the magic square has developed quite simply and notably into
> the Altar of Sacrifice. Look! The letters are just the same: S.W.L.F. But
> the altar is based on Faith, by which we live: it is supported by wis-
> dom and strength; and it is crowned by sacrifice, which is the highest
> form of love.[58]

Kipling's own son, John, had been listed as 'missing' after the Battle
of Loos in 1915. The origin of the theme of sacrifice can be found in
the inability of the bereaved to comprehend a more immediate military or political justification for their loss.

On battlefield sites and at the cemeteries laid out by the Imperial
War Graves Commission, memorials to the missing were erected.
Many regiments and divisions also erected individual memorials to
their fallen comrades on the sites of their military actions. The local
associations with these memorials were strong. Sites for memorials to
the missing were selected in France and Belgium by the Imperial War
Graves Commission, together with other sites in Italy, Salonica,
Gallipoli, Egypt, Palestine and Mesopotamia. The memorials to the
missing were the only national battlefield memorials. The Dominions
also erected national memerials on the Western Front and elsewhere,
recording on them the names of the missing. The dedication of these
memorials and sites provided another thread of continuity for
remembrance throughout the inter-war period.

The first memorials to the missing were those commemorating the dead of the Royal Navy, which were unveiled at Chatham, Plymouth and Portsmouth in 1924. The great cemetery at Tyn Cot in Belgium and the memorial to the missing at Ypres (the Menin Gate) were dedicated in 1927. The Arras memorial and Luytens's massive construction at Thiepval on the Somme were unveiled in 1932. The last major memorial, at Villers-Brettoneux, also designed by Lutyens, was unveiled as late as July 1938. Each dedication or unveiling provided opportunities to reinforce the notion of sacrifice for the greater good. By the end of the 1930s a vast construction of cemeteries and memorials to the British and Dominion dead of the Great War had been erected in all of the major theatres of operation.[59]

The psychological impact of this vast undertaking was considerable. At the Thiepval Memorial dedication ceremony in 1932, the Prince of Wales emphasized the novelty of the enterprise:

> Never before in History have nations shown so tender and tenacious a determination . . . to honour the memory of each one of their dead soldiers. We have shown this not merely by spoken words, which so often take flight and are forgotten, but by giving material expression to that determination as enduring as human hands and human art can make it . . . I am proud of the result – probably the biggest single piece of constructive work we have accomplished since the war.[60]

Not the construction of homes fit for heroes in post-war Britain, but the construction of vast cities of the dead, was to preoccupy the attention of British society throughout the period before the Second World War.

A decade earlier, during his visit to cemeteries in France and Flanders, King George V also alluded to the purposes of the constructions. His visit – termed the 'King's pilgrimage' in 1922 – was a profound expression of national grief, as the vast majority of British people would never be able to visit the graves of their dead. At Terlincthun Cemetery, he reminded his audience that,

> Never before in history have a people thus dedicated and maintained individual memorials to the fallen . . . We cannot but believe that the existence of these visible memorials, will, eventually, serve to draw all peoples together in sanity and self-control . . . standing beneath this Cross of Sacrifice, facing the great Stone of Remembrance, and compassed by these sternly single headstones, we remember, and must charge our children to remember, that, as our dead were equal in

sacrifice so are they equal in honour, for the greatest and the least of them have proved that sacrifice and honour are no vain things.[61]

The dead were commemorated without patriotic fervour or triumphalism but with reference to the equality of sacrifice and the hope of world peace. This was the deliberate construction of remembrance.

The King's visit in 1922 preceded the popular tours which Masefield envisaged in 1916 and which were bitterly satirized by Philip Johnstone in his poem 'High Wood'.[62] Yet only a relatively small number of people could afford to travel to France and Belgium and even fewer to battlefields in the Mediterranean and the Middle East. One early visitor was Stephen Graham. For him, the pilgrimage was sacred and the battlefields were holy places. At Ypres, he saw the wooden crucifix, apparently miraculously spared in the shelling, 'with its riven agonised Lord looking down'. Visiting the Somme, he added to the language of remembrance in his description: 'It does not matter that tourists whirl past without pause in a car. Let each and everyone come and dip a corner of a handkerchief in the blood of the war – for remembrance. Come to the sacrament of the young man's blood which was shed instead of yours.' He also referred to the 'Somme Altar'.[63]

Guidebooks were published from as early as 1919 and the number of visitors grew, particularly after the tenth anniversary of the war's ending.[64] In 1928, the British Legion organized a 'Battlefield Pilgrimage' under the banner 'revisit the land you helped to save'. The aim of these visits was not nostalgia but remembrance. 'We pilgrims are going to offer homage to the million dead of the British Empire', proclaimed the British Legion Great Pilgrimage guide,

> the great majority of whom lie buried in those beautiful cemeteries in France and Flanders. And in this act itself we shall be bringing consolation to the widows and orphans, the mother who lost her boy, the maiden the man of her choice. Those who are not able to come themselves will learn, from those who have seen, how comforting is the serene beauty of those white headstones.[65]

The idea that those who could visit the cemeteries overseas should do so, not just for themselves or their relatives but also for those who could not visit the graves, was also expressed during the King's pilgrimage of 1922. The mother of a Sergeant Matthews had written to the Queen with a bunch of forget-me-nots, and had asked that these might be placed on the grave of her son in Etaples Cemetery. The Queen could not be present for this part of the visit, so it remained for the King to undertake this duty. It was reported that 'He had brought with him the letter, and carried out reverently, dutifully, the pious task, taking care . . . to find the grave, and, kneeling down in homage, to place upon it the mother's flowers.'[66] This remarkable piece of theatre, whether consciously staged or a spontaneous act, was a microcosm of the whole visit. The King was seen to do homage to the dead, for himself and on behalf of a grieving nation. Individual and particular men made up the myriad of the dead and the King's pilgrimage aimed to recognize each loss.

As a language of remembrance developed, so a new liturgy was also required. By 1928, the recommended liturgy for Armistice Day services avoided patriotic statements. 'Even a casual glance', wrote a student of liturgy, 'at the order printed below will make it evident that there is no trace of boasting in victory . . . This omission is made partly because it is becoming increasingly evident that whatever victory there was in the war was a Pyrrhic victory, but more because paeans of victory seem to modern ears particularly out of place in worship.'[67] Commemorative services earlier in the war had had no such difficulty or doubt as to the suitability of a language of heroism and the traditional image of military glory. For example, at a service of Commemoration for the dead of the 1st/23rd Battalion of the London Regiment held in June 1915 in memory of those lost at Festubert the previous month, an address was delivered by the vicar of Battersea, the Reverend Foster Pegg, who was also the Chaplain of the Regiment. 'My feelings', he wrote, 'are those of a non-commissioned officer whose duties lay in the rear, and who, on seeing the gallant way in which the men charged, was melted into tears of joy, and then tears of sorrow as he saw so many fall . . . No English soldier', he concluded, 'has ever fallen fighting in a cleaner, holier, nobler cause, than the men whose loss we mourn today.' The National Anthem was sung and themes of heroism, nationalism and patriotism were prevalent.[68] In 1915 the Bishop of Stepney produced a memorial service liturgy at the request of the Bishop of London. He began with texts from St John's Gospel, including Christ's famous 'greater love' injunction. The bidding prayer enjoined the congregation to seek 'God's help and guidance' for the crowned heads of all the Allies.[69] The Reverend J. Burns also produced an 'Order of Memorial Service' in 1917 which included the following: 'Do not think of your sons . . . as sinking into the grave but as ascending radiantly into life, winning in that high moment the crown of their earthly sacrifices.' Finally, Burns included an address on the reconsecration of memory: 'The ministry of Death is not to sever but to bind.'[70] Between 1915 and 1917 the preferred liturgy had become one of sacrifice and redemption rather than triumph and victory.

After 1918, national acts of remembrance were constructed which drew on this liturgy of remembrance. The process was not fully completed until 1923 and the key question of mood was not decided until 1925. Should Armistice Day be marked by joy and celebration in victory or by dignified and sombre remembrance in contemplation of the dead?

The idea of a national memorial having been rejected, popular attention centred on two forms of remembrance: the commemoration of the dead at the Cenotaph in Whitehall and the services around the tomb of the Unknown Warrior in Westminster Abbey. The origin of these two centres of ritual lay in the contemplation of the extent of British and Dominion losses in the Great War. In the public mind there was no contradiction between the Cenotaph (the empty tomb) with its promise of resurrection and the Unknown Warrior (the full tomb).[71] The distinction was explained in the following terms: 'The Unknown Warrior's grave commemorates the average of the men who died – the Cenotaph in Whitehall commemorates the whole of these men.'[72] Likewise, the British public saw no contradiction, despite J. B. Priestley's criticism, between Kipling's 'Lest we forget' and his choice from Ecclesiasticus of 'Their name liveth for evermore.'[73] The rituals which developed around the two centres functioned in different ways and took shape in different timescales. One commemorator expressed it thus:

> If there be any distinction between the symbolism of the Cenotaph and that of the Grave of the Unknown Warrior, it is the fact that while the former represents, as an entity, the noble army of those who died for their country, the latter represents one individual and the mystery as to whose son he was makes him the son and brother of us all. The Cenotaph, it may be said, is the token of our memory as a nation: the Grave of the Unknown Warrior is the token of our memory as individuals.[74]

Sir Edward Lutyens's stone pylon emerged from a conversation with Lloyd George and first appeared in Whitehall, as a temporary structure in fibrous plaster, for the peace celebrations on 19 July 1919.[75] It remained there for the first anniversary of the Armistice on 11

November 1919, when the two-minute silence was first instituted. After some debate on the permanent site for the stone Cenotaph, it was decided that it should continue to occupy its position in Whitehall. On 11 November 1920, the permanent Cenotaph was unveiled and the two-minute silence was repeated. The King was present for the first time and a short religious service, introduced by the Archbishop of Canterbury, was held.[76]

In 1919 a service of Remembrance had been held at Westminster Abbey; here in 1920, the Unknown Warrior was buried. The idea had been promoted by the Dean of Westminster on the suggestion of David Railton, who had served during the war as Chaplain with the 47th (London) Division.[77] The powerful symbolism of selecting, in secret, a representative of all the British and Dominion dead and laying him to rest with full state honour in Westminster Abbey found immediate popular favour. At the same time, the notion that Armistice Day should be declared a public holiday, as had been the case for the peace celebrations in July 1919, was rejected. Lord Curzon, who was given the task of organizing the ceremony in 1920, stated that, 'In the first place, a public holiday will involve a great dislocation of business. Secondly, a public holiday is an occasion for public rejoicing, and is therefore hardly suitable for a day on which so solemn and impressive a ceremony is to take place.'[78]

Every aspect of ritual associated with the Unknown Warrior was of a special character. Elaborate and secret procedures were taken to select the body; the coffin was specially designed and constructed; the coffin, drawn on a gun carriage, was followed by the King as Chief Mourner, and was buried with 100 sandbags of French earth; a guard of honour was provided by holders of the Victoria Cross; and the flag used to drape the coffin – the so-called Padre's flag – had been used by Railton for a variety of purposes while on active service, including use as a Communion Table cloth and during burial services.[79] In the spirit of remembrance, the flag was regarded as a sacred flag because it had been dipped in the blood of the fallen. The Unknown Warrior was both a 'plain man' and a 'representative man'.[80]

Despite earlier protest in 1919 by the unemployed, the impact of the twin ceremonies in 1920 – the unveiling of the Cenotaph and the burial of the Unknown Warrior – was dramatic. For many days afterwards queues of the bereaved formed to place wreaths at the Cenotaph and to pass the tomb in Westminster Abbey. By the time the grave was finally sealed on 18 November, it was estimated that 1.25 million people had passed the Cenotaph.[81] The events were spoken of in terms of a national pilgrimage. The following year, 1921,

saw the institution of the sale of Flanders poppies by the British
Legion which had emerged as the sole ex-servicemen's organization
after unification under the leadership of Field Marshal Haig.[82] The
Padre's flag was placed in the Abbey above the grave of the
Unknown Warrior and remembrance of the living as well as commemoration of the dead was urged. This theme had been institutionalized the previous year, when Armistice Day was designated as
Obligation Day and employers were urged to find jobs for all ex-servicemen.

The King's wreath in 1920 and 1921 bore a quotation from the
second Epistle to the Corinthians: 'As Unknown, and yet well
known; as dying and behold we live.'[83] These lines carried the hope
of resurrection which lay at the heart of the meaning of the
Cenotaph. The Army Council approved the intention to cease, after
six complete searches since the Armistice, the scouring of the
battlefields for unknown graves.[84] At the unveiling of the Ypres
Memorial to the missing, Lord Plumer had given comfort to many
when he declared: 'He is not missing, he is here.'[85]

The Flanders poppy had not met with universal acceptance as a
symbol of remembrance. General Sir G. M. Macdonagh, when
unveiling the memorial to the fallen at Beaumont College, Old
Windsor, stated publicly that the poppy was 'a pagan flower, it was
the emblem of the dead and the last thing they wanted to do was to
forget them'.[86] Not for him the poppy's associations with the battlefields of France and Flanders and John McCrae's celebrated poem,
'In Flanders Fields'. The British Legion pointed out that its choice
was deliberate and that the flower should now become the flower of
remembrance.[87] Eight million poppies were sold in 1921,[88] when the
rituals of remembrance were renewed despite further disturbances.
The unemployed sang 'Bubbles' and carried placards stating 'The
Dead are remembered, but we are forgotten.'[89] Yet public support
for remembrance was again marked by lengthy queues to deposit
wreaths at the Cenotaph and visit the grave of the Unknown
Warrior. That the Cenotaph had become a central part of the symbolic life of the nation was demonstrated at the wedding of Princess
Mary in February 1922 when, on her return from the Abbey, her
coach stopped in Whitehall and, at her request, a piece of her wedding bouquet was placed at the base of the Cenotaph.[90]

By 1925, some anxiety was being expressed as to the maintenance
of the two-minute silence. There was concern that the ritual could
not continue indefinitely; it was bound to become less certain of popular observance and should be set aside now, at the height of its

power. In fact, the 'Great Silence' was retained throughout the inter-war years.[91] Other concerns were also expressed. The unveiling of the Royal Artillery Memorial in 1925 caused some controversy and reopened debate on the purpose of war memorials. But a more powerful challenge was mounted by 'Dick' Sheppard, Vicar of St Martins-in-the-Fields, on the spirit of celebration which still marked Armistice Day in some quarters, particularly the annual charity ball at the Albert Hall on Armistice night. After some public discussion, the ball was cancelled and Dick Sheppard was given the Albert Hall for a festival of remembrance.[92] After a promotion by the *Daily Express* in 1927, the British Legion Festival of Remembrance became a fixed point of reference for Armistice Night. Originally designated a 'Festival of Empire and Remembrance', the ceremony included, by 1929, the central image of a shower of poppies in which each poppy represented a life. As one observer commented, this spectacle 'conveyed in the most significant fashion – far beyond the power of mere figures – something of the enormous losses suffered by the Nation in the war'.[93] Finally, the tenth anniversary of the Armistice was broadcast by the BBC. Apart from the institution in 1928 of the Field of Remembrance at Westminster Abbey by Major George Howson, Director of the British Legion Poppy factory, the rituals were complete.[94]

That remembrance retained its power throughout the inter-war period can be demonstrated not only by the fact that the rituals themselves became a focus for protest, particularly the attempted disruptions of the two-minute silence, but also by the attempt of the growing peace movement to dominate the proceedings at the Cenotaph.[95] War memorials were referred to as peace memorials.[96] The sacrifice of the 'million dead', it was argued, could have meaning only in the context of world peace. White 'peace' poppies were sold by the Peace Pledge Union to rival the sale of blood-red Flanders poppies by the British Legion. A major peace meeting was held, for example, at the Albert Hall on the night before Armistice Day 1931, under the banner 'No More War', at which Dick Sheppard spoke.[97] During the Munich Crisis in 1938, Armistice Day again took on a powerful meaning in the context of 'Peace in our time'. Ironically, *Kristallnacht* took place on the previous night. The attempt to take over remembrance as an exclusive language of peace was specifically rejected by those who wished to see the sacrifice of the dead in terms of a victory and the salvation of the world.

The national model for remembrance, its language, form and content, was replicated in a thousand towns and villages throughout

Britain between the wars. The functions of these rituals were many. First, those who stood before local war memorials or who queued to place wreaths at the foot of the Cenotaph or to view the Unknown Warrior's tomb did so as mourners. It was an act of personal remembrance. Others, who had served during the war, inevitably experienced a sense of relief at having been spared the fate of their comrades. This was also marked by a sense of guilt. Many of those who chose to write of their experiences, whether in fiction or as autobiography, during the ten years after the war which saw a rush of published accounts following the phenomenal success of Remarque's *All Quiet on the Western Front*, referred to this curious sensation. One wrote: 'I must return to my old comrades of the Great War – to the brown, the treeless, the flat and grave-set plain of Flanders – to the rolling, heat-miraged downlands above the river Somme – for I am dead with them, and they live again in me.'[98]

The experience of remembrance for the survivor was a lonely one. 'These phantoms', the same commentator wrote, 'were more real to him than the living. One must never go back among the living: One must forever say goodbye to old comrades, so that one might always see them with young faces, gay and carefree, in those scenes of the vanished world of the Western Front which could only be entered in silence and alone.'[99] Annual national mourning could not make these individual re-entries into memory less painful for survivors, but they could offer comfort and solace to the bereaved. Ex-servicemen had to find other ways to assimilate the experience in the company of their comrades in ex-service organizations, regimental associations and the world of private thoughts. The vast majority did not record those thoughts.

That the dead had given their lives for the living and that the living should, therefore, not dishonour the sacrifice of the dead, and should lead better lives as a result, was a moral theme which the language of remembrance sought to articulate. The better world, paid for by the blood of the dead, should begin with each individual. This was the theme of the Anglican Lambeth Conference of 1920. In particular, it was argued, class strife betrayed the dead. 'The light must be let in on all the dark places at once, the muddy pools of class selfishness must be cleansed; the self-sacrifice of our soldiers and sailors must find its counterparts in our industrial life.'[100] Archbishop Randall Davidson proffered a world of international classlessness:

> In every national army, comradeship, novel and intense, united men of different classes and most various traditions. Thousands gained quite a

new impression of what human nature might be, when they experienced the fellowship of man with man in danger and death. Conradeship ennobled war. Today men are asking, can it not ennoble peace?[101]

Some war memorials attempted to allegorize this sentiment. Cornhill War Memorial, unveiled by the Lord Mayor of London in November 1920, depicted the Archangel St Michael, with flaming sword, 'repelling strife in the form of two beasts tearing one another as they perish, and leading in Brotherhood and Love in the form of a group of children'.[102] Many war memorial inscriptions quoted Christ's words at the Last Supper (John 15:13: 'Greater love hath no man than this, that a man lay down his life for his friends').

The rituals of remembrance were seen as universal. The two-minute silence, for example, was observed throughout the Empire. The significance of this ritual was seen as a unifying one which emphasized the equality of loss. Remembrance also acted as a rite of passage, conducting British society through the ending of the war and the beginning of peace. A process of social reintegration was accomplished by the rituals. Returning servicemen were reincorporated into society. British social values were reaffirmed and a vision for the future was offered. Equally important, an interpretation of the war was constructed which was strengthened annually as a sustaining ideology for British society. Whatever the motivations and justifications of 1914, the post-war world of 1919 saw the war in larger terms than the petty jealousies of nationalism which had caused Britain's involvement at the outset. Belgium was seldom mentioned in press editorials and even the defeat of Germany was located within a frame of reference which saw world fellowship as the real prize of victory. Figures 1 and 2 attempt to illustrate the structure of remembrance and the transformation of sustaining ideologies between 1914 and 1919.

Remembrance conferred immortality on the dead and gave an apolitical context to their sacrifice. Despite being rooted in the language of the Eucharist and the Passion of Christ, remembrance was also strangely areligious. This derived in part from the strongest efforts of those involved in organizing the rituals of remembrance to avoid specific reference to the Established Church in order not to offend other faiths whose representatives had been killed in the war; but it came about also because much of the theological basis for the rituals themselves and their meaning would not have been acceptable as orthodox Christian belief. That the soldier's sacrifice in the war,

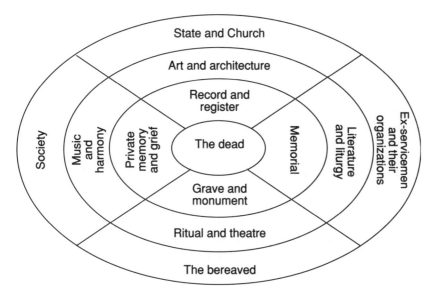

Figure 1 Remembrance

equated with that of Christ, could redeem the living; that death in battle could expiate sin; that the fallen were sanctified by death; that the dead died in an automatic state of grace – these notions, which underpinned much of the language of remembrance to be found in press and pulpit, could not actually stand close theological scrutiny. The peace of mind of the living took precedence over theology in 1919 and, although the rituals of remembrance were bathed in religious and specifically Anglican sentiment and attendant liturgy and hymnody, they were religious occasions in form only.

The presence of the King, the Prime Minister and the Head of the Established Church at the Cenotaph acted as a symbol of the State's obeisance before the dead. As was noted in 1925, remembrance alone 'could have brought together the King, the heir to the throne, and five prime ministers of widely divergent political views, on the same few square feet of ground'.[103] The special collect recited by the King on that occasion makes clear the spirit of remembrance: 'Grant, we beseech thee, O Almighty God, that all who here do honour to the memory of our brothers' sacrifice, may so be filled with the spirit of their love and fortitude, that forgetting all selfish and worldly aims they may live only to the glory of God and to the sacrifice of their fellow men . . .'[104] The notion of unity through remembrance was

particularly marked the following year when Armistice Day succeeded the experiences of the General Strike. Such division was condemned in the context of remembrance: 'Their lives were not given,
those sufferings were not undergone, to leave open the way for strife
and for "class war". There was no class – there is none – for the
dead who sleep side by side in Flanders or on the Somme.'[105]

Throughout the inter-war period British society witnessed an
annual event in which social and political unity was reaffirmed.
Other views and criticisms of the Great War were regarded as doing
dishonour to the dead. The chronology of remembrance was a powerful thread of continuity which linked individual and collective
memory. The emergence of a language of remembrance had the effect
of enhancing and enshrining the experience of the war, thereby
removing it from the sphere of normal social and political debate and
elevating it to a level of spiritual significance from where its memory
for peacetime British society was of a special, supranational and
sacred quality. In this language of remembrance, the notion of

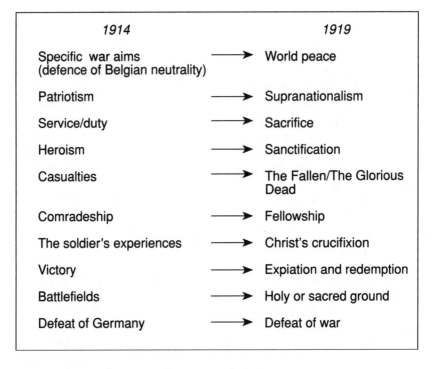

1914		1919
Specific war aims (defence of Belgian neutrality)	⟶	World peace
Patriotism	⟶	Supranationalism
Service/duty	⟶	Sacrifice
Heroism	⟶	Sanctification
Casualties	⟶	The Fallen/The Glorious Dead
Comradeship	⟶	Fellowship
The soldier's experiences	⟶	Christ's crucifixion
Victory	⟶	Expiation and redemption
Battlefields	⟶	Holy or sacred ground
Defeat of Germany	⟶	Defeat of war

Figure 2 The transformation of sustaining ideologies

sacrifice transcended those of duty and patriotism as a justification for British losses in the war, and the residual sense of comradeship, which might have been problematic for the established social order, was isolated to the private world of ex-soldiers and the bereaved. In Britain, soldiers might go on strike in 1919 to achieve more rapid demobilization, and the unemployed might demonstrate for work, but they rarely became revolutionaries. Britain's potential *Freikorps* was loosed in Ireland rather than against revolutionaries in Glasgow.

Armistice Day became a point of reference for British society. The festivities of victory gave way to the sombre mood in which the sacrifice of the dead was renewed and to which Church, state and Crown did reverence. Through the annual act of remembrance the demons of discontent and disorder were purged and the mass of British society was denied access to a political critique of the war by Kipling's universal motto 'lest we forget'. The rituals of remembrance defined what was to be remembered in post-war Britain.

NOTES

1 I should like to thank members of the Social History Seminar in the Department of Modern History at the University of Birmingham and the Graduate Seminar, the University of Sussex, for their comments and contributions when earlier versions of this paper were presented. In particular, I should like to thank John Bourne, Carl Chinn and Mick Reed for their continued interest and stimulating discussion of the theme of remembrance. Any faults are, of course, my own.

2 For Ireland, see David Fitzpatrick (ed.), *Ireland and the First World War*, Trinity History Workshop Publications (Dublin, 1986); in particular, Jane Leonard, 'Lest We Forget', pp. 59–67. The Irish National War Memorial was completed in 1938 but was never officially opened. For Ulster's experience of the Great War, see Philip Orr, *The Road to the Somme* (Belfast, 1987).

3 For Anzac Day see Michael McKernan and Peter Stanley (eds), *Anzac Day: Seventy Years On* (Sydney, 1986).

4 The debate on British war casualties began during the war and continued unabated thereafter, centring on the role of Field Marshal Earl Haig. John Terraine refers to the 'Great Casualty Myth' in *The Smoke and the Fire: Myths and Anti-Myths of War, 1861–1945* (London, 1980), pp. 35–47.

5 *War Graves of the Empire*, reprinted from the special number of *The Times*, 10 November 1928, p. 10.

6. Ibid., p. 14.

7 A full history of the work of the Commission and its predecessors is given in Philip Longworth, *The Unending Vigil: A History of the Commonwealth War Graves Commission, 1917–1984* (first published 1967; new edition London, 1985). See also Sidney C. Hurst, *The Silent Cities* (London, 1929) and Sir

Fabian Ware, *The Immortal Heritage* (Cambridge, 1937), and 'The Work of the Imperial War Graves Commission', *Journal of the Royal Institute of British Architects*, November 1928–October 1929, vol. 36, pp. 507–19. Ware was the Commission's founder.

8 F. Homes Dudden, *The Heroic Dead and Other Sermons* (London, 1917), p. 11.

9 *Soldiers Died in the Great War 1914–1919*, The War Office (London, 1920–1) (these rolls were based on information obtained through the official casualty lists); Imperial War Graves Commission, Cemetery Registers (London, 1920 onwards). *Officers Died in the Great War, 1914–1919* (London, 1919) was published earlier; *The National Roll of the Great War, 1914–1918* (London, 1920) was published by the National Publishing Co. Earlier in the war, the Anglo-American Publishing Company published L. A. Clutterbuck's *The Bond of Sacrifice: A Biographical Record of all British Officers who fell in the Great War*, vol. 1 (London, 1916).

10 *The Studio*, 1918, vol. 73, p. 136, *The Architectural Review*, 1918, vol. 43, pp, 84–5. The King's words are taken from the scroll commemorating Pte Frederick Jacobs DCM, Royal West Surrey Regiment.

11 See, for example, The Revd Francis Irwin, *Stonyhurst War Record: A Memorial of the Part Taken by Stonyhurst Men in the Great War* (Derby, 1927), which is the Roll of Honour of one public school; also Sir William H. Bowater (ed.), *Birmingham City Battalions Book of Honour* (London, 1919) which lists Birmingham's recruits to its three 'Pals' battalions but also lists the rolls of honour of local firms.

12 Captain Guy Paget, *History of the Raising of the 7th (Service) Battalion Northamptonshire Regiment* (Aldershot, 1915).

13 Ibid., pp. 35–47. After the war, an active service history was produced: see H. B. King, *7th (S) Battalion Northamptonshire Regiment 1914–1919* (Aldershot, 1919). Recent work has called attention to this kind of source for the study of the impact of the Great War on post-war British society. See Keith Grieves, 'Making Sense of the Great War: Regimental Histories, 1918–23', in *Journal of the Society for Army Historical Research*, Spring 1991, vol. 69, no. 277, pp. 6–15.

14 See *The Sphere*, 31 July 1915, p. 105 for the 'Duty Card' prepared by the Publicity Department of the War Office and ibid., 21 August 1915, p. 183 for an example of a roll of service from Woldingham near Croydon.

15 David Lloyd George, *War Memoirs*, vol. 1. (London; first published 1933–4, popular edn 1938), p. 220.

16 *The Sphere*, 19 August 1916 p. 154.

17 Michael MacDonagh, *In London During the Great War: The Diary of a Journalist* (London, 1935), pp. 146–7.

18 A. A. Hunter, *The Old Cheltonian South African War Memorials* (Cheltenham, 1904).

19 These examples are illustrated in Sir James Gildea, *For Remembrance: And in Honour of Those who Lost their Lives in the South African War 1899–1902* (London, 1911). See also W. J. Reader, *At Duty's Call: A Study in Obsolete Patriotism* (Manchester, 1988), esp. ch. 1, 'Their Name Liveth for Evermore', pp. 1–16.

20 This memorial was designed by W. R. Colton.

21 Designed by Charles Sargeant Jagger. See James Stevens Curl, 'The Royal

Artillery Memorial at Hyde Park Corner', in Ann Compton (ed.), *Charles Sargeant Jagger: War and Peace Sculpture* (London, 1985), pp. 81–99. For the controversy caused by Jagger's masterpiece – perhaps the finest memorial of the First World War – see *The Times*, 19 October 1925, p. 15 col. 5; 24 October 1925, p. 15, col. 4; 26 October 1925, p. 10 col. 4. The best source for London war memorials is Lord Edward Gleichen, *London's Open-Air Statuary* (London, 1928).

22 Sir J. A. Hammerton (ed.), *A Popular History of the Great War*, vol. 6 (London, n.d. *c*.1933) p. 498. Ch. 26 of this work is concerned with war memorials (pp. 497–534).

23 *The Spectator*, 5 February 1916, vol. 116, pp. 183–4; *The Architectural Review*, 1916, vol. 39, pp. xvii, 112; ibid., 1916, vol. 40, pp. 35–40; *Country Life*, 5 February 1916, pp. 188–9.

24 John Masefield, *The Old Front Line: or, The Beginning of the Battle of the Somme* (London, 1917), p. 11.

25 *The Builder*, 4 February 1916, pp. 102–3.

26 See Lawrence Weaver, *Memorials and Monuments: Old and New. Two Hundred Subjects Chosen from Seven Centuries* (London, 1915); *The Architectural Review*, 1915, vol. 37, pp. 26–30, 44–50, 63–71, 96–104; 1915, vol. 37, pp. 26–30, 44–50, 63–71, 96–104; 1915, vol. 38, pp. 7–12, 73–8, 106–13; 1916, vol. 40, pp. 101–9. Lawrence Weaver delivered a series of lectures at the Royal Society of Arts in November 1917; see *Journal of the Royal Society of Arts*, 1917, vol. 65, pp. 817–39, 846–51.

27 Royal Academy, 'Suggestions For The Treatment of War Memorials', *Journal of the Royal Institute of British Architects*, 3rd series, vol. 25, pp. 143–4, 208–9.

28 *The Architectural Review*, 1919, vol. 45, p. 20. A further circular was issued at the approach of peace to reinforce the need for 'competent guidance'; see *Journal of the Royal Institute of British Architects*, 3rd series, 1919, vol. 26, p. 93.

29 *The Year's Art – 1925: A Concise Epitome compiled by A. C. R. Carter* (London, 1925), pp. 6–7.

30 Sir Reginald Blomfield, *Memoirs of an Architect* (London, 1932), p. 181.

31 For the work of the architects, see Blomfield, *Memoirs of an Architect*; Herbert Baker, *Architecture and Personalities* (London, 1944); Christopher Hussey, *The Life of Sir Edwin Lutyens* (London, 1953); Clayre Percy and Jane Ridley (eds), *The Letters of Edwin Lutyens to his wife, Lady Emily* (London, 1985). For the design of the cemeteries as gardens, see Captain A. W. Hill, 'Our Soldiers' Graves', *Journal of the Royal Horticultural Society*, 1919–20, vol. 45, pp. 1–13. The overall conception was explained in the Report to the Imperial War Graves Commission by Sir Frederic Kenyon, Director of the British Museum; see Sir Frederic Kenyon, *War Graves: How the Cemeteries Abroad will be Designed* (London, 1918). For comment on the proposals, see *Country Life*, 1919, vol. 45, pp. 398–9. The Stone of Remembrance was the conception of Sir Edwin Lutyens; Sir Reginald Blomfield designed the Cross of Sacrifice.

32 *The Times*, 11 November 1924, p. 16, col. 4.

33 *Hansard*, House of Commons, 4 May 1920. Most public concern was with the principle of uniformity of treatment, particularly regarding the headstones.

34 For 'Recessional', see Rudyard Kipling, *Rudyard Kipling's Verse: Definitive Edition* (London, 1940) p. 328. The phrase 'lest we forget' had been used on the title page of Gildea, *For Remembrance*. The poem was written in 1897 and was published in *The Times*. For Kipling's own description of its composition see Rudyard Kipling, *Something of Myself* (London, 1937), pp. 147–8, and Charles Carrington, *Kipling: His Life and Work* (London, 1955), pp. 263–8. It is likely that Kipling's inspiration was to be found in the following passage from the Old Testament (Deuteronomy 4:23): 'Take heed unto yourselves, lest ye forget the convenant of the Lord your God; which he made with you.' The poem was included as a hymn in *The English Hymnal* (London, 1906), no. 558, with the tune 'Folkingham'. The poem had been set to music by G. F. Blanchard in July 1898 and was included as hymn no. 889 in the *Methodist Hymn Book* (London, 1904).
35 The Apocrypha, Ecclesiasticus 44:14.
36 *Journal of the Royal Society of Arts*, 1917, vol. 65, p. 817.
37 For headstone designs, see Ware, *The Immortal Heritage*, pp. 28–31. For Kipling's role, see Carrington, *Kipling*, p. 442.
38 For the Royal Academy War Memorials Exhibition, see *Country Life*, 1 November 1919, pp. 567–8; *Journal of the Royal Institute of British Architects*, 3rd series, 1918, vol. 25, pp. 208–9; *The Town Planning Review*, April 1917, vol. 7, no. 2, pp. 148–51; *The Studio*, 1920, vol. 78, pp. 59–64; *The Architectural Review*, 1919, vol. 45, pp. 20, 129; 1919, vol. 46, pp. 44–5, 163–4. For inscriptions see Victoria and Albert Museum, *Inscriptions Suggested for War Memorials* (London, 1919).
39 Victoria and Albert Museum, *Inscriptions Suggested for War Memorials*, pp. 5–6.
40 *The Times*, 11 November 1919, p. 15, cols 5, 6.
41 British Legion Circular no. 32, October 1928, item 12.
42 A. C. Benson '"Lest We Forget": A Word on War Memorials', *Cornhill Magazine*, September 1916, p. 299.
43 Ibid., p. 300.
44 W. R. Lethaby, 'Memorials of the Fallen: Service or Sacrifice?', *The Hibbert Journal*, 1918–19, vol. 17, p. 621.
45 Ibid., pp. 623–4.
46 Ibid., p. 625.
47 A full account of the Colchester War Memorial is found in Edgar A. Hunt (ed.), *The Colchester War Memorial Souvenir* (Colchester, 1923).
48 Ibid., p. 17.
49 Ibid., p. 18.
50 Ibid., pp. 23–9.
51 Sergeant O. F. Bailey and Sergeant H. M. Hollier, *'The Kensingtons' 13th London Regiment* (London, 1935), pp. 383–4.
52 Captain E. W. J. Neave, *History of the 11th Battalion, 'The Queen's'* (London, 1931) p. 98.
53 For general studies of British war memorials, see Arnold Whittick, *War Memorials* (Glasgow, 1946); Derek Boorman, *At the Going Down of the Sun: British First World War Memorials* (York, 1988); Colin McIntyre, *Monuments of War: How to Read a War Memorial* (London, 1990). For an interesting local study of street memorials, see Alice Goodman, *The Street Memorials of*

St Albans Abbey Parish, St Albans and Hertfordshire Architectural and Archaeological Society (Hertford, 1987).

54 Stephen Graham, *A Private in the Guards* (London, 1919), p. 13.

55 Arkwright's hymn was first published as a poem in John S. Arkwright, *The Supreme Sacrifice and Other Poems in Time of War* (London, 1919), pp. 17–18. Along with Cecil Spring-Rice's 'I Vow to Thee, My Country', it became the most famous remembrance hymn. It was included in *Hymns Ancient and Modern* (no. 584) set to music by Dr Martin Shaw. See Maurice Frost (ed.), *Historical Companion to Hymns Ancient and Modern* (London, 1962), pp. 439, 534. Arkwright's son was killed on active service in 1943 and Shaw's brother was reported missing in the Great War. The hymn was included in the order of service for the burial of the Unknown Warrior at Westminster Abbey on 11 November 1920. Remembrance also saw older hymns take on a new popularity, such as 'Abide With Me' and 'O God our Help in Ages Past'.

56 Siegfried Sassoon, *The War Poems* (London, 1983), p. 16; Wilfred Owen, *War Poems and Others*, ed. Dominic Hibberd (London, 1973), p. 70. *Rudyard Kipling's Verse*, p. 98; E. B. Osborn (ed.), *The Muse in Arms* (London, 1917), p. 22. See also the excellent collection, Dominic Hibberd and John Onions (eds), *Poetry of the Great War: An Anthology* (London, 1986), pp. 89–98.

57 Simms's painting was exhibited at the Royal Academy Summer Exhibition in 1917; see *Royal Academy Illustrated Annual 1917* (London, 1917), p. 22.

58 Rudyard Kipling, *A Book of Words: Selections from Speeches and Addresses Delivered between 1906 and 1927* (London, 1928), p. 153.

59 For memorials to the missing, see *War Graves of the Empire*, pp. 35–40, and T. A. Edwin Gibson and G. Kingsley Ward, *Courage Remembered* (London, 1989), pp. 153–71, 279–80.

60 Hammerton, *Popular History of the Great War*, vol. 6, p. 534.

61 Frank Fox, *The King's Pilgrimage* (London, 1922), part 4, p. 8.

62 Printed in Brian Gardner, *Up the Line to Death: The War Poets 1914–1918* (London, 1964; repr. 1976), p. 157.

63 Stephen Graham, *The Challenge of the Dead: An Impression of the Battlefields of France and Flanders Just after the War* (London, 1921; repr. 1930), pp. 35, 82. Ypres was referred to as sacred ground, see Lieut.-Col. Beckles Wilson, *Ypres – The Holy Ground of British Arms* (Bruges, 1920).

64 A good example is Captain Atherton Fleming, *How to See the Battlefields* (London, 1919).

65 British Legion, *Battlefields Pilgrimage 1928* (London, 1928), p. 23.

66 *The King's Pilgrimage*, part 4, p. 4.

67 Thomas L. Harris, *Christian Public Worship: Its History, Development and Ritual for Today* (New York, 1928), p. 194.

68 Captain Albert Larking, *History of the 23rd London Regiment* (London, c.1912), pp. 13–14.

69 The Bishop of Stepney, *A Memorial Service for Those Fallen in the War* (London, 1915), pp. 1–11.

70 Rev J. Burns, *Order of Memorial Service for Those Fallen in the War* (London, 1917), p. 13.

71 Full accounts of the two rituals are to be found in *The Times*, 3 November 1920, p. 12, col. 2, p. 13, col. 5.

72 Hammerton, *Popular History of the Great War*, vol. 5, p. 499.

73 For Priestley's critical view, see J. B. Priestley, *English Journey* (first published London, 1934; repr. 1977), p. 160.

74 *British Legion Journal*, November 1929, p. 118.

75 See Hussey, *Lutyens*, pp. 391–2.

76 See *Country Life*, 1919, vol. 46, pp. 1O1–2, 131–2, *The Architectural Review*, 1919, vol. 46, pp. 128–35; G. K. A. Bell, *Randall Davidson: Archbishop of Canterbury* (first published London, 1935; 2nd edn Oxford, 1938), p. 1037.

77 Revd David Railton, 'The Origin of the Unknown Warrior's Grave', *Our Empire*, November 1931, pp. 34–6; Revd Maurice H. Fitzgerald, *A Memoir of Herbert Edward Ryle* (London, 1928), pp. 311–13. For Railton's war experiences, see Alan H. Maude (ed.), *The 47th (London) Division 1914–1919* (London, 1922), pp. 76–7.

78 *The Times*, 6 November 1920, p. 10, col. 1.

79 *The Times*, 10 November 1920, p. 14 cols 2, 3. The flag is referred to as the 'Hallowed Shroud'.

80 *The Times*, 11 November 1920, p. 15 col. 3; 11 November 1921, p. 11, col. 6.

81 *The Times*, 19 November 1920, p. 10, col. 5; Ronald Blythe, *The Age of Illusion: England in the Twenties and Thirties 1919–40* (first published London, 1963, repr. 1964), p. 20.

82 For the beginnings of the British Legion and the Flanders poppy, see Graham Wootton, *The Official History of the British Legion* (London, 1956) pp. 37–41; Antony Brown, *Red for Remembrance: British Legion 1921–71* (London, 1971), pp. 76–88; Venetia Newall, 'Armistice Day: Folk Tradition in an English Festival of Remembrance', *Folklore*, 1976, vol. 87, part 2, pp. 226–9.

83 *The Times*, 11 November 1920, p. 10, col. 4.

84 *The Times*, 10 November 1921, p. 14, col. 4.

85 *The Times*, 25 July 1927, p. 14 col. 2.

86 *The Times*, 14 November 1921, p. 5, col. 3.

87 *The Times*, 15 November 1921, p. 6, col. 4.

88 *The Times*, 11 November 1921, p. 6, col. 2.

89 *The Times*, 11 November 1921, p. 6, col. 5.

90 *The Times*, 1 March 1922, p. 4, col. 3.

91 *The Times*, 27 October 1925, p. 10, col. 3.

92 H. R. C. ('Dick') Sheppard's letter, 'An Armistice Night Ball?' was published in *The Times*, 20 October 1925, p. 15, col. 4. See other correspondence in *The Times*, 21 October 1925, p. 17, col. 5 and 22 October 1925, p. 13 col. 5. The Victory Ball, in aid of charity, was postponed; and this was announced by Lord Northampton, chairman of the Hospital Committee which was due to benefit, in *The Times*, 5 November 1925, p. 14, col. 6. 'Dick' Sheppard's replacement festival was reported in *The Times*, 11 November 1925, p. 14, col. 3.

93 *British Legion Journal*, December 1929, p. 150.

94 See *British Legion Journal*, December 1938, p. 199, for the origins of the Field of Remembrance.

95 See, for example, F. Britten Austin, 'Let us be Proud!', originally published in the *Sunday Pictorial* and reprinted in the *British Legion Journal*, December 1929, p. 157.

96 See Arthur Mee, *London* (London, 1937), pp. 4l7, 785, 805, 834.

97 R. Ellis Roberts, *H. R. L. Sheppard: Life and Letters* (London, 1942), p. 2l4.

98 Henry Williamson, *The Power of the Dead* (London, 1963; repr. 1985), p. 80.

99 Ibid., p. 341.
100 *The Lambeth Conferences 1867–1948* (London, 1948), p. 65.
101 Ibid., p. 19.
102 *The Times*, 2 November 1920, p. 9, col. 3.
103 *The Times*, 12 November 1925, p. 15, col. 3.
104 *The Times*, 12 November 1925, p. 16, col. 2.
105 *The Times*, 11 November 1926, p. 15, col. 2.

7

DISCRETION, SOBRIETY AND WISDOM: THE TEACHER IN CHILDREN'S BOOKS
Margaret Kinnell

The teachers of early childhood, so different in their degree of involvement from those encountered later in what is deemed 'higher' education, have been the truly memorable influences on many of us. First of all, for me, there was Miss Sinclair; hawk-nosed and black button-eyed, she possessed a tawse as well as a serious determination (this in a Calvin-inspired Scottish primary school) that held the promise of measured retribution for inattentiveness or other such serious misdemeanours. We learned our tables well. Later, there was the Brodie-like Mrs Miller, whose twin delights in pink Parisian gloves and the novels of Dickens held me in her thrall.

For the child, teacher really does know best; and not only best, but just about everything – knowledge is a seamless web that includes choosing the perfect gloves to match an outfit as well as all that mundane stuff about quotients, percentages and the linoleum industry of Kirkcaldy. Why, then, are teachers no longer the all-wise feared/revered figures that we knew them to be as children? One answer lies in the fact of growing up, realizing the fallibility of every adult, even teacher. But there is more to it. Teachers play an ambiguous role in society: still looked to as dedicated professionals, they are at the same time disdained as lacking the intellectual and business skills of a lawyer or accountant. The salaries say it all; but so too does the lack of authority they can now command both in and out of school. The extent to which this ambiguity pervaded past attitudes to teachers was the starting-point for this essay. Children's books are particularly apt vehicles both for delineating society's expectations of authority figures – they are, after all, seeking to explain and justify such expectations to their audience – and for highlighting adult flaws and weaknesses to delight their readers.

Teachers have been described, defined and sometimes pilloried in our national children's literature since it originated in the eighteenth century – a literature which developed earlier and with greater self-confidence than in other countries. So, more quickly and more impressively than elsewhere, English children's books embedded the myths surrounding teachers and schooling in our national consciousness. The genre of the English school story has no parallel in either European or American children's fictions; their interpretations of school and teachers developed much later and looked to English models. For an eleven-year-old emigrant from a Scottish primary to an English public school it was English rather than Scottish literature which provided the hugely entertaining mythology of this strange new environment.

The ways in which English children's books have depicted the teacher chart the uneasy relationship between what society wants from its teachers and what it is prepared to give in return, in terms of status, financial reward and the satisfaction of a professional job well done. From the beginning these were peculiarly national expressions of the teacher's role, which have not only permeated our culture but have become icons of Englishness worldwide. Teachers started out in English children's books in the way John Locke intended: 'discreet, sober, nay wise'. Locke, though, quickly recognized his own wishful thinking, and highlighted the problem that remains to this day: these were 'qualities hardly to be found united in persons that are to be had for ordinary salaries; nor easily to be found anywhere'.[1] Children's literature was founded on the Lockean principle of rationality, as well as on discretion, sobriety and wisdom: the business of teaching was too important and too profitable just to be left to teachers, and publishers eagerly provided items to lighten the tedium of lessons.

Books for children were, however, primarily intended to teach them; and the language of instruction, together with the ever-present figure of the instructor/ess pervaded even the small chapbooks that were published extensively in the late eighteenth century and sought to provide amusement alongside the moralizing passages. As educational opportunities expanded in the late eighteenth century, so teachers were everywhere in children's books. 'Toby Teachem', 'Mrs Teachwell' (Eleanor Fenn), 'Timothy Teachwell' – all made the point well enough. 'Teachem's' *Entertaining History of Little Goody Goosecap*,[2] containing 'a variety of adventures calculated to amuse and instruct', a poor imitation of Newbery's *Goody Two-shoes*, was one of many attempts to popularize the discreet and sober, kindly but firm teacher figure.[3]

Completely dedicated to the task in hand, Mrs Margery Meanwell, the Two-shoes, was the heroine of a moralizing fable[4] that despite its narrowness of conception was one of the first books for children to marry *amusing* original fiction with an instructional element, a book that fixed the teacher in popular imagination as a kindly and worldly-wise creature whose educational philosophy had to do with middle-class mercantilism and the impression of values, not the expanding of young horizons.[5] The didacticism was explicit; how Margery turns from a 'trotting tutoress' to 'principal of a country college' and finally wins wealth and married respectability, is related through a series of adventures in which good sense prevails over the kinds of foolishness that 'are the frolicks of a distempered brain'.[6] Margery was a 'very humane and compassionate' teacher – even of animals, who are credited with more good sense than their masters. Treating wild birds decently was therefore the only reasonable action; 'As these and other animals are so sensible and kind to us, we ought to be tender and good to them.' She also 'knew the great use and necessity of teaching children to submit chearfully to the will of providence',[7] as well as drilling them in their letters, and of developing a sense of 'coolness and moderation' as 'an universal cure for wrong-headedness'. The teacher's role was burdensome – no less than preparing children for the cut and thrust of society, but a limited kind of society, whose bounds were the merchant's house for boys and the parlour for girls. Good schooling meant setting examples through a moderate, reasoning and well-regulated approach to learning. The teacher's attitude was everything.

Expectations of the teacher's role in implementing society's standards of behaviour for children had been set much earlier. Both Sir Thomas Elyot's *The Governor* (1531) and Roger Ascham's *The Schoolmaster* (1570) were concerned to educate an aristocracy able to take on their social and political duties, setting patterns of behaviour for the lower classes and administering the state wisely. 'Truth of religion, honesty in living, right order in learning' were Ascham's principles, but not to be achieved through the kind of beating of pupils that caused Eton scholars to flee their College at the time he was writing.[8] He would have rather 'cheerful admonishing and heedful amending of faults, never leaving behind just praise for well-doing'.[9] This approach on the part of the teacher was the key to pupils' successes, and the teacher was viewed as the necessary mediator of values. Neither Elyot nor Ascham promoted especially original ideas; their significance lay in making them available to the lay Elizabethan reader for the first time and in setting up expectations of good teachers in terms of embodying those virtues they were to cultivate in their pupils. Expectations of teachers were high, and provided the benchmarks against which an anonymous sixteenth-century poet measured the master who 'peppered my tail with good speed' in 'The Unhappy Schoolboy':

> I would my master were a hare,
> And all his books greyhounds were,
> And I myself a jolly hunter;
> To blow my horn I would not spare
> For if he were dead I would not care!
> What availeth it me though I say nay?[10]

Dryden similarly remembered how his teacher at Westminster, Master Busby, 'used to whip a boy so long till he made him a confirmed blockhead'.[11] Life in schools, then, was rather different from the ideal, and writers were concerned to exhort teachers to a more reasoned approach to their pupils. Early children's books depicted a norm of teacher behaviour quite different from the reality of these birching masters, a reality caught in the amber of children's nursery rhymes and skipping games:

> Doctor Faustus was a good man,
> He whipped his scholars now and then;
> When he whipped them he made them dance
> Out of Scotland into France,
> Out of France into Spain,
> And then he whipped them back again.[12]

The application of calm discipline in an ordered, well-regulated schoolroom was the kind of teaching advocated by Locke and his forerunners; and children's writers were eager to promote these theories and to depict teachers as reasonable, industrious and, that most important of virtues, 'sensible'.

The foundation for these sympathetic, yet normative accounts of teacher/child relationships lay partly with the popularity of Lockean ideas, but also, more pragmatically, with the direct experience eighteenth-century children's writers had of running schools and governessing. Publishers had quickly targeted the growing school market and those parents with money for books and tutors; what better than employing school teachers and proprietors themselves as authors of the moralizing tales? We therefore have the interesting spectacle of teachers – all female – moulding their own stereotypes for the children they would dominate.

Sarah Trimmer was an influential example. As well as writing copiously for children she edited the *Guardian of Education* (1802–6), one of the earliest and most important reviewing journals of children's books, and started three Sunday schools in Brentford (the 'Green School' still stands in Brentford High Street). By 1786 they consisted of '37 boys and 122 girls . . . and all my family and three ladies attend every Sunday to assist in instructing the children'.[13] In *The Servant's Friend* (1787), 'an exemplary tale designed to enforce the instructions given at Sunday and other charity schools', she set out the practices and principles by which teachers should operate. Rules were to be 'exactly' conformed to, and included lessons beginning at seven in the morning in summer and eight in winter, 'no toys or play things to be produced in school hours', and not just mere deference but total subservience to the teacher: 'Every boy must make a bow at coming in and going out of the school, and is advised to behave with humility and respect to persons in supervision at all times.'[14] In this as in everything else she considered in relation to childhood, Sarah Trimmer was immensely practical. She emphasized the value of children exercising their limbs when ever possible, including teachers allowing them 'to run about part of the school hours in the open air'.[15] But her imagery of teaching within the classroom setting is that of repression and of misery; the system was one in which both teacher and pupil were trapped into the repetition of stale exercises from the kinds of books that she herself produced – her *Charity School Spelling Book* was used in schools up and down the country from its first publication in 1798 and, in a simplified version, in the schools of the Society for the Promotion of Christian Knowledge at least as late as 1827.[16] Here was a chilling vision of the teacher, impregnable in her classroom (whether male or female made little difference to Mrs Trimmer). Teachers were austere, humourless creatures, no doubt with impeccable values but lacking in any warmth or humanity towards their pupils.

Many early children's books were written by women trying to make a living from teaching as well as from the small sums they got from publishers. Their depiction of teachers was inevitably therefore directed as much at parents as at their child readers; writers were

sensible of the need to portray teaching as both rational and important. Anna Barbauld, who had to support herself after her husband
went mad and drowned himself,[17] no doubt found that running a
school provided the experience of children that helped mark her
books out for their directness of expression, the beauty and simplicity of her style, and the value with which she was able to imbue the
whole process of teaching even the youngest of children. (Her
Lessons for Children from Two to Three Years Old (1778) was
extremely popular with parents and remained available into the mid-
nineteenth century.[18]) Yet despite this, her concept of teaching was
not very different from that of Sarah Trimmer: both believed in the
importance of drilling a child in the basics and providing only
morally acceptable tales, on the Lockean principle that the blank
sheet of the child's intellect required material suited to immaturity: 'a
grave remark, or a connected story, however simple, is above his
capacity; and nonsense is always below it; for folly is worse than
ignorance.'[19] The contribution of these writers to the status of the
teacher was not their development of new ideas in teaching, but their
bringing to the public the significance of early childhood education
and the consequent value to society of good teachers.

Mary Wollstonecraft, another teacher and early writer for children,
as well as philosopher and novelist, was similarly austere in her attitude to teaching, despite her radical credentials. This acknowledgement of the expectations of parents resulted from her experiences as
a governess to Lady Kingsborough's daughters. Her *Original Stories
from Real Life* (1788) appeared about a year after her arguments for
improving the education of women in *Thoughts on the Education of
Daughters*; but they conveyed a less than ideal version of the kind of
schooling she had advocated there. Mrs Mason, the uncompromising
schoolmistress, whose intention was 'to eradicate these prejudices,
and substitute good habits instead of those they had carelessly con-
tracted', never let her charges out of her sight; and the 'stories' of the
title are the tales she recounts as moral lessons. Her teaching was as
didactic as the best of Mrs Trimmer's Sunday school teachers, but
she also aimed at winning a pupil's friendship, and her 'farewell
advice to her young friends' admitted them at last to her circle – a
dubious reward for their tolerance of her. This, then, was the pinna-
cle of her and their achievement; teaching and learning effectively
meant not only the imparting and acquiring of knowledge but also
sharing a value system: 'You are now candidates for my friendship,
and on your advancement in virtue my regard will in future
depend.'[20]

Eleanor Fenn, another writer popular with parents, followed the same principle that teacher knows best, and is entitled therefore to friendship from her pupils.[21] More philanthropist than teacher by trade, she set up Sunday schools in her Norfolk village and, in addition to producing many lesson books, designed 'schemes for teaching', such as 'figures rendered pleasant to children' as counters 'in a bag',[22] to enliven the standard method of teaching by rote learning. Friendly persuasion best describes her philosophy; one of her early books, *School Occurrences: Supposed to Have Arisen among a Set of Young Ladies, Under the Tuition of Mrs Teachwell* (1782), has a 'Miss Friendly' and a 'Mrs Care' teaching the Misses Sprightly, Pert, Cheat and Pry.[23] Their methods were similar to those of Mrs Mason, and drew inspiration from the same source.

All of the women writers concerned with teachers and teaching in the fifty years or so after children's book publishing took hold followed in a tradition begun just as John Newbery (the first publisher of children's books on any commercial scale) and his imitators were starting to exploit the burgeoning interest in education. The importance of these writers lies in their development of the image of the teacher and their widening of the debate on educating children, through providing simple materials for use by both teachers and parents. Their popularity with parents and with teachers in private academies and in the growing numbers of charity schools ensured the spread of the Trimmer–Barbauld–Fenn versions of teaching. However, they, and Mary Wollstonecraft, owed a considerable debt to a novelist whose single work for children became a model for many of the later school stories.

Sarah Fielding was the first writer to make use of the schoolroom itself as teaching aid, with the omnipresent moralizing teacher as guiding spirit. But unlike later writers, she had apparently neither professional nor philanthropic contact with children, and as she remained unmarried only her nephews, nieces and friends' children served as an audience. Hers was in many ways a more dispassionate view of teaching, although equally bound up with the Lockean educational principles that she described in *The Governess: or Little Female Academy* (1749; probably written for her niece Harriet). In this, the earliest recognizable girls' school story, its narrator 'Mrs Teachum' became the first and also one of the most influential teachers in children's fiction.[24] The credibility of the setting that was evident in the later accounts of teachers and teaching, a credibility that sprang from direct experience of schools and children, is not so readily arguable for this series of tales, loosely strung, like the later school stories, around a teacher who embodied all the Lockean teacherly virtues. Nevertheless, Sarah Fielding was able to draw on her own schooldays at Mrs Mary Rookes's boarding school, to which she and her three sisters were sent 'in order to be educated and to learn to work and read and write and to talk French and dance and be brought up as gentlewomen',[25] the very accomplishments that Caroline Bingley in *Pride and Prejudice* saw as the marks of breeding and good taste.

If only *The Governess* had included scenes of the teaching of 'music, singing, drawing, dancing, and the modern languages', that a woman must have to be 'really esteemed accomplished', or, as Erasmus Darwin recommended, grammar, arithmetic, geography, history, natural history, 'the rudiments of taste', drawing and embroidery, 'the heathen mythology', and 'polite literature'.[26] Instead, Mrs Teachum is obsessed by her pupils' behaviour over trifles; their squabbling over sharing out apples and the ensuing moral tale is overdone, and even her inclusion of diverting tales like that of the 'cruel giant Barbarico, the good giant Benefico, and the pretty little dwarf Mignon', were elaborately qualified by a concern for any possible impact on a pupil's moral sensibilities:

> . . . here let me observe to you (which I would have you communicate to your little friends) that giants, magic, fairies, and all sorts of supernatural assistances are only introduced to amuse and divert . . . neither this high-sounding language, nor the supernatural contrivances in this story, do I so thoroughly approve, as to recommend them much to your reading; except, as I said before, great care is taken to prevent your being carried away, by these high-flown things, from that simplicity of taste and manners which it is my chief study to inculcate.[27]

Nevertheless, she did at least attempt to entertain her pupils, rather more so than Mary Wollstonecraft's unremittingly stern Mrs Mason.

Sarah Fielding's work appeared at just the time when children's books were beginning to be a significant specialism in the publishing trade, and coincided with the huge growth in all kinds of schools and schoolteachers. Innumerable boarding schools for young ladies and academies for boys were springing up all over the country; and the village schools run by clergymen, the product of many generations of parish concern for educating the local poor, became more numerous and better endowed. In Leicestershire, at least twelve new schools were established between 1700 and 1736, and a further twenty-six received fresh endowments from local benefactors, while *The*

Northampton Mercury contained notices from more than 100 schools
of various types from 1720 to 1760 and *The Norwich Mercury* from
sixty-three schools between 1749 and 1756.[28] *The Governess* was
significant as the first example of a new genre, the girls' school story.
She survived well into the nineteenth century, with Sarah Fielding's
idea of an academy as the setting for a series of loosely connected
moral tales copied by several writers; Sarah Trimmer recommended
her to readers in the June 1802 number of *The Guardian of
Education* and Mary Sherwood reworked her into a new, but much
duller edition in 1820.[29] It was left to her later imitators, though, to
embed the stereotype of the teacher most throroughly in the popular
imagination by the spread of their tales and class-books into these
schools and homes where newly literate children were eager for reading matter.

Who were the various teachers encountered by children in reality in
the hugely disparate schools of the late eighteenth and early nineteenth centuries? There was certainly no formal professional class of
teachers, just as there were no architects, land agents or civil servants;
the only qualification appeared to be a willingness to take on a village
school for pay of as little as £12 a year,[30] or to set up a plate for an
academy. Goldsmith described one ill-prepared schoolmaster who had
served as quartermaster under Marlborough and read 'only tolarably
[sic] for an Irishman', but who nevertheless found himself as 'country
schoolmaster to a country parson'.[31] A few children's books did indicate the inadequacies of these village teachers, their recourse to the
rod as a favoured way to winning respect and the narrowness of their
educational horizons. Children couldn't wait to escape them: 'Tis holiday . . . and e'en the village school pours out its little inmates . . .
noisy, wild and void of care; from toilsome task releas'd and tongue
of lecturing dame; and, happier still, from dread of birchen rod,
terrific shook high o'er the doltish head. They shout, they leap, and in
the fervour of tumultuous joy, forget their humble meal, neglected
left, unpack'd, in tiny basket . . .'[32] However, the inadequate dame of
this village school, the 'deaf, poor patient widow' described by
Crabbe,[33] or the butcher's wife whose 'children were like the Harleian
miscellany, by different authors' and yet ran a flourishing school
attended by Robert Southey's aunt,[34] bore little resemblance to the
capable teachers of the earliest children's books – creatures who had
a long life in children's fiction. The village teachers in children's
books were sensible and wise, embodying the rational virtues that
Locke had recommended; they all knew best and their qualification to
teach and to demand their pupils' respect went unchallenged.

Those running boarding schools or day academies were equally well served by authors; no doubts were expressed in early children's books as to the teaching methods on offer, the curriculum or the experience of being schooled. The kind of worries that James Lackington had for the 'dreadful depravity of boarding schools'[35] were not available to child readers. Dorothy Kilner did attempt an attack on supposedly lax morality in her *Anecdotes of a Boarding School; Or an Antidote to the Vices of those Useful Seminaries*, but she failed. The gossipy dialogue and accounts of schoolgirl naughtiness were more likely to attract than to deter children.[36]

The stereotype of the teacher that was embodied in *The Governess* was safe for some time into the nineteenth century. There were, however, distinct shifts in emphasis, with the emergence of alternative models of teaching. The Lockean image of a teacher able to develop 'prudence and good breeding' in a pupil – qualities essential for 'a gentleman's calling'[37] – was giving way to a more child-centred view of education, which brought with it a very different approach to the relationship between teacher and taught. Here was the first crack in the solidarity of children's authors on the subject of teachers and teaching, the first major shift in the school story genre since *The Governess* had set female writers and a female view of teaching firmly as the model for teachers.

In Rousseau's *Emile*, first published in French in 1762, and quickly taken up by English educationists, as cause for both praise and condemnation, the tutor (male) had followed rather than led the child, albeit in a controlling and controlled environment. Children were not only *allowed* to question their teacher, they were expected to do so; freedom to explore their world, to imagine and to dream dreams were part of the process of learning. 'If he asks questions let your answers be enough to whet his curiosity, but not enough to satisfy it.'[38] Teachers were even to engage the child in imaginative play: 'Let him think he is Robinson himself; let him see himself clad in skins wearing a tall cap, a great cutlass, all the grotesque get-up of Robinson Crusoe, even to the umbrella which he will scarcely need . . . This is the genuine castle in the air of this happy age, when the child knows no other happiness but food and freedom.'[39] The peculiarity of Rousseau's vision was his insistence on a pupil knowing only his tutor; social intercourse in a school setting did not form part of his educational system. This presented some difficulties for those who so enthusiastically took up his ideas; Richard Edgeworth's first attempts at educating his son on Rousseauist principles resulted in failure as the boy, somewhat inevitably, grew into an uncontrollable brat dependent on his father who, on visiting the great man himself, was exceedingly rude and chauvinistic.[40] There had to be some acknowledgement of the role of the school setting and the society for which children were being educated to accommodate Rousseau's educational ideas to the practical needs of childhood.

In their *Practical Education*, Maria and Richard Edgeworth therefore adapted Rousseau's views for the benefit of 'every well informed parent and every liberal schoolmaster'. Their shift to a male image of teacher, to a new and more socially self-conscious concept of teaching, was perceptible. They were concerned that 'too little attention is paid to the general improvement of the understanding and formation of the moral character' and in particular that few girls had been 'taught to any purpose, who have not been their own teachers'. An emphasis on the superficial acquisition of a few, female accomplishments had devalued the coinage of teaching: 'Stop at any good inn on the London roads, and you will probably find that the landlady's daughter can shew you some of her own framed drawings, can play a tune upon her spinet, or support a dialogue in French of a remarkable length, in the customary questions and answers.'[41] Any teacher worth *his* salt had to be 'properly qualified to teach' – he 'must have the power of recollecting exactly how he learned; he must go back step by step to the point at which he began, and must be able to conduct his pupil through the same path without impatience or precipitation'.[42]

Children's writers took up this image of the reflective teacher, even if they largely ignored the male teacher model; Charles and Mary Lamb's *Mrs Leicester's School*, while owing its structure to Sarah Fielding's Locke-inspired *Governess*, took from Rousseau in its portrayal of the relationship between Mrs Leicester and the young ladies of Amwell School. The teacher is shown as thoughtful, considerate of her pupils' emotional states and eager to develop a method of teaching to suit their individual needs:

> During our first solemn silence, which, you may remember, was only broken by my repeated requests that you would make a smaller, and still smaller, circle, till I saw the fire-place fairly inclosed [*sic*] round, the idea came into my mind, which has since been a source of amusement to you in the recollection, and to myself in particular has been of essential benefit, as it enabled me to form a just estimate of you my young pupils, and assisted me to adapt my plan of future instruction to each individual temper.[43]

Other writers similarly adapted Rousseau to their own, more pragmatic approaches to teaching: the Comtesse de Genlis, for example, opposed his view that a tutor be dedicated to a single pupil, and in *Adelaide and Theodore* was equally interested to provide an education applicable to girls as well as boys, a conscious repudiation of Rousseau's male-dominated educational system.[44]

Writers of school stories also became more interested in using the relationship between teacher and pupil as a means of developing both plot and characterization. The former stereotyping began to give way to recognizable characters, teachers were no longer sacrosanct beings to be neither criticized nor doubted. Pupils could actually be seen to ridicule them as childhood became more and more respected: 'At the moment that Miss Frivol congratulated herself upon her refractory pupil having become quiet and submissive, she was busily employed in working a figure of that lady with large ass's ears and a pair of goggle eyes at each side of the head, whilst from her mouth proceeded the words, "I may not see nor hear, but I can still think."'[45] Early children's books had allowed no room for manoeuvre. A teacher's place was secure; omniscient and omnipresent, teachers held total sway over their charges. During the early nineteenth century this view of the teacher as infallible didact began slowly to give way, as pupils were shown to fight back.

The school settings experienced by children became more varied and so, consequently, did the range of types of teacher. In the early books, in common with the experience of children, schools were generally small – Mrs Teachum presided over only nine girls and Mrs Leicester over ten, but as schooling for the poor developed in the early nineteenth century increasing numbers of children experienced the factory-like schooling systems of Lancaster and Bell, or the schools of industry set up to prepare pauper children for domestic servitude or simple factory work. There are, however, few imaginative representations of teachers in these schools. Eliza Fenwick's *Lessons for Children* romanticizes a factory school, in which children rise at four in the morning to get in two hours of schooling under an oak tree before arriving at the mill for a six o'clock start. Joseph, their teacher, is one of them, not an outside authority figure.[46] This is a rare example, but indicates how far the average child's educational experience was from the genteel schooling of the academy, and how different the role of the teacher. Although little known, this book is important for its portrayal of the developing democratization of education and the shifting towards a perception of the teacher as a participant in the educational process rather than just an authority figure.

A further model was available in the growing numbers of Sunday schools (by 1818 educating around 450,000 children[47]) and in the schools of the British and Foreign Schools Society and of the National Society. Educating children at minimal cost meant using monitors to spread the most basic of skills. Teachers in these schools were largely redundant, many children would hardly see their teacher: 'It is not proposed that the children of the poor be educated in an expensive manner, or even taught to write or to cypher.'[48] This had been exactly Hannah More's approach to teaching the poor in her Sunday and day schools for the poor of Cheddar: 'My plan for instructing the poor is very limited and strict. They learn of week-days such coarse work as may fit them for servants. I allow of no writing. My object has not been to teach dogmas and opinions, but to form the lower class to habits of industry and virtue.'[49] In schools such as these, the teacher's role, paradoxically, was very much more constrained than in the small, do-it-yourself academies where propri-etors suited their curricula to the dictates of fashion and the market. Large numbers of pupils and a growing demand for educational emancipation saw the end of a simplistic view of the teacher's medi-ating, socializing role. Syllabuses were defined through the reading and spelling systems invented by Bell and Lancaster, and for this work a teacher could be largely irrelevant. It was with some pride that Lancaster calculated how 100 boys spelling 100 words for 200 mornings could spell two million words.[50] Until 1825 only reading, writing, arithmetic and needlework were considered appropriate sub-jects for children in the British and Foreign schools; in that year a geography book was introduced for the first time for older children.[51] During the nineteenth century, therefore, the schism between the schooling experiences of the majority of children and their depiction in children's books widened considerably. The village teachers in popular chapbooks of the *Goody Two-shoes* kind or the discreet and sober governesses following on from Sarah Fielding were a world apart from the experience of children in the vast factory-like schools, or indeed of those children being taught the rudiments of literacy by their fellows.

Similarly, the small academies had little in common with the teach-ing and learning experiences provided in the large public schools that were also coming into their own at this period, schools that empha-sized the manly educational virtues and for which the largely female imagery of teaching in children's books up until then had little rele-vance. The gulf between the social settings of the various kinds of teachers at this time was more marked than at almost any other period. There were a few similarities: the harshness of both public school and charity school regimes, and an increased emphasis on social discipline. Brutality of a kind it is now hard to imagine had preoccupied the public schools in the late eighteenth and early nineteenth centuries: Robert Southey produced a magazine called *The Flagellant*, based on his experiences at Westminster,[52] and there were frequent rebellions by pupils. The Brougham Committee's criticisms, which appeared between 1816 and 1818 and followed on from furious attacks in the press of the day on the brutality and inefficiency of public schools, together with a collapse in numbers attending several of the great schools, prompted reform and a reappraisal of the teacher's role. Brutality by teachers to their pupils, and by pupil to pupil, was still in evidence, but now controlled and excused by reference to a social as well as moral and religious code. 'The schoolmaster is abroad!' declared Lord Brougham in the House of Commons in 1828, 'And I trust to him, armed with his primer, against the soldier, in full military array.'[53]

Disciplining the individual entailed disciplining the school, and, as Arnold believed, winning over the senior boys to the teacher's viewpoint was an essential part of the exercise; a direct parallel with the monitorial system.[54] But first, teachers had to be respected. It was necessary for masters to be 'a proper model for imitation' and of equal social status with their pupils. When asking a colleague about the newly appointed Head of Rugby, a master in 1895 queried: 'Tell me, is James a gentleman? Understand me, I don't mean, Does he speak the Queen's English? but – had he a grandfather?'[55] The new genre of school stories set in the boys' public schools stressed the equality in manliness of these boy–boy and boy–teacher relationships and for the first time portrayed the school as a complex social system. The significant teacher-figures in eighteenth-century children's books were women, usually controlling their charges totally within the simple and absolute despotism of the girls' school. In the first fictionalized account, with accurate characterization, of a recognizably real boys' school, *Tom Brown's Schooldays* – Thomas Hughes' account of Arnold's Rugby School – the teacher was no longer a lone authority figure. Overt moralizing apart, Hughes accurately conveys the complex pecking order and intricate web of relations in a school such as Rugby, where Arnold was the ultimate court of appeal, but where other relationships played an important role. Masters and senior boys exerted powerful moral and physical control over boys – East and Tom smart at the injustice of a master sending them to the Doctor for a flogging, while letting off *his* boys with lines, but this was the code of the school: loyalty to friends, and to the boys in your charge, was a powerful ethic. Their own housemaster, 'a model young master', pleaded with the Doctor on their behalf, speaking in terms that belied his superior position: 'Well, they are not hard workers, and very thoughtless and full of spirits – but I can't help liking them. I think they are sound good fellows at the bottom.'[56] Being judged 'a good fellow' by a master was sufficient to outweigh rule-breaking. There was little sense of distance between a young master and the older boys of the school; all measured and were measured by the same ethical scale, and all stood or fell by it. The boys themselves set much of the discipline in the school – unheard-of in the tales of eighteenth-century schooling, where teachers ruled supremely: 'In no place in the world has individual character more weight than at a public school . . . Now is the time in all your lives, probably, when you may have more wide influence for good or evil on the society you live in than you ever can have again.'[57]

Eric's experiences of masters in Farrar's less acclaimed but more successful *Eric; or Little by Little* were initially less happy; Mr Lawley's grammar school, where he was first sent, operated on a monitorial system, with the upper class hearing the little boys' lessons, so that 'Eric managed to get on pretty much as he liked' without much in the way of teaching. The Head was a sour-faced old master, and 'a little wrong in the head', so wrong that he ended up in a lunatic asylum: 'Often did he tell the boys "that it was an easier life by far to break stones by the roadside than to teach them".'[58] Here too, there is a considerable distance between this vision of the embittered old teacher and the bright infallible models in the earlier school stories. Farrar insisted on the reality of Eric's experiences, claiming for them in the preface 'the merit of truthfulness'. He was himself a schoolmaster, at Harrow and then as Head of Marlborough. The concept of teacherliness is doubly evident in *Eric*; through the descriptions of teacher behaviour and attitude that Farrar sets down in the narrative, and also by the themes and tone of the book, which emanate purely from the 'teacher' that he was himself. In that sense, he was writing in the same spirit as those eighteenth-century school story authors whose experiences of schooling provided the foundation for their writing, but here there is at least acknowledgement of the occasional awfulness of teachers, particularly disillusioned teachers. The moral tone is also strong throughout the book, and Eric is as tiresome as any of the earlier boy prodigies; but just as clearly as in *Tom Brown's Schooldays* a teacher can be a true friend to a boy, even when appearances are against him: 'You have many faults, but I feel sure that I cannot be mistaken in supposing you too noble-minded for a revenge so petty and mean . . . I *trust you*, Eric, and will use every endeavour to right you in the general estimation.'[59] However, the realism should not be overestimated. This idealistic view of the teacher–pupil relationship was in part fantasy, for teachers *were* still feared, and school, particularly boarding school, held real terrors for children:

> Where is the boy, who has ever left his parents to attend a boarding school, who has forgotten the first moment when he entered the school-house? . . . There is a dismal foreboding of long lessons and unknown punishments, and the young urchin is consigned to his schoolmaster, with about as much cheerfulness in his face, and happiness in his heart, as if he were placed under the care of a jailor.[60]

The savagery of warped and unrelenting teachers, and the miseries of the smaller boarding schools in the early to mid-nineteenth century, were being recorded by Dickens and Charlotte Bronte. Squeers is one of the more powerful of fictional teachers in adult literature, all the more so for reawakening memories of schooldays long past, but his type of master was also being written about and ridiculed in contemporary literature for children. There was something infinitely ludicrous in the cruel antics of a Wackford Squeers; teachers like him might be fearsome, but they were also 'old and cunning and slow'.[61]

In the boys' school stories of the later nineteenth century much less respectful images of the teacher became more prevalent: boys were no longer so co-operative nor so patient with the shortcomings of their masters, and the respect accorded to teachers by children's writers could no longer be guaranteed. Kipling's worldly-wise boys of *Stalky & Co* spent many of their schooldays in seeking ways to outwit the masters.[62] Begun as 'tracts and parables on the education of the young', these stories, 'for reasons honestly beyond my control, turned themselves into a series of tales'.[63] In fact, they were a conscious reaction, really a skit, against the compliant schoolboy–master relationships in the school stories of forty years earlier. Kipling's housemasters are shown as pompous and imbecilic, and easily outsmarted by boys who scorn the merely 'naughty Eric' of Farrar's tale. Supposedly based on Kipling's schooling at the United Services College in Bideford, Devon, this was a brutal vision of boys' behaviour in the rarefied environs of the public school, and of the challenges posed to teachers when high-spirited and ruthless adolescents developed their own ethos and pitted themselves against the establishment. However, *Stalky & Co* is at least as interesting for what it fails to record as for its so-called realism, for Kipling's old school was liberal in comparison with the old public schools – 'fagging' was unknown and the use of the cane very limited. The masters helped Kipling in his development as a writer, and sport was not accorded anything like the significance it held in other public schools of the day. Price, Kipling's headmaster, a friend of his parents and very unlike the jingoistic guide and friend to potential heroes of the Empire depicted in the Head of the book, was of left-wing political persuasion. As Quigly argues, Kipling was preaching rather than reflecting the reality he had experienced: *Stalky & Co* was about the kind of school he wanted, not the school he actually attended.[64] Kipling's school story was a work of literature that relied heavily on the earlier stereotypes of teachers as the butt of his heroes' wit, rather than an attempt at sociological verisimilitude. The reality of changed teacher attitudes and the new breed of public school Heads failed to challenge his fictionalized images of teachers that were a direct legacy of the early school stories – images of pomposity, narrowness and ineptitude. But for the reader, as in most children's literature of the later nineteenth century, the authority figures in children's books were anyway no longer of significance other than as foils for the real heroes – the children in the book. Even if they escaped being figures of fun and ridicule, teachers could not but be of lesser significance in the struggle between child and adult worlds.

Girls' public school stories were slower to appear – girls' schools were only just emerging as significant educators of middle-class girls in the late nineteenth century – but when they did they portrayed no more truly realistic views of school relationships than did the boys' stories. Angela Brazil's *Fortunes of Philippa* was first published in 1906, and was as far removed from reality as *Stalky & Co.*, although nowhere near as skilfully written nor in the least critical of the system. Her heroine is put to school in England (as she herself was) from a childhood spent in Rio de Janeiro; and her father's preference in curriculum bears an uncanny resemblance to that of Caroline Bingley, or indeed of Sarah Fielding: 'You've not been taught a note of music, you can't speak French or dance a quadrille, and if it came to a question of fine sewing, I'm afraid you'd scarcely know which was the right end of your needle.'[65] The schools that Angela Brazil attended had none of the excitements of her fictionalized schools, and the teachers were similarly of another age, with clear echoes of the early girls' school stories. Mrs Marshall, the Headmistress, received only forty pupils; her 'right hand in discipline' was a Miss Percy, 'a lady of uncertain age, and even more uncertain temper':

She seemed to regard schoolgirls with perpetual suspicion, and to have a perfect genius for pouncing down upon us on the most inopportune occasions. Were we indiscreet enough to talk in bed, Miss Percy was sure to be passing the door at the identical moment; were we late for prayers, hoping to shuffle in unnoticed among the servants, she was certain to be waiting for us in the hall. She had a very lynx eye for missing buttons or untied shoe-laces, her long thin nose smelled out directly the chestnuts we endeavoured to roast by the school-room fire, and she could catch the lowest whispers in the preparation hour.[66]

Those writers following in the genre (Bessie Marchant, Ethel Talbot, Dorita Fairlie Bruce, Elinor M. Brent-Dyer *et al.*) were equally limited in their depiction of girl–mistress relationships. There were the occasional chaste crushes on pretty young mistresses, but the older teacher harridans were still a prevalent image; Miss Bullivant, 'the Bull' of Charles Hamilton's Cliff House, who enjoyed putting down any unfortunate man who crossed her by means of her hockey-stick or golf club, is a memorable example. The intricate power relationships of the boys' school stories of the nineteenth century were much less in evidence, and the debt to earlier teacher–pupil exchanges much clearer.

However, all of those immensely popular boy and girl school stories of the late nineteenth and early twentieth century were about as far removed from the experience of schooling as could be imagined; many of their readers were in any event out of school by the time they got round to reading them.[67] The slide towards pure fantasy in the St Trinian's and Greyfriars teacher stereotypes began in this period – fantasy because they were never intended to capture the reality of the kinds of teachers to be found in the elementary and secondary schools in which most of their readers were taught. Writers no longer had to portray teachers to an *adult* audience in children's books; children would glory in the assault on authority figures in school stories, while their parents viewed teachers from afar – usually literally, as parents seldom visited school premises, whether the public schools or, for most of the population, the local elementary school. Teachers in these schools were sometimes as harassed as their pupils. One struggling elementary schoolmistress recorded in her school log how a recalcitrant truanter, on being caned, 'turned round and tried to kick me, in fact he did kick me, though he did not hurt . . . At noon the boy being kept in, his mother came in a frightful passion, fetched her boy and abused me in a frightful manner.'[68]

Elementary teachers were not always the respected paragons of earlier story books, and indeed, at the beginning of the nineteenth century they were largely untrained and themselves poorly educated, but by the 1830s some were at last receiving some training through apprenticeship in the central schools of the British and Foreign and National Societies, and in the Church schools. Only with the creation of training colleges in 1839 did a proper training become available for teachers; thereafter the standard of recruits could begin to rise. The introduction in 1846 of the pupil-teacher scheme to encourage more entrants into teaching, and then in 1854 the imposition of uniform syllabuses on teacher training colleges, marked increasing state intervention in the development of a teaching profession – although with the result that teacher training merely repeated many of the arid teaching practices of the Lancasterian system rather than providing a more liberal and advanced education for intending teachers.[69] Despite enhanced opportunities, elementary school teachers were still seen as social inferiors by the graduate teachers in the secondary and public schools; most elementary school teachers were, like their pupils, of working-class origin, and usually female. The assumption that only girls would be interested in this lowly profession continued up to the 1920s and beyond.[70] Unsurprisingly, therefore, elementary teachers did not figure as important characters in children's popular literature, and when they did appear were treated lightly and with little in the way of moral or intellectual significance to the child: 'Jimmy had come to school with dirty hands. His teacher was shocked. "James", she said reprovingly, "your hands are very dirty. What would you say if I came to school that way?" "I wouldn't speak about it," said Jimmy. "I'd be too polite".'[71] Child autonomy had come a long way since the teachers in early children's books had terrorized their pupils. No early nineteenth-century child would have dared address a teacher thus – *The Rebellious School-girl* had at least kept her own counsel.[72] Professional training for secondary school teachers developed more slowly than for elementary teachers; a master's social status, scholarship and moral authority were his most important attributes.[73]

There was thus no concept of a unified teaching profession, and no single image of teaching upon which children's writers could focus other than that developed by the public school. And so the popular imagery of teaching remained fixed, with those fossilized elements of an outdated system in which a master was defined by his mortarboard and a mistress by her pince-nez and bun. Quelch's authority at Greyfriars was grounded solely in his sarcasm and fierceness; only the Head, 'Dr Locke', had any claim to scholarship. The circle from

John Locke to Greyfriars was complete – but only the Head, modelled on Thomas Arnold, laid claim to sobriety and wisdom; the masters were generally a simple lot, with raw cunning as their favoured weapon. Their names indicate their status – Prout, Hacker, Capper, Wiggins and Twigg – and all were mere fodder for Bunter's pranks.[74] In *The Hotspur*'s series of Red Circle School stories there were similar stereotypes: Mr Alfred Smugg was the unpopular master of the Home House, with Dixie Dale as a favourite teacher who eventually makes it to Head.[75]

These fixed images of public schools and their teachers that dominated English popular children's fiction from the early years of the twentieth century up to the 1950s were, in Orwell's words, 'safe, solid and unquestionable'.[76] The readers of comic-book school tales and of the school stories that poured off the presses during the same period took them for the fantasies they were; most children were stuck with the daily grind of an elderly, under-resourced state school. And yet . . . there was sufficient truthfulness in the portraits of grim-faced and eccentric masters and mistresses to engage a child in empathetic understanding of a Bunter's predicament. Edward Blishen's account of his schoolteaching days in London schools in the early 1950s catches the various degrees of oddness, viciousness and incompetence that children encountered, and their uncomfortable closeness to fiction:

> In the first half [of the morning] I saw a man totally at a loss. He dashed at his teaching like someone plunging into a thick and hostile crowd in search of something he had dropped. Driven back by muttering amazement and a chaos of elbows, he stood at the edge of it, his voice on squeaking tiptoe . . . After break I was handed over to a young man with an amused, cool face and very large teeth. 'I like the Socratic method', he told me . . . In the lowest class, a youngish man with strained eyes . . . Face purple, he would bend down to some little offender – chosen at random, so far as I could see – and bellow: 'I didn't tell you to do that, did I? You're daft, aren't you?' Then he would shake the child until his legs were skidding about the floor, bang away at the boy's bottom and return to me.[77]

Some teachers had travelled no distance at all from their birching forerunners; no wonder then that children's books and comics should parody them so mercilessly.

The shift in teacher portraits over the centuries since children's books were first published was conditioned largely by the enhanced significance of the child as reader, and by the 1950s as consumer, of a burgeoning child-centred literature. In the beginning, teacher knew best; discretion, sobriety and wisdom were what a parent, and society, expected of both the teacher and the book. As the literature developed and attitudes towards children changed, and when children began to choose and eventually to buy books for themselves, then the depiction of traditional authority figures changed – for good. The parent's view of the teacher in children's books was no longer of any account. From their role as guide, friend and moral guardian, teachers evolved in twentieth-century children's stories into the butt of jokes; they became stock figures against which a hero could test his mettle. William's struggles for supremacy over 'ole Markie', and his triumph over the 'temporary history master' confirmed his heroic qualities of defiance and quick-wittedness in the battle with a spurious adult intellectual superiority and authority.[78]

In the face of enfranchised childhood, early ideals of the discreet, sober and wise teacher as a moral beacon in children's stories were doomed; the democratizing of education that accompanied this change meant the end of the school story. Only the mortar board remains in comic strip cartoons. Reverential memories of pink Parisian gloves or similar such remembrances of teacher heroes do not find their way now into the collective fictions of childhood; nostalgia for teachers long gone has become personal reminiscence.

NOTES

1 J. Locke, *The Educational Writings of John Locke*, ed. James L. Axtell (Cambridge, 1968), p. 187.

2 'Toby Teachem', *The Orphan: Or, the Entertaining History of Little Goody Goosecap* (London: John Marshall & Co., c.1780). This was also published in a later version by John Harris (1828); other editions were published in Exeter in 1795 and in York in 1803. See M. Moon, *John Harris's Books for Youth 1801–1843* (Winchester, 1987), p. 53 and J. St John, *The Osborne Collection of Early Children's Books: A Catalogue*, 2 vols (Toronto, 1958–1975), p. 949. John Marshall issued a further imitation in c.1785, *The Renowned History of Primrose Prettyface*, 'who by her sweetness of temper and love of learning, was raised from being the daughter of a poor cottager, to great riches, and the dignity of the lady of the manor'.

3 *The History of Little Goody Two-shoes* (London, J. Newbery, 1765). The publishing history of this first edition is set out in J. Roberts, 'The 1765 Edition of Goody Two-shoes', *British Museum Quarterly*, 1965, vol. 29, pp. 67–80. Later Newbery editions are described by S. Roscoe, *John Newbery and his Successors 1740–1814* (Wormley, Herts, 1973), pp. 135–7, while F. J. H. Darton, *Children's Books in England*, 3rd edn (Cambridge, 1982), pp. 130–1, assesses

nineteenth- and even twentieth-century versions which were available up to as late as 1940.

4 S. Pickering, *John Locke and Children's Books in Eighteenth Century England* (Knoxville, 1981), p. 49.

5 F. J. H. Darton, *Children's Books in England*, 3rd edn (Cambridge, 1982), pp. 128–31.

6 *The History of Little Goody Two-shoes*, 3rd edn (London, 1766; facsimile edn, published by Griffith and Farran, 'successors to Newbery and Harris', 1881, p. 56.

7 Ibid., pp. 104, 81.

8 R. Ascham, *The Schoolmaster (1570)*, ed. L. R. Ryan (Ithaca, 1967), pp. 6–11.

9 Ibid., p. 16.

10 I. Opie and P. Opie, *The Oxford Book of Children's Verse* (Oxford, 1973), p. 11.

11 John Dryden, quoted in W. De La Mare, *Early One Morning in the Spring* (London, 1935), p. 372.

12 I. Opie and J. Opie, *The Oxford Dictionary of Nursery Rhymes* (Oxford, 1951), pp. 168–9. 'Doctor Foster' waved his stick in another version: I. Opie and P. Opie, *The Oxford Nursery Rhyme Book* (Oxford, 1955), p. 101).

13 S. Trimmer, *The Oeconomy of Charity* (London, 1787), p. 162; and D. M. Yarde, *The Life and Works of Sarah Trimmer* (Hounslow, 1972), p. 33.

14 S. Trimmer, *The Servant's Friend* (London, 1787), pp. 13–14.

15 S. Trimmer, *Instructive Tales*, 2nd edn (London, 1812), p. 238. Trimmer's 'Rules for the Management of Children' first appeared in *The Family Magazine*, 1788–9.

16 J. M. Goldstrom, 'The Changing Content of Elementary Education as Reflected in School Books in Use in England 1808–70', PhD thesis (Birmingham University, 1968), p. 40.

17 A. L. Le Breton, *Memoir of Mrs Barbauld* (London, 1874), pp. 121–2.

18 A. L. Barbauld, *Lessons for Children* (London, 1834). Richard and Maria Edgeworth had admired her work and Darton considered that her 'masterly command of English has been matched by few other writers for children' (p. 153).

19 A. L. Barbauld, *Lessons for Children from Two to Three Years Old* (London, 1787), 'Advertisement'.

20 M. Wollstonecraft, *Original Stories from Real Life; With Conversations Calculated to Regulate the Affections, and Form the Mind to Truth and Goodness* (London, 1791), p. 177.

21 Eleanor Fenn also wrote under the pseudonym of 'Mrs Lovechild'; her books first appeared around 1780, and were still being published as late as *c.*1848, when her *Infantine Knowledge* was issued in a 7th edition by Grant and Griffith.

22 Listed in a catalogue to E. Fenn, *The Child's Grammar, Corresponding with Parsing Lessons and Forming Part of a Series for Teaching*, 25th edn (London, 1819).

23 E. Fenn, *School Occurrences: Supposed to have Arisen among a Set of Young Ladies, under the Tuition of Mrs Teachwell; and to be Recorded by One of Them* (London, 1782).

24 S. Fielding, *The Governess; Or Little Female Academy, being the History of Mrs Teachum and her Nine Girls* (London, the author, 1749; facsimile edn, ed.

J. E. Grey, Oxford: Oxford University Press, 1968). Richard Edgeworth recounted how as a child he 'had no resource but Newberry's [*sic*] little books and Mrs Teachum'.

25 Ibid., p. 7.

26 E. Darwin, *A Plan for the Conduct of Female Education in Boarding Schools* (London, 1797), p. 128.

27 Fielding, *The Governess*, p. 68.

28 B. Simon, (ed.), *Education in Leicestershire, 1540–1940* (Leicester, 1968); G. A. Cranfield, *The Development of the Provincial Newspaper 1700–1760* (Westport, 1978), p. 215.

29 M. M. B. Sherwood, *The Governess; Or, the Little Female Academy* (Wellington, 1820). There was no acknowledgement of Sarah Fielding by name, and the fairy stories were replaced by moral tales and biblical quotations.

30 R. Porter, *English Society in the Eighteenth Century* (London, 1982), p. 91.

31 O. Goldsmith, *Collected Works*, 5 vols, ed. A. Friedman (Oxford, 1966), vol. 4, p. 295; V. Neuburg, *Popular Education in Eighteenth Century England* (London, 1971), pp. 17–38.

32 W. Holloway, *Scenes of Youth* (London, 1803), p. 84.

33 G. Crabbe, *The Borough* (London, 1810), p. 329.

34 C. C. Southey, *The Life and Correspondence of the Late Robert Southey*, 6 vols (London, 1849), vol. 1, p. 21.

35 J. Lackington, *The Confessions . . . to Which are Added Two Letters on the Bad Consequences of Having Daughters Educated at Boarding Schools* (London, the author, 1804), p. 207.

36 D. Kilner, *Anecdotes of a Boarding School; Or an Antidote to the Vices of those Useful Seminaries* (London, c.1783).

37 Locke, *Educational Writings*, p. 197.

38 J-J. Rousseau, *Emile*, trans. B. Foxley (London, 1911), p. 135.

39 Ibid., p. 148.

40 G. Summerfield, *Fantasy and Reason: Children's Literature in the Eighteenth Century* (London, 1984), p. 118.

41 M. Edgeworth and R. L. Edgeworth, *Practical Education*, 2 vols (London, 1798), p. 532.

42 Ibid., p. 542.

43 C. Lamb and M. Lamb, *Mrs Leicester's School: Or, the History of Several Young Ladies, Related by Themselves* (London, 1809), p. iv.

44 S. F. Ducrest de Saint-Aubin [Comtesse de Genlis], *Adelaide and Theodore; Or Letters on Education* (London, 1783), p. 11: 'The deepest study of the human heart, with every talent united, which is so essentially necessary in a tutor will avail nothing without that experience which alone can be acquired by long practice.'

45 M. Robson, *The Rebellious School-girl* (London, 1821), p. 33.

46 E. Fenwick, *Lessons for Children, or; Rudiments of Good Manners, Morals, and Humanity*, 2nd edn (London, 1811).

47 T. W. Laqueur, 'Working Class Demand and the Growth of English Elementary Education', in L. Stone (ed.), *Schooling and Society* (Baltimore, 1976), p. 42.

48 Andrew Bell, quoted in H. B. Binns, *A Century of Education, being the Centenary History of the British and Foreign School Society* (London, 1908), p. 56.

49 Hannah More, quoted in M. G. Jones, *Hannah More* (Westport, 1968), p. 152.

50 J. Lancaster, *Improvements in Education as it Respects the Industrious Classes of the Community* (London, 1803): 'a method of teaching to spell and read, whereby one book will serve instead of six hundred books'.

51 J. M. Goldstrom, *The Social Content of Education 1808–1870* (Shannon, 1972), p. 46.

52 J. Gathorne-Hardy, *The Public School Phenomenon 597–1977* (London, 1977), p. 42.

53 Quoted in De La Mare, *Early One Morning in the Spring*, p. 342.

54 Gathorne-Hardy, *The Public School Phenomenon*, p. 72.

55 J. R. de S. Honey, *Tom Brown's Universe: The Development of the Victorian Public School* (London, 1977), p. 326.

56 T. Hughes, *Tom Brown's Schooldays* (Cambridge, 1857), ch. 9.

57 Ibid., ch. 8.

58 F. W. Farrar, *Eric; Or, Little by Little. A Tale of Roslyn School* (London, 1858), ch. 1.

59 Ibid., ch. 11.

60 *The Boy's Week-day Book*, 4th edn (London, 1842), ch. 5.

61 'The broken window', in *The Misfortunes of Toby Ticklepitcher* (London, c.1850), p. 5.

62 H. G. Wells called them 'mucky little sadists' in his autobiography: see G. Trease, *Tales Out of School*, 2nd edn (London, 1964), p. 108.

63 R. Kipling, *Stalky & Co* (London, 1899); Rudyard Kipling, quoted in R. L. Green, *Tellers of Tales*, 4th edn (London, 1965), p. 228.

64 I. Quigly, *The Heirs of Tom Brown* (London, 1982), pp. 113–14.

65 A. Brazil, *The Fortunes of Philippa* (London, c.1924; first published 1906), p. 8.

66 Ibid.

67 Quigly, *The Heirs of Tom Brown*, p. 219.

68 The log book of Harlton School, Cambridgeshire, June, 1884; quoted in A. Digby and P. Searby, *Children, School and Society in Nineteenth-Century England* (London, 1981), p. 167.

69 Ibid., p. 41.

70 *Teaching as a Profession: A Guide for Parents and Guardians* (London, 1922), p. 7: 'The standard of education required is not as high as is necessary for a secondary teacher.'

71 *The Children's Treasury of Pictures and Stories*, No. VII (London, c.1909), p. 49.

72 Robson, *The Rebellious School-girl*.

73 Digby and Searby, *Children, School and Society in Nineteenth-Century England*, pp. 43–5.

74 'F. Richards' [Charles Hamilton], *Billy Bunter's Own* (London, 1953). Greyfriars first appeared as a named school in *Smiles*, 1907, vol. 47.

75 W. O. G. Lofts and D. J. Adley, *The Men Behind Boys' Fiction* (London, 1970), pp. 11–14.

76 George Orwell, quoted in E. S. Turner, *Boys will be boys*, 2nd edn (London, 1957), p. 200.

77 E. Blishen, *A Nest of Teachers* (London, 1980), pp. 17–18, 52.

78 R. Crompton, *William's Crowded Hours* (London, 1958; first published 1931).

8

AUTHORITY IN THE UNIVERSITY: BALLIOL, NEWNHAM AND THE NEW MYTHOLOGY

Reba N. Soffer

Myths about late nineteenth-century Oxford and Cambridge endured for at least half a century because they preserved the memory of innocence long gone and because they contained just enough truth to remain persuasive.[1] Graduates, who had actually lived in an unsanitary, bleak, interminably grey and damp miasma, recalled their college experience as sunny and satisfying. Many adults, looking back from the influential careers their college degree had guaranteed, cherished idealizations of college as a sanctuary where they prepared for serious lives. In the university, and particularly in the college, the most important of Victorian institutions for forming men and subsequently women, the figure of potentially greatest authority was that head of college who convinced undergraduates to dedicate themselves to the greater public good. Neither religion nor family could compete with the university's systematic cultivation of opportunities for maturation and independence. The authority of the heads of houses, and the subsequent myths which surrounded them, were given credibility by their graduates' continuing successes in the world. Those graduates were proud of their public records, not only because of what they actually achieved, but because they fulfilled the Master's elevated expectations of them. As their work prospered, the myth of the Master's prescience and wisdom grew.

When the new women's colleges began in the 1870s, they had very little to offer their graduates. Men moved easily into careers controlled increasingly by former graduates. But women often discovered that independence ended rather than began with graduation. Women graduates also remembered a luminous college refuge; but their life after college was restricted by domestic duties, cultural stereotypes and the limited number of appropriate careers available to them. Given these constraints, a very different mythology might have developed among women about the purposes of their education and about their heads of college. Instead, the myths held by women and men were nearly identical. It never occurred to the women students, let alone to the founders of their colleges, that a university education should provide unique sensibilities and circumstances suitable to women's unique needs and wants. The informing principles of one of the most influential of the new women's colleges, Newnham in Cambridge, when compared to one of the most influential men's colleges, Balliol in Oxford, reveals that late nineteenth-century educational reformers of both sexes thought about women, with some reservations about feminine endurance, as if they were almost men. When university education for women was discussed, many ends competed for primacy. But in Newnham, as in Balliol, the social obligations of university graduates mattered far more than the insufficiencies of individuals. Higher education in both colleges was meant to fit graduates for public service. Instead of developing education for women as women, Newnham deliberately adopted the dominant university culture of civic, national and imperial responsibility.

Among the colleges at both ancient universities, Balliol and Newnham played unprecedented roles in their student's futures. The new standing of both colleges began with their government by distinguished figures – Benjamin Jowett at Balliol and Eleanor Balfour Sidgwick at Newnham – with important academic, political, intellectual and social connections, who gave their colleges unity and purpose. A style of living and thinking came to be identified with each of them. What was taught and learned in each college met the ambitions of an aspiring elite and the needs of an expanding society for leaders. Jowett and Sidgwick provided their colleges with conspicuous identities which persisted because the colleges came to have their own inertial tendencies, perpetuated by intellectual and social traditions, rites of passage and return, and a powerful sense of community. Even during their lifetimes, Jowett and Sidgwick became mythic figures whose authority perpetuated their goals well beyond their time. Both created colleges that connected higher education to an ethos of national obligation and both identified their tenures with the broad world of new scholarship and the narrow world of effective power. Balliol, consecrated by Jowett to the higher seriousness, produced the most graduates of any college at either Oxford or Cambridge destined for the loftiest echelons of public service at home and abroad. Newnham, the first women's college to become integrated into a traditional university, had to establish its autonomy as an intellectual community with aspirations comparable to the best of the men's colleges. Although Newnham's standards and accomplishments could hardly compare initially with those of Jowett's Balliol, Sidgwick created a serious collegiate life for women which stressed, as did Jowett, mind, character and duty. Perhaps the most important of the qualities which Jowett and Sidgwick shared was that each believed that their colleges must represent the highest standards of individual and national life. And, even more important, they made that ideal irresistibly compelling for their teachers and students.

As heads of houses, Jowett and Sidgwick created a tenacious sense of loyalty to place and people greater than even the most devoted families could achieve. They each constructed a parental persona that allowed them to develop and extend influence and to manipulate power within and without the universities, and they provided for their colleges as if they were immediate families. Sidgwick spoke of Newnham's 'children' and of the college, which proudly kept detailed records of their subsequent careers and lives, as their constant home.[2] Without a family of his own to rely upon, Jowett produced a surrogate family of eminent Balliol graduates who promoted Balliol principles, partly by finding places for new graduates. Jowett made the 'life of the College' the Master's life and his money 'the money of the College. He is married to the College and has a duty to support his family.'[3] Those precepts were carried out for the rest of his life. A considerable part of Sidgwick's money went to the expansion and maintenance of Newnham.

Unlike the independently wealthy Eleanor Sidgwick, Jowett had no inheritance. He arrived at Balliol on an open scholarship from St Paul's School in the City of London in 1836 and never left; he died as Master in 1893. As an undergraduate, Jowett divorced himself from his relatives, and the college increasingly became his psychological as well as physical home, with an expanding family of graduates whom he consistently advised throughout their careers and to whom he appealed successfully for the support and development of the college. It is revealing of his domestic concerns that within a month of becoming Master in 1870, with a staggering agenda of reform to be accomplished, he completely reorganized the kitchen, gardens and laundry facilities.[4] The progeny of Jewett's union with the college included the public men Amery, Asquith, Curzon, Grey, Lansdowne, Milner, Samuel, C. P. Ilbert, M. E. Grant Duff, A. Godley, R. B. D. Morier, Cecil Spring-Rice, Midleton, Arthur Hardinge, Louis Mallet and A. Ponsonby; ecclesiastics such as Cosmo Gordon Lang, who became Archbishop of Canterbury, and the more problematic Charles Gore, eventually Bishop of Oxford; Lord Chancellors such as Loreburn; literary figures such as Swinburne, Gerard Manley Hopkins and J. A. Symonds; journalists such as St Loe Strachey and Sidney Low; scientists such as A. Vernon Harcourt; mathematicians such as C. H. Hinton; the founder of the National Trust, H. D. Rawnsley; and academics and civil servants at home and abroad. As the Balliol Registers demonstrate, the dominant people in every profession included Balliol men.[5]

Sidgwick, the second principal of a new college for women, could not depend upon well-situated graduates for either patronage or financial assistance because women were restricted largely to school-teaching, which they entered at the bottom or, occasionally, somewhere in the middle. But she did have an important family at the highest levels of Church and state and considerable connections within the reforming interests in Cambridge which enabled her to strengthen her college and its future prospects. The exceptional Balfour family included Eleanor's sister Evelyn, Lady Rayleigh, whose husband was appointed in 1880 to the Chair of Experimental Physics in Cambridge; her brother Francis, a Fellow and lecturer of Trinity; her brother Gerald, who became a fellow of King's; and her youngest brother Eustace, a painter and architect who entered on a military career and married Frances Campbell, daughter of the Duke of Argyll and a leader in the suffragist movement. Lord Salisbury, her uncle, became Prime Minister and he was succeeded by her brother Arthur Balfour. Before and after marriage, she drew upon her family and a large circle of extraordinary friends, made even larger and more extraordinary by the Sidgwick connection, already involved in Newnham activities, administration and finances. When on the governing body of Newnham Hall, Eleanor Balfour met Arthur's former tutor, Henry Sidgwick, an eminent philosopher and the organizer of Newnham. Henry Sidgwick had a loyal following of Cambridge students, Cambridge and Oxford graduates, and other friends. His sister Mary married E. W. Benson, Bishop of Truro in 1877 and later Archbishop of Canterbury. Their son was A. C. Benson, a master at Eton before becoming Master of Magdalene College, Cambridge, in 1904. Henry's brother William was a Classical fellow of Merton and later a lecturer at Oriel, and the father of Nevil Vincent, the distinguished scientist and professor of chemistry at Oxford. Henry's other brother, Arthur, was reader in Greek at Oxford. After their marriage, Henry and Eleanor Sidgwick's circle of friends included every important political, academic and literary figure of the day – the

Gladstones, the Lytteltons, the Albert Diceys, the Tennysons; Frederic Myers, Jowett, Stubbs, Ruskin, G. M. Trevelyan, Roen Noel, Graham Dakyns and T. H. Green. An important part of Newnham life, for students and their teachers, was enlivened by tennis games and Sunday evening parties, attended by many of these friends, including Henry Sidgwick, J. R. Seeley, the mathematician Cayley, R. C. Jebb, Alfred Marshall, R. D. Archer-Hind,[6] F. W. Maitland, A. W. Verrall, H. S. Butcher, Henry Cust (later an MP and editor of the *Pall Mall Gazette*) and Arthur Balfour. Among the Newnham women who became dons, Mary Paley, M. de G. Merrifield, Miss Crofts and Miss Martin married some of those visitors and other Cambridge dons.[7]

Within the intellectual and social community in which Jowett and Sidgwick lived, special understandings without sexual content were common among friends such as Lord Acton and Mary Gladstone or Mark Pattison and Meta Bradley, or married couples like the Edward Carpenters or the Bernard Shaws. These intimate friendships provided sympathy, encouragement, approval and the pleasure of shared causes and beliefs for lives that were energetic and productive. Both Sidgwick and Jowett were sustained by this kind of alliance. Eleanor Balfour married Henry Sidgwick when he was 38 and she was 31. Even though he was supposedly sexually impotent,[8] she adored and respected him for the rest of their life together and endured a 'horrible loneliness' after his death in 1900.[9] Together, they pursued education for women and psychical research. Jowett considered marrying Margaret Elliot, the daughter of the Dean of Bristol, but he abandoned the idea in 1862 because it would have required him to resign his college fellowship.[10] That year, when he was 43 and she 40, Jowett began a confidential attachment to Florence Nightingale centred on religion, the reform of India, education and public health. A year before his death, he sent her 'my love on New Years day if you won't think this language is too sentimental. I often think of the long years in which we have known each other & of the great piece in my life which your friendship has been.' And he concluded that, for both of them, 'work is the law of our existence & that the best conditions of work are the best conditions for us, and "the greatest happiness of principle" of which we are capable.'[11]

Jowett's promotion of Nightingale's intellectual work was consistent with his active advocacy of educational, political and economic rights for women. When a new university college was proposed for Bristol, one of the conditions for Balliol's provision of support was that the college be open to women as well as men. He wanted able women to 'work at higher things' and encouraged George Eliot to write on moral philosophy just as he discouraged Nightingale from using a style that might be dismissed because it was 'a woman's writing.' Less than a month before Jowett died, he asked Nightingale a question that Sidgwick would have extended, without any opposition from Jowett, to women: 'Does not half the good of the world . . . arise from putting the best men in the best places?'[12] Jowett used his college and its graduates to put Balliol men in the most powerful places.

Balliol and Jowett were indivisible during his lifetime and his image there persists in seven portraits, six cartoons, two pieces of sculpture, one photograph and a stuffed owl, which looks uncannily like the Master. Eleanor Sidgwick, who preferred to remain in the background while developing the independence of her college, is commemorated by one reticent portrait. Jowett became Master in 1870, after running the college successfully from 1866 in opposition to its beleaguered Master, Robert Scott. Jowett set out to make 'Balliol into the model college of his dreams, a sort of heaven on earth, complementing his concept of Heaven as a kind of Balliol in the sky'.[13] A generation before attaining the authority of office, Jowett was a leading Oxford reformer aovocating competitive scholarships for entrance to all colleges and for the Home and Indian Civil Service. An Anglican clergyman, he opposed religious tests for university entrance and subordinated clerical influence in his college to a Christianity exemplified by national service. While a Balliol tutor, and in the same year that Gladstone appointed him Regius Professor of Greek, he applied the higher criticism he had learned in Germany to *The Epistles of Paul to the Thessalonians, Galatians, Romans* (1855). Four years later, he contributed to *Essays and Reviews* (1859), the manifesto of liberal Anglicanism and perhaps the most important book on religion in the second half of the century. Although a religious, educational and social rebel, Jowett devoted most of his life to the wealthy and prominent because they were destined for the greatest influence. He believed that eventually class distinctions would disappear, but while 'they remain', he wrote with characteristic practicality, 'I wonder at anyone not taking advantage of them'.[14] When Master, he introduced new statutes for the college that substituted for religious tests the declaration, still used by fellows today, that they will be 'true and faithful to the College and will endeavour to promote its interest and studies'.[15] It was not that Balliol took precedence over God for Jowett, although it may often have appeared so, but rather that God and humanity were both best served by the best men produced by the best education. Before and after becoming Master, he lobbied for a national system of education for everyone who showed ability from every part of the world. Hundreds of students from Siam, Japan, the Middle East and the Indian subcontinent learned to govern their countries according to the Balliol interpretation of individual and public good. Jowett even tried to influence the heirs to European thrones. In 1876, he suggested to his friend R. B. D. Morier, then in charge of the Bavarian legation, that the young Prince of Prussia visit Jowett to learn English and possibly become a member of Balliol. 'You know the sort of people who visit me at Oxford,' he reminded Moirer, 'and what I can do for him and what I can't.'[16]

Increasingly, under Jowett's direction, the college became the cultivated, urbane and lively home he had never known. In a university hostile to new influences, Jowett gave Balliol laboratories, scientific teaching, athletics, music and drama. He encouraged teaching fellows to take leaves at two-thirds of their pay every fourth year so that they could study at a 'foreign university' and keep pace with the changing state of knowledge.[17] And he provided for poor students, often from his own pocket. Perhaps most poignantly, the year he became Master, he took the unprecedented step of allowing half the fellows to marry. Although he governed Balliol through a series of committees of fellows, he sat on every one until 1885, when A. L. Smith, appointed in 1878 to carry out Jowett's ideals within the college, began increasingly to act as his deputy. Jowett sacrificed himself and his teachers to the work of making Balliol students an unprecedented force for good within the world. After 1870, about forty-seven men came to college each year as compared to twenty-eight in the 1860s, and by 1899, there were about 165 undergraduates, including twenty-eight scholars and twenty-six exhibitioners who had won financial support through competitive examinations. There were also a few graduates and some Indian Civil Service probationers. Jowett's small college turned out a disproportionately large part of those governing country, empire, business and the professions.

Jowett's favourite rhetorical style, in speaking and writing, was the admonitory exhortation, an invocation of a Christian life lived for the well-being of others. Aside from the force of his personality, he touched students effectively from three concurrent sources of authority. The translator of Plato and Aristotle and a classical tutor, he furnished the definitive texts studied in *Literae Humaniores*, or Greats, the most popular honours degree course in Oxford during the last quarter of the nineteenth century, and transformed Greek studies into didactic lessons for nineteenth-century English leaders. The Greek philosophers became prototypical Victorians facing the same issues of private and public obligation that Balliol men would meet. The life of Socrates demonstrated that there was no 'essential difference between the lives of the Great Men of antiquity and of our own contemporaries'. Jowett imagined Socrates as an Oxford colleague, 'walking into the clubs and courts of law, appearing in society, talking with our statesmen, instructing our artists, reasoning with our divines and men of science, ready to argue about all things human and divine with young men everywhere'[18] and showing that 'a man ought to be improving his time'.[19] The ancient polis, whose heir was constitutional England, taught the 'noble' lesson that 'ethics and politics are inseparable; that we must not do evil in order to gain power; and that the justice of the state and the justice of the individual are the same'.[20] The life and organization of the state were inferior to that of the individual because the state was concerned essentially with law and politics, while the individual was governed by morality and religion. States were no 'mere organization of individuals', but, like individuals, they were capable of acting from 'higher motives than interest' because they had a 'national life'.[21] The 'true life of a nation, as of an individual' consisted in 'righteousness and serenity, in intelligence and education, in the love of truth and justice, in the fulfillment of the destiny which God has assigned to her in this world'.[22]

Jowett disapproved of modest ambitions, while Sidgwick found them virtuous by necessity. Using his authority as a clergyman to teach the widest possible audience, he preached to Balliol undergraduates twice a term and to large evening congregations at Westminster Abbey once a year. His subjects included the national role of Balliol; the development of character, conduct and Christian duty; the responsibilities of money; the pleasures of good society; and an analysis of new theories in science and religion. Freshmen were recruited for their productive after-lives by his sermons on the college as a place of transition from youth to the responsibilities of manhood. In his first sermon as Master, he developed the themes he had instilled in his pupils as a tutor and to which he remained committed. The mature sons of the college would transform the world, and, when they needed renewal, the college would be there as a permanent hearth and haven. Balliol was to be 'the nursery of Christian and noble thoughts which have in them some seeds of human improvement, to which eminent men may look back as the cherished home of the early days, in which those who are returning from distant lands, India or the Colonies, or who from any cause are friendless or isolated, may receive a welcome; and that those who are present here today may recognize that in this place something of value was contributed to the formation of their character and their usefulness in after-life'.[23] In Balliol, study was not the 'mere acquisition of knowledge' but the 'enlargement and improvement of the mind'. The 'great society' of the college, he often told undergraduates and the nation, rested on a tradition of university honours and successes but even more on 'unity, and friendship, and loyalty, and public spirit, and intellectual energy, and a high standard of character and manners' which has always generously preferred 'public interests' to 'private ones'.[24]

As Master, the third source of his unusual authority, he continued his earlier role as a tutor, supervising every Balliol student's moral and intellectual evolution. When William Anson, the future Master of All Souls, came to Balliol as an undergraduate, his tutor Jowett gave him a glass of wine and told him that he should 'read ten hours a day' and 'coach with one of his most objectionable proteges, and finally that I should take a walk with him every Monday and breakfast with him every Friday, that he may see how I am getting on'. Conceding that it was 'very kind of Jowett to take so much trouble about me', Anson found the whole plan unacceptable. But he did take a first class in Greats, win a fellowship to All Souls and follow a career which satisfied Jowett's principles.[25] A. L. Smith, the history tutor at Balliol who taught the greatest number of history honours students in the university and became Master in 1916, remembered Jowett as asking Balliol men 'to do your best and be your best, and . . . this is why men were commonly "afraid" of him as of a conscience'. Of all Jowett's disciples the most loyal in principles and practices, Smith appreciated Jowett's insight into character and into the proper careers for individuals, but he recognized that 'this rapid judgment of character became, in his later years, almost too rapid, and led him to see men as types rather than as individuals'.[26] But his judgement was often good, and his advice was accepted even by figures such as Curzon who had long outgrown his tutelage. Jowett warned Curzon about his prolixity when he was an undergraduate in the Oxford Union in 1882, after he left Oxford in 1884, and again in 1889. Curzon was always grateful for his old Master's advice.[27]

Jowett's legacy came close to extinction in the internal struggle to appoint his successor. But even from the grave he set the agenda. Philip Lyttelton Gell and Curzon wanted someone like Jowett who would 'live for the College'. Gell wrote to Sir John Conroy that it was not 'originally social position nor scholarship that made Jowett a great Master. He owed the first to the College primarily, and to the respect of the men who had known him there. In the second he was inferior to half the Balliol Tutors.' The 'secret lay', Gell continued, in the 'concentration of his whole life and affection and sympathy and judgment upon the welfare of the College'. Milner, too, believed that the most important thing was to 'have someone who is *part of Balliol*, who forms a link between its past and its present, between the College at home and its loyal alumni all over the world'.[28] Jowett was not succeeded by J. L. Strachan Davidson, the internal candidate that Gell, Milner, Curzon and Conroy wanted. Instead, A. L. Smith led a minority who wanted to bring in someone of intellectual distinction whom they felt Jowett would have respected. The Balliol graduate Edward Caird, Professor of Moral Philosophy at Glasgow, was elected Master and he carried on Jowett's spirit and traditions as did his successors, Strachan Davidson in 1907 and A. L. Smith in 1916. The enduring myth that Jowett constructed was not himself but his college.

When Eleanor Sidgwick became Principal of Newnham in 1893, she had already been a decisive figure in the running of her college for a generation, but without the opposition Jowett faced. The first Principal, Anne Jemima Clough, began in 1871 as a chaperone and elevated housekeeper in charge of five women. In some bewilderment, she found herself administering a rapidly growing college which opened with thirty residents as Newnham Hall in 1875. In that nearly incestuous world of the Victorian intelligentsia, A. J. Clough was the sister of the poet Arthur Hugh Clough, an undergraduate contemporary of Jowett's at Balliol who married Florence Nightingale's cousin, became Nightingale's secretary and introduced Jowett to Nightingale, before dying, prematurely, the following year in 1861. Before the 50-year-old A. J. Clough came to Cambridge, at Henry Sidgwick's invitation, she had been a schoolteacher for girls and an organizer of schemes for university lectures for women. Blanche Athena Clough, who became Principal in 1920, admitted reluctantly that her aunt 'was not learned, and her way of talking was rather confused', and she seemed to the early women students 'fussy and nervous, and inclined to interfere unnecessarily with what they chose to do'.[29] When a new residence was built in Newnham in 1880, later called Sidgwick Hall, the Sidgwicks moved into it; Eleanor became Vice-Principal and helped administer the growing college until 1882 when Helen Gladstone succeeded her. There were eighty-five undergraduates at Newnham then, and in 1881, for the first time, the university admitted women to the honours degree exams, listed their names by the class they received and gave them certificates – while denying them degrees until after the Second World War. Four years later, the Newnham Council decided to expand further so that the new college could house some 150 students in about eight acres. Just before her death in 1892, Clough advised the students leaving college to take 'the little pleasures of life, watch the sunsets and the clouds, the shadows in the streets and the misty light over our great cities'.[30] Eleanor Sidgwick's farewell addresses typically sent students to fill their 'place', their 'post of duty – We must *serve our generation* in our way.' Even those who did not follow a profession but remained at home were told to take responsibility for the welfare of the people around them and 'a share in the social work'. No one was to be a 'mere sojourner in the land'.[31] Although Henry Sidgwick guided Newnham's early days and sat on the governing council of Girton College, from at least the time ot their marriage Newnham's expansion and policies were increasingly left 'all to Nora'.[32]

Unlike Jowett, Eleanor Sidgwick had to work against a variety of objections, from women as well as men, to the existence, growth and ends of her college. Emily Davies, the founder of Girton, also advocated equal education and equal opportunities for women, but it is not clear that she genuinely liked the noisy and independent-minded young women who came to the college.[33] Without a subject that might have provided intellectual excitement for her and which she could have taught in college, she never developed the love of learning or the sensitivity of a teacher to a student that were so evident in Eleanor Sidgwick's direction of Newnham. Larger principles were more manageable for Davies than the undergraduates for whom she fought. In the controversy over whether women needed to learn classical languages, she explained perceptively that women should not study Greek and Latin simply because men did, but because men and women needed a 'common culture . . . in the interest of sympathy and human fellowship' instead of living apart and generally in opposition.[34] Eleanor and Henry Sidgwick were prepared to relinquish Greek and Latin not only for women, but also for men, because they believed that more modern languages would serve them all better in the real world. But they were especially willing to delete ancient languages as a requirement for women's matriculation in the university since it served essentially to exclude intelligent girls who had never been to preparatory schools where the ancient languages were taught. Eleanor Sidgwick pursued particular objectives, immediately attainable, as an incremental strategy for dealing with issues of principle.

When the Education Act of 1903 allowed women, including married women, to sit on educational committees, she urged women to run for School Boards and to allow themselves to be co-opted on to county councils since they could not be elected to those bodies.[35] She was always aware, perhaps too much so, that since the 'natural caution and conservatism of human nature' predisposes people against change, leaders needed 'good judgment – a sound political instinct as to what it is wise to press at any given moment'.[36]

In 1895, the university again considered the issue of women's degrees. Davies responded with an historical account of the progress of women's education in refutation of the position that degrees for women would harm the university. It is interesting that this 45-page pamphlet never mentions why university education was important for women, or the university, or the larger society; nor does it examine the specific advantages a degree would confer.[37] Eleanor Sidgwick was also furious about Cambridge's denial of degrees to women, but her more measured reply took the form of a comparison of university education in Britain, in the USA, and on the continent, 'in as uncontroversial a manner as possible and without direct relation to the questions now before the University'. She tried to show that universities were evolving from a purely liberal education which produced cultivated human beings towards 'the acquisition of the special knowledge' which would be useful to the 'majority of the serious students' in their 'future career'. Since the university turned out either transmitters or advancers of knowledge, the object for both sexes was 'preparation for the work in life that is to follow'. The 'symbol' of a degree was important for professional purposes, Sidgwick argued, but much less important than 'the substance' which existed in the form of common 'education and examination'. The university's slowness to recognize women fully was 'one of the anomalies and inconsistencies, the result of gradual development and adaptation, which appears to be natural in old institutions'.[38] Sidgwick negotiated with the realities of her time. Helen Gladstone was especially welcomed at the Sidgwicks' as an out-student of Newnham, not only because of the friendship between the two families but because 'it was useful that a daughter of Mr. Gladstone's should enter the College'.[39]

Davies, who never married, believed women ought always to be independent, but Sidgwick argued still in 1912 that a 'happy marriage is the happiest career for a woman' and that while a university education does not 'discipline' a woman for marriage, 'a cultivated mind and developed intelligence is likely to make her a better companion to a man similarly endowed, and a better guide and helper for her children'.[40] A man's professional life continued after his marriage, but a woman who married 'generally finds it best to give up her profession, unless she can carry it on in a kind of partnership with her husband'. Even among women who preferred to marry, the excess of women to men of at least 6 per cent, or more than one million, with a higher percentage from the professional and upper classes, meant that those who could not marry should be able to earn their living.[41] But it was also important that women have independent careers 'because nothing can be more depressing or demoralising than waiting for a marriage that may never come' or marrying unhappily because marriage is seen as a career. Beyond personal needs, 'society' had 'a right to expect that women, unmarried as well as married, should take a share in the work of the world . . . and the women themselves have a right to the kind of happiness which can only come from work'. Women, like men, should 'make up their minds what they mean to do in the world apart from marriage, and prepare themselves'. In the university, men and women learned 'thoroughness and the habit of independent and strenuous work' which fitted them for any calling.

Sidgwick recognized that higher education would provide economic independence for many women, and she urged those graduates who were financially independent to experiment with new commercial or industrial enterprises that would employ and train other women. Just as Balliol graduates helped each other enter the world, Sidgwick saw her graduates joining the 'little army of Newnhamites already scattered over the world, . . . fighting on the right side of knowledge against ignorance, good judgment against sentimentality, light against darkness, public spirit against selfishness and good against evil'.[42] Both Sidgwick and Jowett saw 'sentimentality' as an enemy, but it was especially so to Sidgwick because of its traditional associations with befuddled femininity.[43] Sidgwick's scientific training and her determination to advance scarce intellectual and professional opportunities for women made her respect cautious strategies more than Jowett, the classical scholar who knew that his graduates' opportunities were assured in the modern polis.

Eleanor Sidgwick's delight in mathematics and physics was reflected in the preponderant interest of Newnham undergraduates in the sciences. She had read mathematics with Lord Rayleigh in 1872 and continued in 1876 with J. W. Ferrers, who believed that she would have been a high Wrangler if permitted to take the tripos examinations.[44] Instead, she married and taught algebra, and in 1888 experimental physics, to Newnham pupils. From 1880 to 1885, when Rayleigh left Cambridge, she collaborated with him in measuring electricity at the Cavendish Laboratory; they published their results in a series of important papers in *Philosophical Transactions*. She consistently advocated scientific training for women in secondary schools as well as at university, and with her sister Evelyn donated the Balfour Laboratory to Newnham in honour of their brother Francis.[45] Fluent in French, German and Italian, she edited the international journal of the Society for Psychical Research, was its honorary secretary from 1907 for twenty-five years and its president in 1908, gave many papers on psychic phenomena and wrote on spiritualism for the *Encyclopaedia Britannica*. Henry Sidgwick, widely considered the most important thinker of his generation in Cambridge, complained when his wife became Principal of Newnham that if he had to take her place in the work of the SPR his intellect would 'be an inferior substitute'.[46] She also produced articles, letters, speeches, statistical research and other testimony on behalf of women, in addition to serving as Newnham's bursar from 1880 to 1919. A member of the Royal Commission on Secondary Education in 1894, she maintained her association with the Board of Education and with the educational work of the Cambridgeshire County Council when she resigned as Principal in 1910. Following Henry, she presided over the Cambridge Central Aid Society and endowed them with twenty-eight cottages in 1911. She was the first woman to preside over the Newnham College Council and, in 1915, over the Educational Science Section of the British Association.[47] Although unsympathetic to militancy, she campaigned for women's suffrage and was president of the Cambridge Branch of the Conservative and Unionist Women's Franchise Association in 1913.

Although Sidgwick always stressed the practical utility of systematic learning as preparation for a domestic or professional life, she encouraged women to study 'for study's sake'. They might not go as far as men because they would 'always be distracted . . . from learned pursuits by domestic duties' more than men are by 'practical affairs' and their physical strength was less than men's. She considered Jowett's plan to make old pupils 'ambitious' to do 'silently a real work' as especially applicable to women, who rarely received credit for what they did.[48] In spite of a marriage of shared work and considerable recognition for her research, writing and administration, she believed that the 'ablest women' were intellectually inferior to the 'ablest men'. But she argued further that if 'all men who are not intellectually superior to the best women were excluded from the universities, these would become – no doubt very elect – but starved and unprofitable institutions. And if this degree of intellectual inferiority is not a reason for denying a university education to men,' it should not be a reason for denying it to women.[49] But even if 'very few women should prove capable' of discovery and research, 'fewer even than the very few men', she expected that 'women will do excellent work in the subordinate fields of science and learning, will do much laborious work that needs to be done, though it is not very brilliant or striking, and will in particular prove excellent assistants'.[50] Was Sidgwick trying to reassure the largely male audience on which she relied for support that they need fear no significant competition, or was she remembering that Rayleigh developed the fundamental explanations while she kept the notebooks on electrical measurements and checked long arithmetical computations? The fourth Lord Rayleigh recalled in 1924 that her 'patient accuracy and neatness of hand were of great value' to his father.[51] Would that have given her pleasure to read? Ironically, it was Sidgwick's misfortune to have worked with Rayleigh, because he had no equals, man or woman. But when Victoria University gave her a Litt. D. in the late 1890s, they said that 'her researches in physics were sufficient to have entitled her to a degree'.[52]

Like Jowett, Sidgwick understood that universities introduced men and women to profoundly satisfying intellectual pleasures they might never have known. Education began with the acquisition of skills and information applicable to life. Then, the mind had to be trained to be 'strong and supple, able to concentrate, to reason, to think clearly and accurately – to enable it to see things from different points of view, to grasp new combinations, to adapt itself to new situations', and, most important, education had to teach 'culture', which enhanced life through appreciation of literature, nature and art and led to a 'sustained, alert, and well-directed desire to increase our knowledge of the world'. The 'test and crown of culture' was that intermittent 'intellectual delight' which punctuated otherwise mundane labour.[53] The self-sacrificing Sidgwick never found a compelling reason to sacrifice 'intellectual delight' for herself or other women, even though she measured happiness by usefulness to others.

Sidgwick and Jowett meant their graduates to take pleasure in doing good, and the settlement for social work in south London, founded by Newnham graduates, was a counterpart to Balliol's Toynbee Hall. But Sidgwick had to demonstrate additionally that Newnham women were good. In her Commemoration talks, she concentrated on the 'corporate feeling and tradition', the work for the 'common good' of the college[54] that led graduates to 'fight against evil, unhappiness, and ignorance' because the 'opportunities' they enjoyed at Cambridge made them 'good citizens' and 'useful members of the community'.[55] When Principal, she dined once a week in each residence hall, and every student in her third year had breakfast with her at least once during the term so that she could know them all. The testimonials she wrote for graduates reveal that the qualities of mind, character and personality that Newnham cultivated were very like those that Jowett encouraged in Balliol: 'plain living and high thinking', 'energetic' and 'sympathetic' work that was disinterested and responsible, and 'public spirit'. She especially praised 'vital power(s) of enjoyment' complemented by 'a reasonable disciplined attitude towards life'. Newnhamites were characteristically 'law abiding, frank and friendly, cheery under disappointment . . . zealous and painstaking' in their work, serious, principled, kind, intelligent, altruistic, serene, humorous, independent, critical, conscientious and ambitious.[56]

These dualities were possible, Sidgwick believed, because Newnham was part of Cambridge University. She agreed completely with Davies that separate universities for women were undesirable, and untenable. When, in 1897, the Governors of the Royal Holloway College were deciding whether to join a federation of women's colleges, Eleanor Sidgwick made it clear that Newnham would never join a university especially for women which would 'condemn itself in perpetuity to be the inferior partners' because it could not 'command the teaching power of the university'. Instead she urged Holloway to be either independent or a constituent part of the University of London.[57] Five years earlier, when Trinity College Dublin was considering whether men and women should be taught together, Sidgwick conducted a survey of mixed classes in Cambridge and sent the results to Dublin. Of the seventeen Cambridge lecturers approached, none had any objection and some, such as H. M. Gwatkin, Dixie Professor of Ecclesiastical History, found them 'advantageous'.[58]

The most compelling argument to Sidgwick for bringing women to universities was the moral and intellectual happiness they received both during and after the actual period of study. Within a college they discovered 'membership in a worthy community, with a high and noble function in which everyone can take part, and at the same time not so vast in extent as to reduce the individual to insignificance', a community that 'expands the interests and activities of its individual members'. In their studies, they learned the 'habit of

reasonable self-dependence' from 'a group of teachers who are thinking for themselves and advancing as well as imparting knowledge'.[59]
To persuade reasonable people that university education was
beneficial not only to the women who enjoyed it, but to the university and society, Sidgwick collected and analysed comparative statistics about university education in general and about Newnham
students in particular.[60] At the end of her first year as Principal, a
comparison of the results of tripos honours examinations placed
Newnham third after Trinity and St John's.[61] The results continued
to be superior to the general average of university honours degrees
during and after Sidgwick's time. In 1890, the university had been
electrified when Philippa Fawcett, the daughter of the Professor of
Political Economy and of the famous suffragist and member of the
Newnham Council, received a class higher than the Senior Wrangler.
Sidgwick had repeated causes for satisfaction in Newnham's women
in every field of study, and she was especially proud of the international reputations won by scholars such as the classicist Jane Ellen
Harrison and the historian Mary Bateson.

Sidgwick's successors, almost as well-connected as she, continued
her intellectual and pragmatic ambitions for Newnham. Katherine
Stephen, Principal from 1910 to 1920, daughter of the famous jurist
Sir James Fitzjames Stephen and niece of Leslie Stephen, had been
Vice Principal of Sidgwick Hall, while Blanche Athena Clough, who
succeeded her as Principal, had been a part of Newnham as a student, don and Vice Principal of Clough Hall. The 'family', in aesthetically satisfying surroundings, were taught by a distinguished group
of tutors, in addition to attending lectures by senior members of the
university, and they found in their college the physical and emotional
support that Sidgwick wanted them to have. After the First World
War, Newnham graduates entered local government and Parliament,
armed with their political experience in the college's active Political
Society, where students debated major contemporary issues as if they
were members of policy bodies. In 1936, a Newnham graduate
recalled, with gratitude, the 'Sidgwick tradition of genuine freedom
and sincere empiricism' and the way in which everyone learned
'something of what existence in and for the community implies' and
learned it 'under the happiest tradition'.[62]

It is very difficult to know what, if anything, members of Balliol
and Newnham learned about the uses of authority from either Jowett
or Sidgwick. But we do know that both were central figures to an
undergraduate for at least the three years of their residence in college, and in many cases, as diaries, letters, and autobiographies sug-

gest, for the rest of their lives. They rarely saw Jowett or Sidgwick handicapped by frailties, doubts and disappointments, because of the carefully guarded Victorian border between private and public lives, sustained even in a crowded college which tended to expose more than to conceal. But the myths associated with each one were often mightier than reality. The undergraduate mind, A. L. Smith wrote, is so 'mythopoeic that it clothes every don with something of a predetermined character'. The Jowett 'of legend' terrified students by being either domineering, 'disconcertingly silent', caustic, or outspoken. But what the legend omitted was his 'bright quizzical humour', his decisiveness, his personal and financial generosity, his ability to nurture the most altruistic qualities in people, and his 'unique open-mindedness'. The character which myth gave Jowett was a type which 'college life tends to develop'. Oxford, 'by a sort of anthropomorphism, created a legendary embodiment and impersonation of its own peculiar . . . spirit of cynical criticism . . . responsible for so much waste of power here'. But Jowett succeeded brilliantly in repudiating for Balliol 'the sheltered nature of academic life', that had become 'a padded cell with few of the responsibilities of the outer world, and little contact with its rough and tumble realities and its demand for practical action, for decision and initiative'.[63]

It might be assumed that 'mythopoeic' stereotypes could not be so readily applied to a Principal in a new woman's college. But Newnham was also an integrated part of Cambridge and the attitudes and values common there and in late nineteenth-century Oxford prevailed in Newnham, too. Sidgwick's ends for her college and its graduates were very similar to Jowett's, and she, too, was practical in pursuing them. Almost all the qualities associated with Jowett were also attributed, with some variations, to Sidgwick. For students who 'worshipped' her, she was 'always remote . . . and one felt . . . the long line of privilege behind her' because of her family and its position. Jowett's 'line of privilege' rested on the worldly success of Balliol graduates. Sidgwick 'was like an exquisite alabaster vase with the soul shining through'. No one praised Jowett's appearance, but his 'soul' was admired consistently. Newnham students found Sidgwick 'quiet and unassuming' but with the 'poise and unselfconscious dignity of a great lady'. Everyone admired her generosity in time and money to the college, and the members of the college imitated her 'simple tastes' and 'unimaginative' dress. But they respected her above all because she was 'the pure intellectual' unconsciously 'making one painfully aware of one's own amateurish inferiority'.[64] Both her thought and conduct 'corrected one's standard of values'. Although Sidgwick was described as a 'masculine intellect', Newnham women thought of her as 'strengthening, bracing, sometimes rebuking, with the delicate intuition of a mother'.[65] In 'the midst' of the 'brilliant' Cambridge 'Academic circle', Eleanor Sidgwick 'shone like a star' with a 'lambent light'. Jane Harrison, like so many other Newnham women, 'adored' both Sidgwick and Newnham because they gave her 'liberty and sanity'.[66] Jowett's Balliol also provided a liberating life for its members.

A shy, diminutive Eleanor Sidgwick consistently thought of herself as Henry Sidgwick's wife rather than as a public figure. But, warning her graduates that marriage was no substitute for an engaged life, she forcefully pushed them into public activity. Newnham's graduates, like Balliol's, were meant to succeed not for their own sakes, but for college and country. By the end of the nineteenth century and the beginning of the twentieth, the ideal of the powerful but selfless person who used authority for the immediate good of others and the greater good of society found its exemplary standard in figures like Jowett and Sidgwick. Their authority began with an office, but it was justified because they each practised the ideals they preached. As their graduates' careers demonstrate, Balliol and Newnham created remarkable communities willing and able to serve society according to the ideals their colleges came to represent.[67] The standards which Jowett and Sidgwick tried to give their 'children' had much more to do with duty than with the development of personalities, let alone gender. While never losing sight of the larger assignments which nature supposedly gave to men and the lesser role reserved for women, both Sidgwick and Jowett argued that the intellectual development of both sexes transformed their lives from the frivolity of random choices to the urgent work of capably serving their nation at home and abroad. Sidgwick led other university reformers in insisting that women must be educated together with men at the same universities and in the same classes. Rather than emphasizing differences between men and women, male and female advocates of higher education for women spent most of their time in demonstrating the intellectual and moral similarities.

Feminism as we have come to know it was not an articulate set of principles for Newnham women in the last three decades of the nineteenth century. Instead, a mythology began in the 1870s, common to both women and men, which created personal and communal memories of debt and obligation that ignored the confining limits of college life and the rigid and myopic qualities which could have been emphasized in both Jowett and Sidgwick. The mythological college pro-

vided freedom, identity and the meaning of life, while the mythological Master or Principal was idealized as the wise parent who compelled his or her charges by precept and example to be better and
more effective than they ever could have been if left to their own
devices. The truth of the myths was not as important as their common currency. They provided sustenance and reassurance for young,
inexperienced men and women who, without any special training,
found themselves in important jobs which often required experienced
judgment. Communal retrospection gave these graduates confidence
by providing them with an intellectual and moral ancestry. They
were the favoured products of an elitist institution, inspired by wise
and competent figures who had provided them with models for their
own wisdom and competence. The first generation to leave the universities and become leaders within burgeoning civil and imperial services, schools, universities, letters, industry and finance, redressed
capricious reality by subjecting it to reliable myth.

NOTES

1 For their kindness and generosity of time and knowledge, I am most grateful
to Penny Bulloch, Librarian of Balliol and her staff; John Jones, Dean and
Archivist of Balliol; John Prest, Admissions Tutor of Balliol; Ann Phillips,
Librarian of Newnham; and Helen Fowler.

2 Eleanor Sidgwick, MS Farewell Addresses, 1905 and 1907, Sidgwick Papers,
Newnham College Library.

3 Quoted in E. Abbott and L. Campbell, *The Life and Letters of Benjamin
Jowett*, 2 vols, 3rd edn (London, 1897), vol. 2, p. 78.

4 The English Register, 1794–1875 (College Minutes), 15 November 1870,
Balliol College Library, p. 244.

5 See Reba N. Soffer, *The Modern University and National Values: The Making
of an Elite, 1850–1930* (forthcoming) for an analysis of the careers of Balliol
first- and second-class graduates in history from the 1870s to 1930.

6 Hope Mirrlees, 'Fragmentary Notes on Early Newnham Days', Jane Ellen
Harrison Papers, Newnham College Library, Box 14.

7 Payley married Alfred Marshall; Merrifield, A. W. Verrall; Crofts, Francis
Darwin; and Martin, James Ward. Ellen Harrison, at 50, would have married
R. A. Neil, but he died unexpectedly.

8 Kenneth Young, *Arthur James Balfour* (London, 1963), p. 40, attributes this
information to 'A Record of the Balfour Family of Whittingehame', by the
Countess of Balfour, wife of the third Earl, based largely on the memories of
Alice Balfour, Eleanor Sidgwick's sister.

9 Eleanor Sidgwick to Eveleen Myers, 9 February 1907, Frederick Myers Papers,
18.7, Trinity College Library, Cambridge.

10 Vincent Quinn and John Prest (eds), 'Introduction', in *Dear Miss Nightingale:*

   A Selection of Benjamin Jowett's Letters to Florence Nightingale, 1860–1893
   (Oxford, 1987), p. xvi, provides a perceptive account of Jowett's life.

11 30 December 1891, in Quinn and Prest, *Dear Miss Nightingale*, p. 320.

12 4 January [1874?], 11 August 1874, 6 September 1893, in Quinn and Prest,
   Dear Miss Nightingale, pp. 250, 162, 323.

13 Quinn and Prest, *Dear Miss Nightingale*, 'Introduction', p. xxvii. See also
   Prest, 'Jowett's Correspondence on Education with Earl Russell in 1867', and
   'Robert Scott and Benjamin Jowett', Supplements to the *Balliol College
   Record*, 1965 and 1966; John Jones, *Balliol College: A History, 1263–1939*
   (Oxford, 1988), ch. 15; and Peter Hinchliffe, 'Benjamin Jowett and the
   Church of England: or, "Why really great men are never Clergymen"' in John
   Prest (ed.), *Balliol Studies* (London, 1982), and *Benjamin Jowett and the
   Christian Religion* (Oxford, 1987).

14 Quoted in E. Abbott and L. Campbell (eds), *Letters of Benjamin Jowett*
   (London, 1899), p. 250.

15 Statutes 9. Statutes of Balliol College. 1871. Approved by the Privy Council,
   21 December 1871, no. 17.

16 3 January 1876, in Abbott and Campbell, *Letters of Benjamin Jowett*, p. 201.

17 The English Register, 1875–1908, 8 June 1875.

18 Benjamin Jowett, 'The Character of Socrates', in *Essays on Men and Manners*,
   ed. P. L. Gell (London, 1895), pp. 5, 20–1.

19 Benjamin Jowett, 'The Place of Socrates as a Philosopher', *The Scotsman*, 3
   March 1866; repr. in *Essays on Men and Manners*, p. 59.

20 *Politics of Aristotle*, trans. with introduction, marginal analysis, essays, notes
   and indices by Benjamin Jowett; vol. 1: Introduction and Translation
   (Oxford, 1885), p. xiii.

21 Benjamin Jowett, 'The State and the Individual', *The Republic of Plato*, Greek
   text. ed. with notes and (unfinished) essays by Jowett and finished ones by
   Lewis Campbell, 3 vols (Oxford, 1894), vol. 3: *Essays*, p. xxxii.

22 Benjamin Jowett, 'General Gordon', a sermon preached at Balliol Chapel, 15
   February 1885; repr. in *Essays on Men and Manners*, p. 177.

23 'The Building up of the College', (October 1870), in W. H. Fremantle (ed.),
   College Sermons by the Late Benjamin Jowett (London, 1895), pp. 57–8.

24 'An Introduction to Oxford', in Fremantle, *College Sermons*, pp. 33, 34, 39.

25 William Anson to his mother, 18 April 1866, in *A Memoir of the Right
   Honourable Sir William Anson Baronet: Warden of All Souls College, Burgess
   for the University of Oxford*, ed. H. H. Henson (Oxford, 1920), pp. 56–7.

26 A. L. Smith, *Reminiscences of Jowett*, repr. from the Blue Book, n.d., Jowett
   Papers, Balliol College Library, pp. 10, 4, 18, 5, 6, 11. For Smith, see Soffer,
   The Modern University and National Values, 'The Honours School of
   History', *The Oxford History of the University*, vol. 7 (Oxford, forthcoming),
   'Nation, Duty, Character, and Confidence: History at Oxford, 1850–1914',
   Historical Journal, 1987, vol. 30, pp. 77–104, and 'The Development of
   Disciplines in the Modern English University', *Historical Journal*, 1988, vol.
   31, pp. 933–46.

27 The Earl of Ronaldshay, *The Life of Lord Curzon, the Authorized Biography
   of George Nathaniel, Marquess Curzon of Kedlestone, K.G.* (London, 1928),
   vol. 1, pp. 44–5.

28 Gell to Conroy, 27 October, Milner to P. L. Gell, 28 October 1893, Conroy
   Papers, Box 12, Balliol College Library.

29 Blanche Athena Clough, *A Memoir of Anne Jemima Clough* (London, 1897), preface; p. 196.

30 Clough, *Memoir*, pp. 343–4.

31 Farewell Addresses, 1905, 1907.

32 Quoted from Henry Sidgwick's diary, 21 November 1885, in Arthur Sidgwick and Eleanor M. Sidgwick, *Henry Sidgwick: A Memoir* (London, 1906), p. 430. See also Ethel Sidgwick, *Mrs Henry Sidgwick: A Memoir by her Niece* (London, 1938), p. 61.

33 See Daphne Bennett's sympathetic biography, *Emily Davies and the Liberation of Women* (London, 1990), for Davies's quarrels with Girton students and her chronic anger towards them.

34 Davies to J. R. Seeley, Regius Professor of History at Cambridge and a staunch supporter of Girton, 12 January 1869, Seeley Papers, Box 2, University of London Library.

35 Eleanor Sidgwick, MS, 'The Education Act as it Affects Women', talk delivered 4 March 1903, pp. 8, 12, Box 6, Sidgwick Papers.

36 Eleanor Sidgwick, *The Progress of the Women's Suffrage Movement*, Presidential Address to the Cambridge Branch of the Conservative and Unionist Women's Franchise Association, 23 May 1913 (London, 1913), p. 2.

37 Emily Davies, *Women in the Universities of England and Scotland* (Cambridge, 1896).

38 Eleanor Sidgwick, *University Education of Women: A Lecture delivered at University College, Liverpool, in May 1896* (Cambridge, 1897), p. 9.

39 Eleanor Sidgwick, 'University Education' (1926), quoted in Ethel Sidgwick, *Mrs Henry Sidgwick*, p. 69.

40 Eleanor Sidgwick, *University Education for Women*, Presidential Address delivered to the Education Society, Manchester University, 21 November 1912 (Manchester, 1913), p. 18. This talk is substantially the same as the Liverpool address in 1896.

41 Sidgwick, *University Education of Women*, preface, pp. 5, 8–10.

42 Farewell Address, June 1899, pp. 5, 8.

43 Jowett prayed to God to 'deliver us from the darkness of prejudice, from the false colours of sentiment': 'Study' (1885) in Fremantle, *College Sermons*, p. 201.

44 Ethel Sidgwick, *Mrs Henry Sidgwick*, p. 66.

45 At Rayleigh's Terling Laboratory, from 1885 to 1914, Sidgwick often helped with problems then occupying him. R. J. Strutt, *Life of John William Strutt, Third Baron Rayleigh* (Madison, 1968), pp. 108–9, 259; Eleanor Sidgwick to Mary Sidgwick, 25 October 1876, Add Ms. c. 105 17(1) 1876, Trinity College Library. In *Family, Love and Work in the Lives of Victorian Gentlewomen* (Indiana, 1989), p. 148 and n. 49, Jeanne Peterson points out that there were approximately fifteen women working in science among the total of 240 at the Cavendish from 1871 to 1910. Since the figure was arrived at by a retrospective inquiry, the actual number may have been greater. See *Report of Proceedings and Address of Mrs Sidgwick*, King Edward's School Birmingham, Opening of the New High School for Girls, 26 November 1896, pp. 14, 20, 21; *Mathematics in the Education of Girls and Women* (London, 1912); and Address to the Students attending the Vacation Course for Women Teachers of Physics at Newnham, 7 August 1915.

46 Quoted from Henry Sidgwick in Ethel Sidgwick, *Mrs Henry Sidgwick*, p. 120.

47 See her Presidential Address, 'Educational Retrospect and Outlook', Manchester, 1915, *Transactions of Section L of the British Association for the Advancement of Science* (London, 1915).

48 Quoted by Sidgwick from a letter Jowett wrote to her, Farewell Address, June 1902, p. 4.

49 MS, 'Women's Colleges', fo. 78, read to the Birmingham Teachers' Association, 5 October 1896, Box 5, Sidgwick Papers.

50 Sidgwick, *University Education of Women*, pp. 11–14.

51 Strutt, *Life of John William Strutt*, p. 108.

52 'Nineteen Years as Principal of Newnham', *Manchester Guardian*, 11 February 1936. She also received honorary degrees from Bimingham, St Andrews and Edinburgh.

53 Sidgwick's central ideas remained unchanged and they reappear in nearly every speech and essay: Address to the Bradford Girls' Grammar School, on the occasion of the Annual Distribution of Certificates, 15 November 1910 (London, 1910), pp. 2, 5–7; *Report of Proceedings and Address of Mrs Sidgwick*, King Edward's School Birmingham (1896); *An Address by Mrs Sidgwick* on the occasion of laying the foundation stone of Roedean School, 26 July 1897 (Brighton, 1897); and *The Place of University Education in the Life of Women*, an Address delivered at the Women's Institute on 23 November 1897 (London, 1897). Sidgwick sat on the Council of the Women's Institute.

54 MS Commemoration talks, Box 6, Sidgwick Papers, 1897, 1899, 1900, 1904, 1907.

55 Eleanor Sidgwick, Farewell Address, June 1897, pp. 8–9; Commemoration, 1908.

56 Testimonials, Box 4, Sidgwick Papers.

57 University Degrees for Women, *Report of a Conference Convened by the Governors of Royal Holloway College . . . 4th December, 1897* (London, 1897), p. 35.

58 Correspondence and replies in Box 2, Sidgwick Papers.

59 Sidgwick, *University Education of Women*, pp. 18–20.

60 See statistical notes on proportion of women to men in American universities and on numbers of women at Girton and Newnham who have taken honours in the various triposes; Appendix A, 'Women in the British Universities', and B, bibliography on higher education for women, in *The Place of University Education in the Life of Women*, pp. 31–51. In 1890, she collected *Health Statistics of Women Students at Cambridge and Oxford and of their Sisters* (Cambridge, 1890) which concluded that women students were healthier than their sisters who did not attend universities (p. 91).

61 Principal's Report, 1893–4, fos. 12–13; Box 7, Sidgwick Papers.

62 Mary Agnes Hamilton, *Newnham: An Informal Biography* (London, 1936), p. 193.

63 A. L. Smith, *Reminiscences of Jowett*, pp. 4, 18, 5, 6.

64 M. A. Wilcox, in residence 1880; C. Crowther Kenyon, 1896; M. A. Quiggin Hingston, 1899; and E. Terry, 1902. Quoted in Ann Phillips (ed.), *A Newnham Anthology*, 2nd edn (Cambridge, 1988), pp. 14–15, 39, 46, 54.

65 Quoted from Helena Powell, who came up in 1881, in Ethel Sidgwick, *Mrs Henry Sidgwick*, pp. 77, 78.

66 J. E. Harrison, *Reminiscences of a Student's Life* (London, 1925), pp. 55–6.

67 For the careers of Newnham graduates, see *Newnham College Register, 1871–1971*, vol. 1: *1871–1923*, 2nd edn (Cambridge, 1979). For Balliol, see *The Balliol College Register, 1833–1933*, 2nd edn and *1916–67*, 4th edn.

9

THE GENTLEMAN AND THE HERO: WELLINGTON AND NAPOLEON IN THE NINETEENTH CENTURY

Iain Pears

Since the earliest guidebooks in the sixteenth century, the English view of the foreigner has changed remarkably little. Despite the rise and fall of several empires, the alliances with and wars against virtually every country on the Eurasian continent, the English have been able to comfort themselves with the view that foreign character is pretty much stable. From the Tudors if not earlier, Germans have been seen as obedient but unimaginative gluttons; Italians as greasy and dishonest; Spaniards as cold and sinister; the French as dandies and egotists; the Dutch as worthy but dull. All, it went without saying, were untrustworthy, most were dishonest and none could match an Englishman.

The constancy of these stereotypes is strange, considering that Englishmen's views of themselves – and hence of the qualities which they considered worthy – have undergone remarkable transformations in the same period. In the sixteenth century, Erasmus commented on their openness, and proneness to kissing everyone. In the seventeenth century, they went through a dour and serious phase before national frivolity broke out once more. While supposedly possessing Bottom, that great ability to endure suffering without complaint, the eighteenth-century English were very much proud of their emotions, which supposedly led them to burst into tears on any occasion, commit suicide with frequency, become melancholy, get drunk and fall in love with noisy panache.

The arrival of the Victorian worship of self-discipline – again in myth if not necessarily in reality – represented an enormous swing of self-perception that was accompanied by the rise of the Great Man cult. The nineteenth century saw the production of innumerable biographies, portraits and statues to give examples of true merit. This was not, of course, an entirely new phenomenon; a 'temple of British Worthies' had been constructed at Stowe in the 1740s and in the early eighteenth century 'heads of eminent men' were displayed to inspire the owners with thoughts of greatness. The difference was that the eighteenth-century hero tended to be long dead, the representative of abstract ideals – courage, patriotism, learning and so on; the nineteenth century revered more recent heroes, frequently ones who were still alive, presenting their lives in close detail through the medium of the well-researched, authoritative and often polemical biography, and stressing the qualities of their personality as much as their deeds.

The visions of the foreigner and the Englishman were embedded in stereotypical characters for simplicity's sake, with the creation of a gallery of stock characters – the mynheer, the burgomeister, the courtly fop, the bravo, the inquisitorial priest – which served to encapsulate each nation and was contrasted with an equally stereotypical Englishman – the squire, John Bull, or whoever. Such characters popped up in cartoons, on the stage and in literature from the sixteenth century to the nineteenth.[1] At the same time, and on a slightly more intellectual level, real characters from history or the recent past could be brought into close proximity, one of the classic combinations being the trio of Henry VIII, Francis I and Charles V: bluff and hearty, frivolous and artistic, serious and pious. Other conjunctions – Elizabeth and Philip, Marlborough and Louis XIV, Buckingham and Richelieu – could all be compressed through the medium of history or biography in a way which illuminated, reinforced and, in some measure, created differences in national character.

Of all the nineteenth century's modern heroes, the Duke of Wellington was by far the most eminent, and the contrast between him and Napoleon Bonaparte was an enduring element in contemporary literature. The importance of this conjunction is no longer obvious; Napoleon is still a perennial topic for biography and continues to exert a fascination, but the reputation of Wellington has faded somewhat. Children are no longer taught about Vittoria, Salamanca or the Talavera, let alone Assaye; his tomb draws only a fraction of the visitors who go to the Invalides. This personal eclipse, however, partly masks the permanent impact Wellington exercised in the way his character, and the qualities he came to symbolize, became built into the national consciousness as part of the essential fabric of Englishness. This is not to assert that Wellington created a new image of what it was to be English; rather, he encapsulated a newly-forming vision of national type which, through his personal success and the way he could be opposed to the personification of foreign threat, provided a form of shorthand by which this notion could be disseminated.

In this essay I will try to lay out the salient elements of Wellingtonian Englishness, and to argue that he represented the prototype of a new model gentleman, fine-tuned to suit the requirements of an industrial but hierarchic society still deeply alarmed at the implications of France's revolutionary legacy. Particularly after his withdrawal from active politics and especially after his death, Wellington-worship was a curious amalgam of diverse elements – xenophobia, modernism, chivalry, patriotism, individualism, classicism. Equally, it was a reasonable reflection of the Duke himself, for he imprinted his character on the English self-image at the same time as he was a vehicle for national aspiration and moulded himself to fit the requirements of others. As he himself said: 'I am the Duke of Wellington, and must do as the Duke of Wellington doth.'[2]

For several hundred years the English had, against all contrary evidence, loudly asserted their superiority over – and to – all comers. It was disconcerting when Waterloo suggested this boasting might be true after all. Being the richest and most powerful nation in Europe was dangerous unless reasons could be found to explain it; unless the sources of superiority could be isolated, they could not be reproduced, and if they were not reproduced England's dominance would prove illegitimate and perhaps also short-lived. Modern scholarship would maintain that the explanation which found favour – one based essentially on an account of character – was entirely erroneous. None the less, it was still strongly held and found its most perfect embodiment in the victor of Waterloo. 'In all that has singled out England from the nations, and given her the front place in the history of the world, the Duke of Wellington was emphatically an Englishman.'[3]

Perhaps of the highest points of extreme 'Wellingtonism' came on the 18 November 1852, when he was given the last heraldic funeral in England.[4] The emphasis on elements of chivalry was unusual; as a writer to the *Gentleman's Magazine* noted, heraldic devices were now rare: 'In the ordinary modern funeral, even of persons of the highest rank, all these various modes of heraldic display are now obsolete.'[5] However much the code of chivalry was attracting renewed attention, Wellington's funeral was unique in being awash with Pennons, Guidons and Banners, Trophies, Atchievements and Bannerols. Similarly, enormous play was made in almost every newspaper and magazine which wrote on the event (and they all did) of the extraordinary list of honours the Duke racked up over his long life, this being read out in full by a herald over his coffin and reprinted almost obsessively by biographers for the next two decades.

Alongside this clear reference to English hierarchy and tradition, however, the funeral also stressed classical parallels and more modern elements of British history. The funeral car itself was a direct allusion to the long line of British worthies who had been similarly honoured – including Cromwell (1658), Marlborough (1722) and Nelson (1806) – but also to the common ancestor of them all, the wagon which had borne Alexander the Great to Alexandria.[6] At the same time, and showing the distinct footprints of Prince Albert, instructions were issued that the car 'should . . . do credit to the taste of the artists of England'.[7] More than this, it was to 'afford an instance of the remarkable rapidity with which the most elaborate works can be manufactured in the gigantic establishments of Sheffield and Birmingham'.[8]

The funeral ceremony itself was also an exemplar of modernism, a state affair which built on the experience of the Great Exhibition the previous year, and had some of the same objects in view. For contemporary commentators, the significance of both was proven by the sheer quantity of people who attended, the mobilization of a mass audience serving as a demonstration of national solidarity and unity. At both, the huge numbers were brought in by rail, with the rail companies organizing special funeral excursions for the latter occasion.[9] Equally, recent practice in handling large numbers of people – the police were organized by the man who had directed crowd control at the Exhibition – enabled the authorities to ensure a dignified ceremony by concentrating forces in the places where experience suggested they might most be needed.[10]

But why was such an enormous effort made to honour Wellington? He was, certainly, England's most distinguished military commander since Marlborough, but it was none the less the case that no general had ever been praised, in life or in death, with the extraordinary generosity he received. Part of the explanation lay not merely in his role in recent events but also in the way in which much of the history of Europe was reconstructed by English writers around the middle of the century. Just as the Whig historians had tended to present a spectacle of progress towards the triumph of constitutional liberty, so now the international past was recast as an inexorable rise towards national hegemony. Sir Edward Creasy's *Fifteen Decisive Battles of the World*, for example, presented a logical progression from Marathon to Waterloo, with the last campaign ushering in an era of universal peace, freedom and prosperity.[11] Wellington was portrayed, therefore, not merely as a successful general, but rather as the culmination of two millennia of strife, and as the man who finally produced the peace of nations under the benevolence of English supremacy. A further stimulus, of course, was the more immediate fear that this happy state might prove short-lived without the sturdy resistance which he represented; his funeral took place less than a year after the *coup d'état* which brought Napoleon III to the French throne, and authors of all stripes linked the death of the English hero and the resurrection of the French one through his nephew as a possibly ominous sign for the future.

More overtly, however, the event was also shaped as an answer to a similar funeral which took place in Paris some twelve years previously, with the 'retour des cendres' and the ceremonial burying of Napoleon Bonaparte's mortal remains under the dome of Les Invalides. From the beginning, comparisons were made with this earlier ceremony. While the French funeral had been sneered at for the gimcrack nature of its decorations, and the flimsy, temporary style of its furniture, the organizers of the Duke's farewell set out to ensure that it contained 'nothing mean, tawdry, theatrical, inappropriate'.[12] While Napoleon's funeral car was of 'pine and papier-maché', Wellington's was of bronze and oak.[13] The funeral was to emphasize substance rather than style, and provide a material contrast between English solidity and the French preference for flashy but empty display.

None the less, caution was required. The English liked to see themselves as a nation pre-eminently able to produce heroes, but peculiarly resistant to the fawning displays of devotion to them that was so dangerous an element of the French character. As the *Illustrated London News* explained, 'The English are said to be a people who do not understand shows and celebrations . . . unlike the French and other nations of the continent, they have no real taste for ceremonial. There is, doubtless, some truth in this. We are a practical people.' The funeral of the Duke was thus not an adulatory farewell for a Great Man, but rather a demonstration that the English could excel even at things for which they had no natural affinity: 'What Englishmen resolve to do, they always do well; . . . this event shall be solemnised as becomes the mightiest nation in the world.'[14] Equally, the Wellington who was entombed in St Paul's had not aroused such emotions when he was Prime Minister in the 1830s; his direct political involvement rather tended to be written off as something of an aberration by authors more concerned with delineating the greatness of his character and concentrating on the magnitude of his military achievements.

Just as Wellington's funeral took place in the shadow of Napoleon's and was in a sense an answer to it, so the depiction of the Duke's character was marked throughout all the biographies by the presence of his great adversary. This was inevitable; Wellington's entire career depended on Napoleon, and the parallels between the two men – born in the same year, educated in French military academies, rising through their abilities, leading their countries' armies, and meeting once in a final showdown – were too obvious and appealing to be resisted. 'There does not exist an epic, the foundations of which are better suited for artistic purposes than the story of Wellington's struggle with Napoleon's power.'[15]

Carefully interpreted, the quarter century of fighting involving the whole of Europe could be reduced to a more simple collision between two countries and two sets of ideas as represented by two men. That they were portrayed in highly different fashions goes without saying, but nothing could be further from the truth than the comment of a French journalist that 'France and England will never agree on the manner of judging Napoleon and the Duke of Wellington'.[16] In fact, French and English commentators agreed almost entirely; it was the meaning read into the judgements which often differed radically.

From the beginning, the biographical approaches to the two men have differed markedly. It is, for example, remarkable how Wellington's *personal* reputation is jealously guarded. While Napoleon's memory has been subjected to innumerable accounts of his somewhat dull love life, the state of his haemorrhoids examined in medical treatises, his relationship with his mother and his marshals scrutinized for the slightest sign of homosexuality, his death analysed for evidence of murder, the personal activities of Wellington – who had as many, if not more, affairs and whose attitude to such matters was much more open than the somewhat prim Bonaparte's – have been treated with the most extreme delicacy.[17]

To a considerable extent, the pair were responsible for their later reputations; certainly few men in the period devoted as much time to the attempt to fine-tune their images. Napoleon laboured away on St Helena writing his memoirs to boost the idea of the peaceful lawgiver; Wellington carefully had others edit vast volumes of his dispatches to strengthen the image of 'a chief, distant, Olympian, severe'. Thus, he was described as being disdainful of honours and titles, despite the enormous collection he acquired, some of which he solicited; mindful only of his duty, despite the vast financial rewards he accumulated; too direct and honest to be a politician, despite three years as Prime Minister and nearly two decades of dominance in the back rooms of power. His military reputation was scarcely touched by the fact that his role in baulking reforms led to disaster in Crimea, his reputation as a defender of liberty unmarked by his willingness to turn out the troops to block reform movements in England.

To list these factors is not to say that Wellington was in fact reprehensible; rather, I merely wish to note that abundant material existed for an unfavourable portrait at the time of his death or afterwards, had anyone wanted to make use of it.[18] It is similarly notable that, however much his memory might have faded in recent decades, his reputation has not changed a great deal. On most important points, the portrait painted in Elizabeth Longford's biography of 1969 is the same as that offered by Brialmont in 1852, or Guedalla in 1931.[19] Biographers create their subjects through the material they choose to use; with Wellington the concern was to present a picture of almost unalloyed virtue embodied in a particular character and outlook. As with many other heroes, too, memorialists were not always content to stay firmly with the record, but were often happy to invent anecdotes to fit the point being made. Some at least of the Duke's reputation for the terse but pungent *bon mot* depends on statements he never actually made or which were improved on afterwards.

For all that many admired him, most French commentators assigned Wellington a very secondary place in the universal pantheon of Great Men. John Lemoinne maintained that 'it will not be said that Wellington was of the true race of Heroes'.[20] Biographies of Napoleon habitually compare the Emperor with the likes of Alexander, Caesar and Charlemagne, that is, with soldier–rulers, rather than with mere generals. Rarely do his admirers even bother to mention the man who beat him at Waterloo. Indeed, they implied that Wellington did not defeat Napoleon; only God was mighty enough to bring him down: 'To the question, was it possible for Napoleon to win this battle, our answer is, No. Because of Wellington? Because of Blucher? No. Because of God . . . Napoleon had been impeached in heaven and his fall decreed; he was troublesome to God.'[21] For admirers of Napoleon, French or English, the Emperor bestrode the continent like a colossus, while Wellington was a mere theatre commander. Any comparison between the two could only reduce the Emperor and, according to one French author, the

Duke was almost unknown in France by the time of his death.[22] In contrast, writers on Wellington rarely adopted the tactic of trying to diminish Napooleon's ability – 'Let him be exalted, on the contrary, for it suffices to have conquered and dethroned him'[23] – rather laying out a series of parallel but opposite qualities possessed by their chosen champion. Waterloo was sufficient demonstration of their superiority.

So what lessons did admirers of Wellington draw from the perusal of the two careers? In the stampede of biographies that followed his death, the contest between the two men was elevated to a battle of giants, a personalized clash in which two opposing forces – good and bad, Frenchness and Englishness struggled against each other. Generally speaking, there was agreement that, if seen in strictly personal terms, Napoleon was infinitely superior as both man and hero: 'It may be conceded that the schemes of the French emperor were more comprehensive, his genius more dazzling, and his imagination more vivid . . .'.[24] In comparison, his opponent was a plodder: most commentators were willing to agree, more or less, with Hugo's statement that 'Wellington was the technician of war, Napoleon was its Michelangelo.'[25] This, of course, meant that Waterloo needed to be explained. None of the constituent elements of Wellington's success was flashy, none would ever excite any but the most diligently patriotic poets to launch into verse. But, demonstrably, they won, and it was in Wellington's very mundaneness, the almost dull doggedness that eschewed personal extravagance, that the source of true greatness was found.

So, in contrast to his opponent's fire and brilliance, Wellington possessed 'patience in action',[26] or 'simplicity sublime'.[27] As the *Times* obituary put it, allying his achievements with the fundamental nature of the nation, 'the chief characteristic of Wellington's mind was that sterling good sense which is said to distinguish the capacities of his countrymen in general'.[28] Common sense was not important merely as a personal quality, but could be seen to have had profound political overtones. Napoleon was the upstart, the man gifted with talents so enormous that they could not be contained and which ended up being perverted and used for personal gain, Wellington was forever the loyal servant, acting for the best of his King and country at all times.

'From the instant I gained a superiority, I have recognised neither master nor laws' – was the confession of Napoleon.

'I am the Prince Regent's servant; and will do whatever he and his government pleases' – was the language of Wellington.[29]

Napoleon was the creation of the revolution, and ended by bringing his country and cause to ruin and defeat. Wellington, the product of Burkean conservatism, boosted his to world dominance and utter security. In the political and social turmoil of the period of reform and Chartism, their careers were also a lesson in the virtues of English political stability:

> With a nation like the French, fond of glory, enamoured more of equality than of liberty, a general like Bonaparte must of necessity arrive at dictatorial power, and next, at the crown. But with a nation like the English, a man of Wellington's mould could aspire but to constitutional and regular greatness. On both sides, men and countries were admirably adapted to each other.[30]

The self-characterization of Wellington as 'nimmukwallah', a man who had 'eaten the King's salt'[31] and was bound to obey him forever, was perhaps the most constant theme referred to throughout biographies, and was again a characteristic accepted as perfectly English by domestic and foreign commentators.

Allied to this theme of service to the state was a contest to gain the moral high ground of classical precedent. On both sides of the channel, Roman memory was important; Napoleon's eagles, legion of honour and triumphal arches are an easy demonstration of French awareness. But whereas admirers of Napoleon preferred to concentrate on the soldier, laying stress on the period before the Imperial adventure, supporters of Wellington concentrated on Napoleon as Emperor: for them, the Englishman was the representative of Roman republican values, with Napoleonic egotism and self-aggrandizement embodying the excesses of Roman decline. Wellington is compared to the likes of Fabius, Scipio and other loyal servants of the ancient Republic – 'In all he seemed the Roman of old, save in pomp.'[32] Equally, ever more stress is laid on Spartan simplicity, again in a fashion which erases something of the true picture. Thus the youthful dandy, or the Wellington of Apsley House and Stratfield Saye, vanishes in favour of the 'abstemious, active, self-denying man' who never tasted wine or spirits, rose at dawn and slept on a couch with a pillow stuffed with horsehair. Moreover, there were few who omitted to draw the appropriate moral lesson that the revolutionary who grabbed for personal supremacy brought the world down on his head, while the loyal servant ended up as Prime Minister, loaded with riches and honours, and died universally admired and loved.

> The emperor fell, the scaffolding crumbled away and he who raised it with heroic temerity only survived his irreparable shipwreck for a few years in exile. His fortunate rival . . . saw open before him another career . . . is not such a lesson a striking proof of the final ascendency of reason and of good sense over all the boldness and all the flights of imagination and of genius?[33]

In military ability also, biographers almost deliberately stressed different aspects of the two men's respective abilities, so that Napoleon appeared a more exciting leader and Wellington a less. While the Emperor's strategic skills and vision in command were constantly referred to – the lighting dashes across half a continent, the tactical flair and imaginative grasp of strategic possibilities – Wellington was singled out for his logistical skills, his caution and his humanity. Such an opposition is forced; Napoleon's success lay above all in his organizational abilities and Wellington was capable of rapid and imaginative moves. The way such a contrast was built up through selection of evidence again illuminates the method by which the Englishman was shown to be superior. Wellington relied little on providence and more on forward planning. Napoleon, beloved of fate, was supported by fortune in the manner of a Greek hero, and when fortune abandoned him he fell. Much of his success, therefore, was owed less to his inherent abilities than to plain good luck:

> Napoleon might be said to have been one of those brilliant, but wild batsmen who with luck in their favour can hit up a century in record time. In his first innings sixes and boundaries flowed from his bat, but with catches dropped all over the field . . . His luck held for a long time . . . but he never attempted to play for his side and in other features of his game he was quite useless. His second innings was short and ignominious, though the bowling against him was easy and his opponents an unpractised and hastily got together team.[34]

English accounts refer frequently to the rapacity of French troops but stress Wellington's attempts to keep his under control. Once again, the contrast is forced. The sack of Badajoz was as violent as anything performed by the Grand Army, and the death of more than

100,000 Portuguese as a result of the Torres Vedras campaign generally fails to be mentioned even in a footnote.[35] Such omissions were
virtually compelled by the idealized opposition created between
Napoleon the egotist and destroyer, and Wellington the selfless protector:

> [Napoleon] marshalled on his side licence, cupidity and expediency
> and transfigured them with a bright haze of glory. Wellington headed
> the protest of law against licence, of conscience against cupidity, of
> justice against expediency, and walked in the plain light of duty . . . In
> Napoleon's case, living men became dead corpses merely to prop his
> throne; in Wellington's they were sacrificed that mankind might be
> delivered from an intolerable yoke.[36]

Thus, the juxtaposition of the two men, and the aspects of their
careers singled out for emphasis, were essential for the task of trans-
forming Wellington – the man who restored the Bourbons in Spain
and France, who opposed the Reform Act and deployed thousands of
troops to protect London against the Chartists – into the champion
of liberty: 'The sword of Wellington was never drawn to enslave, but
to liberate. He was never the oppressor, but always the friend of the
nations among whom he appeared.'[37]

For all that Wellington was presented as a saviour, however, the
picture presented was not one of a typical hero; rather, biographers
were at pains to leave such characteristics to the Emperor and define
their subject almost in deliberate opposition to them.[38] However elec-
tric and fascinating, heroes were dangerous people to have around in
a quiet, peaceful, law-abiding country. Heroes, especially romantic
ones, had particular qualities that enabled them to be recognized.
Above all there was the notion of destiny, of being touched by God
and preordained for great things. While biographers of Napoleon
successfully isolated incidents from his youth which presage the
actions of the man – for example his leading a snowball fight at
school – writers on Wellington gave up and confessed that he was
not a 'heaven-born general'.[39] Quite the opposite, in fact; in his
youth, even his mother remarked that 'anyone can see he has not the
cut of a soldier'. Wellington's achievements came from hard work,
study and practice. While he earned greatness, Napoleon did not, in
the sense that the Frenchman had no option but to be great – the
implication being that Wellington was in some way more meritorious
and industrious.

A second aspect of heroes is that they leave everything changed after them, their presence in the world pushing it in a new direction. The hero is a man who upsets the status quo.[40] Wellington's impact was less dramatic; Napoleon tore the world to pieces, and Wellington's task was merely to put it back together again.

> Having battled for the established order as a soldier, he fought a rear-guard action against change as a politician. Calculating and grudging retreat was scarcely the stuff of the hero; Wellington and his ilk were not creators, inventors, parents of ideas. The world cannot live upon negations; it requires faith, as lungs require air. Man must love liberty as an absolute good, not submit to it as a necessary evil.[41]

A third characteristic is that heroes have, to use the modern term, charisma; their uniqueness is instantly sensible to those who come into contact with them. Again, Napoleon, portrayed as Jove, the man who struck like a thunderbolt, had this quality and he 'dazzled the world'. Wellington's personality never dazzled anyone; Nelson took him for some junior officer until told who he was. At the opposite end of his life he was accosted in the street by someone who thought he was 'Mr Smith'. The anecdotes themselves would be trivial, but for the fact that they were repeated countless times by biographers who sensed in them something characteristic of a man who, although inordinately vain about his position, liked to present himself as ordinary. The image also comes through in art: Ingres showed Napoleon as Jupiter or touching soldiers for scrofula; David's portrayal of Napoleon crossing the Alps shows an elemental hero. The parallel depiction of Wellington crossing the Pyrenees looks more like an English gentleman out for an afternoon's exercise in Kent. In his life and in the way he was represented, Wellington was portrayed in a consciously unheroic fashion.[42]

Similarly, heroes inspire enormous love and loyalty in those who will pick themselves up and follow. Napoleon was said to have generated enormous passion among his army and among the French, driving his hungry and ill-equipped soldiers in Italy on to ever greater deeds through his personality, oratory and example. The image of the *petit caporal* was carefully preserved throughout the period of Empire, as one of the few remnants of revolutionary fraternalism. Wellington inspired little devotion in those who served him. While Napoleon talked to his soldiers in the familiar *tu*, Wellington pointed at his with a cane and called them scum.[43] Napoleon liked to give his

troops a fraternal embrace, Wellington recommended flogging them.
'He was not a loveable character,' said one historian, while another
noted that he acquired a reputation for being unsympathetic, ungen-
erous and ungrateful to his subordinates.[44] He never spoke of glory
to his army, and took no interest in soldiers once his task was done;
the army was packed up 'like a machine', and unlike other generals
Wellington associated afterwards only with his old officers.[45] Again
this was taken as a reflection of national character:

> The English soldier does not like to feed upon imagination, and with
> empty stomach he would not care much about being contemplated by
> forty centuries. But with such high-sounding words as those you will
> make the French soldier go on to the end of the world . . . it is quite
> enough to talk to him of victory and glory; he will readily die for the
> sake of a rhyme.[46]

A further element of nineteenth-century heroism was individualism,
and the way biographers treated both men in this respect presents
one of the most intricate tinkerings with conventions in the portraits.
Napoleon's genius marked him as an individual *par excellence*;
Wellington's contentment with serving militated against such isola-
tion. But from another perspective there was an attempt to reverse
the picture: Napoleon's achievement was seen as the result of the
mass mobilization of an entire country, and indeed an entire continent; his victories were ascribed to the vast resources he had at his
disposal and represented as the ultimate expression of French central-
ism. Wellington, on the other hand, was presented as the lone voice
in the wilderness, fighting almost forgotten in the Peninsula, the only
person who could see that victory was possible and having to defeat
not only the French but also the British government in order to
achieve his ends. His triumph was the embodiment of the confused
and ramshackle approach in which the English have always taken
such inordinate pride.[47] Again this point was raised almost to a key
tenet of military theory to explain his victory. Wellington's professionalism was downplayed in favour of pragmatic improvisation so
that it could be contrasted with the rigidities of a Cartesian devotion
to grand plans: 'They planned their campaigns just as you might
make a splendid piece of harness. It looks very well; and answers
very well; until it gets broken; and then you are done for. Now I
made my campaigns of ropes. If anything went wrong, I tied a knot;
and went on.'[48] Wellington himself stressed his indispensability: 'I am

obliged to be everywhere and if absent from any operation something goes wrong.'[49] Later authors also concentrated on the idea that the British government was more of an obstacle than a help to his progress. 'Napoleon was never . . . so harassed by the French, as Wellington was by the English, Spanish and Portuguese governments.'[50] The point was of some importance, and it was the only one in which French and English biographers differed, each trying to demonstrate that their hero was the more personally responsible for his achievements. Hugo maintained that the victory of Waterloo was the victory of the army, not of the general, while also implying that Napoleon's triumphs were his own. An obituary in the legitimist *L'Union* maintained that, far from the government impeding Wellington, he was merely 'the instrument of British policy'.[51]

Finally, the true hero resembled a human meteor; such people 'burn quickly and die young'.[52] Alexander, the greatest of them, conquered the world and died by his mid-thirties; more recently the likes of Shelley, Byron and Schubert, romantic artists all, died before middle age. Nelson, the opposite of Wellington in many ways, and Wolfe, died at the point of ultimate victory.[53] Wellington neither burned himself out nor ended his career in exile, poverty or misunderstood disgrace. He 'had none of that compulsive anxiety, or of that theatrical melancholy, which often leads heroes to private asylums'.[54] Or, it could be added, leads them to exile. While Napoleon ended as Prometheus, chained to the rock of St Helena, Wellington's iron control of his talents and passions enabled him to outlive his rival by thirty years and end his days strolling in Hyde Park surrounded by grandchildren and universal adulation. Napoleon in death was shown in apotheosis, the heavens rent by an enormous thunderstorm; the illustration of Wellington dying showed him comfortably asleep in his armchair, surrounded by friends and family, to the accompaniment of typically English drizzle.[55] In all, one was depicted through allegory, the other was shown in comfortable, affluent domesticity.

The post-mortem contest and contrast of Napoleon and Wellington was given many meanings by those who used it. It typified the contest of order against revolution (or freedom against feudalism for the Napoleonists); of method against madness (or caution against genius); of modesty against ambition, of civilization against anarchy and even of gentlemen against players. It is notable, for example, that while English writers stressed Napoleon's professionalism to the point of describing him virtually as a mercenary, Wellington's equally professional outlook on soldiering was played

down. In the context of the English tradition that very much dis-
trusted the narrowing effects of specialization, preferring the general-
ist as the more appropriate embodiment of gentility, this is not,
perhaps, altogether surprising, especially when combined with a long-
standing suspicion of standing armies and a preference for local mili-
tias too incompetent to pose a constitutional threat. However
inappropriate, the notion that Waterloo represented the triumph of
the gentleman over the professional was another major element in
Wellington's Englishness.

While Napoleon's genius made him an aberration who could be
admired but not imitated, the qualities of a Wellington – acquired
rather than innate, human rather then godlike – could serve as a useful example for others. Biographers were at pains to point out that
the abilities of Wellington were such that he would have been successful at any task to which he turned his hand, great or small. The
qualities of a Napoleon, in contrast, could only come through in the
deeds he performed: without an entire continent at his disposal and
an empire to run, he rapidly became absurd. For Wellington's biographers it was a note of praise to assert that he many of the qualities
of a good book-keeper, and to mention that his post-Waterloo career
was longer than his time as a serving soldier. Napoleon could not do
anything but be himself; he withered and died after power was taken
from him, and his efforts to drill a couple of hundred troops on
Elba, or cultivate his garden on St Helena, became a symbol of personal decline.

The elaborate construction of the two men had the strange effect
of making the defender of hierarchy more of a 'man of the people'
than was the son of revolution. As servant of the Crown he acted
more in the interests of the people than Bonaparte as the self-
appointed protector of 1789. However high his achievements raised
him, Wellington was merely a man and a subject, and so others
could follow the path he took without endangering everyone else. His
career and success were moral object lessons for those who came
after him, the main point being that staying within the system was
both more honourable and more rewarding than trying to change it.
'Children of England, great and noble as Wellington was, here are
qualities you can all imitate. This is the stuff of which heroes are
made . . . This path of duty is the *Queen's* highway open to both
sexes and to all ranks and conditions . . .'[56] The difficulty was, of
course, that it could have been reasonably pointed out that relatively
few women, hand-loom weavers or coal miners had much of a
chance of being elevated to the peerage, let alone being placed in

command of an army or made Prime Minister. To counter such arguments Wellington was recast in such a way that he became both the epitome of hierarchy and an example of the new meritocracy, a mingling of two conceptions of personal value that had been effectively opposed for at least a century. In this respect his origins as a member of the somewhat lowly Irish aristocracy was useful. While his aristocratic forebears enabled genealogists to stretch his lineage back to the English warrior King Edward I,[57] and enormous stress was placed on his place in the social hierarchy,[58] he was also presented – indeed he developed the impression himself – as a form of self-made man, who rose through talent rather than connection: 'He possessed interest enough to make merit available, but not enough to dispense with it. On a remarkable occasion in after times he spoke, in the House of Peers, of having "raised himself" by his own exertions to the position he then filled.'[59]

Since the sixteenth cemtury, gentility in England has been described in terms of both birth and merit. While Wellington was more than aware of the former – his tendency to prefer members of the aristocacy for officers has been widely noted – the public presentation emphasized the latter. He became the ultimate definition of gentility, of social and political position justified by merit rather than as a right, and thus helped modify the concept which, throughout the nineteenth century, was the English ideological answer to the revolutionary notion of equality. As a response to the Citizen, the English placed greater stress on the Gentleman, and found its most perfect embodiment in the man who was 'far prouder of being an English gentleman than of all his honours and titles'.[60]

While in the context of English politics Wellington could be presented as a self-made man, in that of international competition, his aristocratic birth was stressed. Wellington had the balance, modesty and moderation of the true gentleman by birth; Napoleon the vulgarity, coarseness and excitability of the Mediterranean *parvenu*. Wellington's measured tone was contrasted with the egotistical propaganda of France, with authors particularly fixing on Waterloo as the ultimate example; very few fail to mention that whereas Napoleon issued a triumphant dispatch announcing victory before the battle had started, Wellington's own account was so underplayed that many thought he was announcing a defeat. Again, the evidence was stretched to make it fit the contrast between English understatement and French bombast. Wellington's army frequently complained that his dispatches failed to mention meritorious conduct and gave the impression that he alone was responsible for victory; where these complaints are referred to, his actions are explained away as arising from his belief that all had acted as a team.

National myths grow out of circumstance and survive even when a substantial body of evidence exists to suggest that they may, in fact, be erroneous. The association of character and power embodied by Wellington not only survived throughout the heyday of Empire; the type he represented may he said to have reached its apotheosis in the Second World War. Once again, the image was of an England standing alone, threatened by a foreign tyrant and nearly defeated by a larger, more aggressive foe. None the less it overcame its civilized distaste for fighting, and won through by sheer persistence when all others had given up. The public school fighter pilots were the descendants of Wellington's aristocratic officers, just as Montgomery's logistical skills and caution were considered sounder than Rommel's dash and flair. Churchill took on the previously Wellingtonian role of the lone outsider convinced that victory was possible and getting on with producing one. As with the Napoleonic wars, the verdict tends to be that England should not have won; that Germany had the greater resources and the better generals and was better able to mobilize an ideologically inspired society, while all Britain had was a dogged determination to defend freedom and civilization. Ultimately, defects of character brought Hitler low, just as they had undermined Napoleon, and British moral superiority enabled the nation to keep its nerve until the foreigner made the fatal mistake which reified his faulty personality. The fact that the crucial error in both cases was to invade Russia made the parallel even more convincing.

Each age needs its myths, and the Victorian age in particular needed its great men. Where the Victorian heroes did not exist, they were invented or, as in the case of Wellington, reconstructed and modified. The picture presented to the public was not false; merely selected, simplified and overladen with authorial comment to stress comparisons and make points. Wellington was a far more complex, contradictory and interesting character than he ever admitted or Victorian adulation allowed him to be.

On his death nearly a quarter of a million people filed before his coffin, and more than that number lined the route to St Paul's on the day of the funeral. Most came from precisely those classes of people he had worked so hard to keep out of political power, and yet they came none the less and gave every indication of genuine sadness on his death. Popular admiration for Wellington existed because he represented a national self-image which was valid even for those who disagreed absolutely with the politics he espoused. For all his innumerable faults, his reputation as the man of honour, the embodiment of power without ambition, courage without ostentation, loyalty without greed, care without distasteful public shows of emotion, had become and remained the essence of how the English liked to see themselves – 'In him England admires her own likeness.'[61] Rather than concentrating on diplomatic negotiations, industrial and economic resources, his victory became a triumph of national and individual personality, and established the pattern for the popular interpretation of later conflicts as well: 'Wellington may have been less gifted in scope and vision than Napoleon, but he was far superior in character, and it is usually character that wins in the long run.'[62]

NOTES

1 Other nations also had their own collections; in France the *milord* has only recently been challenged by the football hooligan as the abbreviated quintessence of Englishness.
2 Quoted by Neville Thompson, 'The Uses of Adversity', in Norman Gash (ed.), *Wellington: Studies in the Military and Political Career of the First Duke of Wellington* (Manchester, 1990), p. 9.
3 *Gentleman's Magazine*, October 1852, p. 423.
4 A good account of the ceremony can be found in Michael Greenhalgh, 'The Funeral of the Duke of Wellington', *Apollo*, September 1973, pp. 220–6.
5 *Gentleman's Magazine*, December 1852, p. 592.
6 Leopold Ettlinger, 'Wellington's Funeral Car', *Journal of the Warburg and Courtauld Institutes*, 1939–40, vol. 3, p. 254.
7 Ibid.
8 *Illustrated London News* (hereafter *ILN*), 30 October 1852, p. 354.
9 Account in *Independence Belge*, reprinted in *ILN*, 27 November 1852, p. 467: 'More than a million and a half men, women and children assembled from the extremities of the kingdom . . . The railways had organised *funeral trains*, which, during all the previous afternoon and night, brought thousands of spectators.'
10 *ILN*, 23 October 1852, p. 335.
11 First published in 1851, the year before Wellington's death.
12 *ILN* 25 September 1852, p. 242.
13 Michael Marrinan, *Painting Politics for Louis-Philippe: Art and Ideology in Orleanist France, 1830–48* (New Haven, London, 1988), p. 193. Napoleon's funeral car was destroyed; the Duke's was for years in the crypt of St Paul's and is now at Stratfield Saye. Not everybody approved; Charles Greville called the Duke's wagon 'tawdry, cumbrous and vulgar', and the reputation for technical expertise it was meant to bolster was damaged when the mechanism for getting the coffin off at St Paul's stuck solid, delaying proceedings for an hour. See Neville Thompson, *Wellington after Waterloo* (London, 1986), p. 263.

14 _ILN_, 25 September 1852, pp. 241–2.
15 E. B. Hamley, _Wellington's Career: A Military and Political Summary_ (Edinburgh, 1860), p. 66. Macaulay, of course, at one stage sketched out a spoof Wellingtoniad.
16 Extract from the _Assemblée Nationale_, repr. in _ILN_, 25 September 1852, p. 266.
17 See, for example, H. Fleischmann, _Napoléon adultère_ (Paris, 1908); L. A. F. de Bourrienne, _La jeunesse de Bonaparte_ (Oxford, 1907) and for more modern works, D. Carrington, _Napoleon and his Parents_ (London, 1988) and F. M. Richardson, _Napoleon, Bisexual Emperor_ (London, 1972). With Wellington, even in 1987 the prospect of a film suggesting he had had an affair with the Duchess of Richmond (which he probably had) drew protests from his descendants and press comment (_Daily Mail_, 27 October 1987).
18 Wellington's heroic reputation settled into orthodoxy more or less with his retirement from politics. During the 1820s, especially, he was more closely identified with current government policies and hence more of a target for factional abuse. Thus, during the passage of the 1829 Catholic Reform Act, opponents blotted out streets named after him, while in the early 1820s radicals like William Cobbett drew strong parallels between the size of the pension given to him and the falling wages of agricultural labourers. See Cobbett, _Rural Rides_, ed. G. D. H. and M. Cole (London, 1930), vol. 1. p. 114.
19 Elizabeth Longford, _Wellington: The Years of the Sword_ (London, 1969); A. H. Brialmont, _Histoire du duc de Wellington_, 3 vols (Paris, 1852–3); trans. and amended by G. R Gleig, 4 vols (London, 1858–60); P. Guedalla, _The Duke_ (London, 1931).
20 John Lemoinne, _Wellington from a French Point of View_ (London, 1852), p. 6.
21 Victor Hugo, _Les Misérables_ (London, 1982), pp. 302–3.
22 Jules Maurel, _The Duke of Wellington: His Character, His Actions and His Writings_ (London, 1853) p. 10.
23 Ibid., p. 102.
24 Lord Roberts, quoted in the _Dictionary of National Biography_, vol. 20 (Oxford, 1921–2), pp. 1081–94.
25 Hugo, _Les Misérables_, p. 314. While the attitudes of many commentators are coloured by their responses to Napoleon III, it is clear that in many cases the Emperor's reputation survived his nephew; Hugo (whose father was one of Napoleon's marshals) wrote his rhapsodies on the Emperor while in exile on Jersey.
26 J. W. Fortescue, _A History of the British Army_, (London, 1920), vol. 10, p. 222.
27 Arthur Griffith, _The Wellington Memorial_ (London, 1897), p. 255.
28 _The Times_, 15–16 September 1852, repr. London, 1852, p. 124.
29 _The Military Achievements of Field Marshall the Duke of Wellington, by a Peninsular and Waterloo Officer_ (London 1854), vol. 2, p. 279.
30 Lemoinne, _Wellington_, p. 20.
31 Wellington's phrase, quoted in Griffith, _Wellington Memorial_, p. 107, and elsewhere.
32 Robert Blakeney, _A Boy in the Peninsula War_ (London, 1899), p. 338; quoted in Longford, _Wellington_, p. 426.
33 _ILN_, 25 September 1852, p. 266.
34 Charles O. Head, _Napoleon and Wellington_ (London, 1939), p. 130. It may be

noted how Wellington received renewed attention around the time of the Second World War. One of the most notable contributors to this revival of interest was Jacques Chastenet, who, writing from Paris in 1944, produced a French-language biography that aimed at 'characterizing British methods and temperament' which, he concluded, had neither 'degenerated nor lost their virtue': *Wellington* (repr. Paris, 1979).

35 It is notable that French accounts (such as Georges Lefebvre's *Napoleon*, 2 vols, Paris, 1935–6) contrast the barbarism of English soldiers and Napoleon's attempts to control his men.

36 Hamley, *Wellington's Career*, pp. 20, 41.

37 *ILN*, 18 September 1852, p. 225.

38 For a good summary of Victorian heroism, see Walter E. Houghton, *The Victorian Frame of Mind, 1830–1870* (New Haven, 1957) pp. 305–40. For heroism in general see J. Campbell, *The Hero with a Thousand Faces*, (London, 1988), esp. 334–64.

39 *The Times*, 1852.

40 Campbell, *The Hero*, p. 337.

41 Lemoinne, *Wellington*, pp. 34–5

42 It is notable that one of the few attempts to portray Wellington in the grand allegorical fashion – by James Ward – was a lamentable fiasco. See J. W. M. Hichberger, *Images of the Army: The Military in British Art, 1815–1914* (Manchester, 1988), pp. 14–30.

43 See Marrinan, *Painting Politics*, esp. pp. 158ff.

44 Fortescue, *History of the British Army*, vol. 10, p. 219; Griffiths, *The Wellington Memorial*, p. 225.

45 Socially speaking this was important in the days before pensions and disability allowances. Large numbers of officers in the army spent time and money before and after actions aiding their old troops. Wellington did little, which is one reason that, while London abounds in pubs called the Marquis of Granby or the Raglan – generally because they helped the original proprietors set them up, there are few named after Wellington. In contrast, he did throw the annual Waterloo banquet for officers – still continued – which helped perpetuate the memory of how much the country owed him.

46 Lemoinne, *Wellington*, pp. 17–18.

47 For which see Correlli Barnett, *Britain and her Army, 1509–1970; A Military, Political and Social Survey* (London, 1970).

48 Sir William Fraser, *Words on Wellington* (London, 1899), p. 37.

49 15 May 1811, quoted in Longford, *Wellington*, p. 318.

50 Sir William Napier, quoted in *The Life, Military and Civil, of the Duke of Wellington. Digested from the materials of W. H. Maxwell and in part re-written by an old Soldier* (London, 1852), p. 420. The English hold the idea of the lone hero saving the nation from the consequences of its own folly very dear. The Second World War, in which nearly all the fondest notions of Englishness reached their highest point, produced a particularly fine crop of the type.

51 Quoted in *The People's Life of the Duke of Wellington* (London, 1852), introduction.

52 Lemoinne, *Wellington*, p. 7,

53 Unfortunately there is not enough space here to dwell on the character of Nelson in English myth. He had some of the attributes of Wellington – above

all the notion of duty – and much of the more charismatic personality of Napoleon. Although he was a more popular figure, Victorian biographers spent less time on the quality of his personality, not least because of the unfortunate existence of Emma Hamilton. Another figure frequently contrasted with Wellington was the Duke of Marlborough, who similarly led allied armies to victory over the French. While some commentators tended to conclude that Marlborough was the superior soldier, most stressed that Wellington's victory was the more complete.

54 Maurel, *The Duke of Wellington*, p. 109. The popular myth of the lunatic who thinks he is Napoleon may be noted here; I have never come across any example, in fiction or reality, of someone mad enough to think he was the Duke of Wellington. In England, at least, wanting to be the Emperor was crazy, wanting to be the Duke was wholly understandable and even to be encouraged.
55 H. R. Evans, *The Napoleon Myth* (Chicago, 1905), p. 36.
56 *The Patriot Warrior*, pp. 277–8.
57 *ILN* 25 September 1852, p. 267.
58 Even his charger, Copenhagen – an important motif again implicitly linking him with Alexander the Great – was described as being of 'distinguished pedigree'; see *The Life, Military and Civil*, pp. 449–50.
59 *The Times*, 1852.
60 Fortescue, *History of the British Army*, vol. 10, pp. 224–5.
61 Lemoinne, *Wellington*, p. 35.
62 Head, *Napoleon and Wellington*, preface, p. x.

10

BRITISHNESS AND PORTRAITURE
Gertrude Prescott Nuding

Portraiture is one department of art in which the British have taken a certain, at times begrudging, pride and which for their ex-colonialists has been a consuming passion. No matter that some of the greatest portraitists were not 'British' in their national origin; many of their greatest statements were made on British soil and have since been subsumed into the British cultural identity. No matter that Sir Joshua Reynolds relegated portraiture to the lower ranks of painting below history painting (that is, religious, historical, allegorical and mythological subjects), along with still life, landscape, and domestic scenes (Discourse IV). His most significant artistic statements were – and continued to be regarded as such – in the genre; further, portrait painting, despite its 'lowly' status, opened the upper echelons of society to its leading practitioners, and dominated Royal Academy exhibitions in the 1780s.[1] No matter that mid-nineteenth-century contemporaries considered *nouveaux riche* industrialists' and merchants' commissioning of portraits as a form of vulgar self-aggrandizement,[2] and the images not appropriate for enshrining in a national portrait collection.[3] With greater historical distance, hearts have grown fonder and twentieth-century museum curators and directors, while remaining wary of self-promoters, have developed a more lenient view of acceptable departments of enterprise.

Indeed, the *nouveaux riches*, the industrialists and their ilk (including their descendants), have contributed greatly to fuelling the heritage market for British portraiture, and thereby perpetuating the myth of national collective identity, both at home and abroad. The image of Britishness and portraiture is not one that was time-encapsulated in the great country houses. It continued as a living entity, reassembled and expressed in different places and in different ways. It found one of its greatest expressions through its institutionalization in Victorian times (the founding of the National Portrait Gallery in 1856) and through its export to Britain's emotionally closest former colonies, America and Australia. To an extent it is the marketplace which tests and reveals the extent to which certain myths retain a currency in popular belief. For collecting taste, particularly where portraits are concerned, is not just aesthetic in its basis, but closely bound up with ideology (what is deemed acceptable, important and impressive to collect). The competitive pursuit of certain British portraits in recent years has helped to enshrine myths about the collective British past, towards which the British, in response, have become increasingly protective.

Portrait collecting and commissioning has been viewed as a British national trait. In November 1989 Alexandra Peers's article in the *Wall Street Journal* (European edition) was headlined: 'Hanging a Poodle over the Fireplace is latest Society Rage . . . Blame it on the English.' While this, of course, referred to animal portraiture (considered historically, by some, as yet further down the rank of aesthetic hierarchy), it eerily echoed a similarly edged comment by the young British artist Benjamin Robert Haydon (who aspired to the higher realm of history painting) in 1817: 'Portraiture . . . is one of the staple manufactures of the empire. Wherever the British settle, wherever they colonise, they carry and will ever carry trial by jury, horseracing, and portrait-painting'[4] – and to this we should add, collecting British portraits.

In no other nation have portrait galleries been so pervasive and possessed such historical continuity as in Britain. By the late sixteenth century, long galleries filled with portraits were incorporated into great country houses (for example Hardwick Hall, Derbyshire, in 1590–7). Portraits were also displayed in the main rooms (at Wilton House, the Double Cube Room, *c.*1649) or interspersed with other art in a long gallery (at Syon House, 1763–4). The proliferation of copies, both spurious and intentional, of major and minor portraits is further evidence of the social and political purposes which portraits filled in the setting of the British house. Even in smaller houses an area might be set aside for miniatures or silhouettes (and, later, photographs and photographic albums),[5] echoing boudoir-like spaces in the great houses devoted to similar collections or else miniaturizing the grand galleries modest owners could not afford. Portrait prints often found a useful purpose in filling wall space on minor stairways or hallways. In contrast to the situation in France, where so many art collections were irrevocably scattered,[6] British collections tended historically to remain intact (even if neglected)[7] or, if dispersed, were often re-integrated into other British private (and later public) galleries.

From the vantage-point of the late 1950s, the historian of the economics of taste Gerald Reitlinger credited much of 'the excessive valuation of the English school' to the Viennese-born Baron Ferdinand de Rothschild, who became domiciled in Britain. Within his French Renaissance-style chateau (designed by Destailleur), Waddesdon Manor, Buckinghamshire, built between 1874 and 1889, Ferdinand de Rothschild gave 'pride of place to English whole-length portraits', according to Reitlinger. For example, following 'the example of the head of the English branch of the family, Lionel Nathan de Rothschild, who had paid £3,150 for Reynolds's *Miss Stanhope* in 1872,'[8] Ferdinand bought Gainsborough's portrait of *Mrs Sheridan* for the same price in 1873. The Rothschilds' interest in Gainsborough and Reynolds portraits was responsible, according to Reitlinger, for pushing prices to new highs.[9]

By the 1890s, Reitlinger relates, the Americans' interest had begun to dominate over Ferdinand de Rothschild's. James Pierpont Morgan celebrated coming into his inheritance by purchasing (through the dealer Samson Wertheimer) Reynolds's *Mrs Delmé and her children* in 1894 for £15,000. Further, American buying was responsible for bringing up the then undervalued (that is, in comparison to Reynolds's and Gainsborough's) prices of Romney, Hoppner, Raeburn and Lawrence. This market was essentially created by the British dealer Joseph Duveen[10] (later Sir Joseph, and patron of the National Portrait Gallery), who was so well able to cater to his clients' aspirations to grandeur and the ambience of British aristocracy through his London and New York galleries. In a sense, it was entirely appropriate that, as S. N. Behrman observed, Duveen made his debut as an art dealer in 1901 by paying the then highest price for any painting sold at British auction: £14,050 for John Hoppner's *Lady Louisa Manners*. While it was subsequently sold at a loss, 'he started paying high, and kept stepping it up higher the rest of his life'.[11]

It was just not the buyers' 'innocent romanticism' which made Reynolds and Gainsborough so attractive and, as Reitlinger had suggested, key to Duveen's successful marketing of portraits to American millionaires.[12] The high visibility that Duveen gained through the expensive purchase of this portrait helped establish an ethos around which he would hang future sales. He was, in a sense, a supplier of British heritage and grandeur, wrapped up in the mythic presence of the British portrait. And such an ethos *should not* come cheap if it was to be seen as exclusionary and desirable. Duveen successfully juggled clients such as Henry Clay Frick and Henry A. Huntington (whom Reitlinger characterized as 'collectors for the sake of prestige and not for love of art') into paying higher and higher prices: Frick, 1913, Gainsborough's *Hon. Frances Duncombe*, £82,700; Huntington, 1915, replica of Reynolds's *Lavinia, Countess Spencer*, £50,000; Frick, 1916, Gainsborough's *The Mall in St James's Park*, £62,000; Huntington, 1921, *Blue Boy*, £148,000;[13] Huntington, 1925, Reynolds's *Lavinia, Countess Spencer* (second version), the *Little Fortune Teller, Lady Bingham*, and *Duchess of Devonshire*, probably each for £50,000–£60,000.[14] Duveen also supplied Gainsboroughs to Andrew Mellon, at what John Baskett (who has been known to buy for his son, Paul Mellon) reflected were 'staggering prices', given current values. Reitlinger suggests that three were purchased for around £100,000 during the 1930s.[15]

As if not to be outdone by his American counterparts, the industrialist Lord Leverhulme paid £19,425 in 1927 for *Lady Anne Fitzpatrick* by Reynolds.[16] Scottish rivalry, too, responded to the American challenge: Reitlinger reported that Dewar (of whisky fame) paid £25,140 for Hugh Lane's Raeburn, *The McNab in the Uniform of the Breadalbane Fencibles*, in 1917; and in 1920 Raeburn's *Macdonald Children* went to Lord Bearsted for £21,000.

Reviewing these purchases in the late 1950s, Reitlinger rightly drew attention to the fact that:

> no other single school of painting has ever achieved such values, and certainly not the French Impressionists. Nor have we seen anything like it in the post-war era. Since the 1940s only two pictures in the salerooms of the world have made over £200,000 each. Possibly a dozen have made such prices outside the saleroom, but they are pictures of *all schools and all periods.*[17]

Yet so much has happened since. Today, the market for British portraits is perceived to be undervalued, left far behind in the great art market race. During the 1980s, records were consistently broken in the Impressionist, Modern and Contemporary fields which dominated public perception of what the art market was. British portraits also failed to keep up with the quieter, more steady rise of Old Masters.

In a sense, the market for the majority of British portraits became isolated from the rest of the market through its earlier extraordinary highs and subsequent doldrums and is being only gradually reintegrated as recently as the 1980s. This can be attributed to a convergence of factors.

As prices in other areas of the market outpace buyers, less highly valued areas, such as British portraits, are perceived to be more desirable. The lower and middle sectors of the portrait market have appreciated more quickly as displaced buyers explore what had been regarded as less 'fashionable', but are now comparatively more affordable, areas. In addition, Christie's specialist Margie Christian observes that private buyers are attracted to portraits because they often include their original eighteenth-century frames: for example, while John Thomas Seton's portrait of Mr Hallowell, seated, full-length, on a plinth against a landscape with classical ruin, might not be classified as the most exciting of portraits on its own, when it is housed in its original George III giltwood frame with splendid expanding Rococo flourishes, the whole effect projects a cohesive period authenticity and an ambience of a golden past in British history. The frame alone might be worth £1,000–£2,000, while the whole ensemble sold for £6,050 in November 1990 at Christie's. To be sure, little of comparable quality in other fields of painting is available for such a price, while recent, barely-known art school graduates' work might be similarly valued. No small wonder, then, that such a painting would hold an attraction to the historically minded: it would be an appropriate companion to a similarly priced and dated settee. The general return to 'period' interior decoration in the 1970s and 1980s has also had an effect on the market in the lower ranges. Furthermore, the marked success of the Polly Peck sale (Asil Nadir's collection, sold at Phillips on 19 February 1991)[18] in attracting a large proportion of private buyers for eighteenth-century English furniture, paying retail prices at auction, might be viewed as all part of the same phenomenon.

Margie Christian sees the recent interest in British portraits as responding to the 'need for stability', 'a surrogacy of ancestry', particularly among *nouveau riche* American, Canadian and Australian private buyers. (Such 'Thatcherite' values came in for typically mild ridicule in Godfrey Barker's dismissive column in the *Daily Telegraph* of 16 July 1990.) According to auctioneers and dealers, Americans like to come to Britain to buy British, even if some bid over the phone. There is a certain mythic feel about buying items with nationalistic trappings on the appropriate *terra firma*. The degree to which buying direct from the native source continues to appeal is evidenced by the fact that British portraits (and British paintings generally) continue, regardless of their source of consignment, to be marketed on British soil. For example, portraits exported earlier in the first decades of this century and purchased by American collectors entered the North Carolina Museum of Art in the 1950s; deaccessioned, they then were reimported back to London for sale at Christie's in November 1990. The portraits seem to have attracted predominantly American and Canadian interest (along with some British dealers, whose clients include Americans) and would therefore, once purchased, undoubtedly have begun yet another transatlantic voyage. Another transatlantic saga occurred in August 1990 when Bonhams held an exhibition and auction of Royal Commemorative China in honour of the 90th birthday of HM Queen Elizabeth, the Queen Mother. The collection of china with royal motifs, spanning fourteen reigns, was put together by the 'anglophile' Pennsylvanian, Herbert Ward, over forty years. The timing of the sale gained it the utmost publicity and on the day the 900 lots realized a total of £285,058, with only fifteen lots, 2 per cent by value, left unsold. Interest was keen on both sides of the Atlantic.

Of course, the North Carolina Museum of Art's deaccessioning might raise the question whether the myth of British ancestry, so important to American collectors in the first decades of the century, continues to hold currency. Yet institutional collecting often exists on a timescale of its own, motivated by rationalizing concerns other than those of the collectors whose bequests the institutions received and of those private collectors actively competing within a very different current marketplace. Since portraits were so avidly collected in the 1920s and many given to public institutions (one of the consignments from the North Carolina Museum of Art had been given to them by Cornelius Vanderbilt Whitney of Lexington, Kentucky), some museums now find their collections to be over-represented in terms of portraiture, according to Jay Cantor, Christie's New York museum services representative; the deaccessioning should therefore be seen as a pruning process in collection management, rather than as a wholesale dispersal of British ancestry.

Indeed, one man's excesses are another man's gains, even in the institutional arena. The sale in London of the group of ten portraits from the North Carolina Museum of Art opened the possibility that some 'national treasures' would be repatriated (the repatriation made easier for British institutions through purchases being in sterling rather than in dollars). One portrait, established prior to the sale as

Staffordshire pottery jug, with central wedding transfer depicting the young
Queen Victoria with Prince Albert, flanked by sheep and fish. On the reverse is
printed Farmer's Arms and 'God Speed the Plough' verse. Animal vignettes are
scattered throughout. From the Herbert Ward Collection of Royal
Commemorative China offered at Bonhams 8 September 1990, the jug sold to an
English buyer for £600.
Photo: Bonhams.

by Robert Peake the Elder and as depicting Queen Elizabeth of
Bohemia (rather than a less historically and nationally important per-
sonage) possessed the provenance of Hengrave Hall, Suffolk; it was
possibly sold by Hamptons Estate Agents in August 1897, subsequently entering two New York collections, beginning in 1916; by
1952 it had been acquired by North Carolina Museum of Art.
Deaccessioned and put up for sale at Christie's, it sold (with Leggatt
Bros. bidding) to the National Portrait Gallery for £126,500 in
November 1990.

As earlier in the century, the transatlantic rivalry continues to stimulate prices. Now, however, this rivalry is bringing some of the best of British portraits on to the market at prices more in line with those for paintings in *other* fields. To some, the price which the

Robert Peake the Elder (fl. 1576–1626), portrait of the Queen of Bohemia, sold by Christie's (16 November 1990) on behalf of the North Carolina Museum of Art and purchased by the National Portrait Gallery.
Photo: Christie's.

nation must pay to keep its portrait patrimony is too dear, the results stimulating allegations of impropriety on the part of the participants. Take the case of Joseph Wright of Derby's *Mr and Mrs Coltman*, offered at Christie's in November 1984. At the time, and subsequently, the sale raised rumblings that the National Gallery had been 'taken'; allegedly the only 'bidder' in the room, it was 'forced' to bid high against a high (by implication extortionate) reserve. Even before the sale, *Private Eye* alleged that Sotheby's had turned down the painting because of the demand for a high reserve (the price set between the auction house and owner below which the painting will not sell), in excess of £1 million. *Private Eye* queried:

> So why are Christie's so confident of getting such a large sum? The answer is that the National Museum directors have let slip, after many a glass of Christie's excellent claret, that the painting must be acquired by a British gallery and under no circumstances will it be allowed to go abroad. Further, the Government-funded National Heritage Fund has also let its eagerness to pour out taxpayers' money to keep the painting in the UK [be] abundantly clear. With all this declaration of interest before the sale, Christie's are clearly confident they can take the picture to an astronomic sum without having to concern themselves about such small details as the genuineness of the underbids.[19]

Incredibly, seven years later, an *Apollo* editorial in February 1991 by Robin Simon (art critic for the *Daily Mail*, appointed editor of *Apollo* in August 1990), brought up the issue again: the National Gallery was the only bidder above £900,000. Further, Simon asserted that the reserve was increased by the owner's agent, Robert Holden, on the eve of the sale, in response to news leaking out that the National Gallery's director (after lunching at Christie's) was determined 'to acquire the picture at almost any price'.[20] To set the record straight, Julian Agnew stated in a subsequent letter to *Apollo*'s editor that they (on behalf of the National Gallery) were actually bidding against John Baskett (who bids, on occasion, for the American collector Paul Mellon – although he could not confirm this was the case for this portrait, given client confidentiality).[21] Baskett affirmed that he had dropped out of the bidding and that the final underbid came from an unknown source. This underbid turned out to be the reserve, rather than a bidder active in the room. The portrait was purchased at a price (inclusive of buyer's premium and VAT) of £1,419,600; the National Gallery received purchase grants of £400,000 from the National Heritage Memorial Fund and £20,000

Joseph Wright of Derby (1734–97), *Mr and Mrs Thomas Coltman*, purchased by
the National Gallery at Christie's November 1984; sold on behalf of Charles
Rogers-Coltman
Photo: Christie's

from the Pilgrim Trust. According to the Fine Art agent Robert
Holden, the painting actually had a reserve of £1.3 million (which
was not, as alleged, raised on the eve of the sale). Prior to the owner
even considering sale, Holden had put a £1.2 million valuation on
the painting; this was the basis for the subsequent decision to sell
and the intensive marketing campaign by the auction house. In
defending the bidding, and thereby the final price, Agnew noted that
the owner had been made an offer prior to the sale in excess of the

auction result, and that therefore the nation had actually done well for itself. Holden observed that this was the case, but that the hypothetical 'offer' of £1.5 million one week before the sale had been preceded by three other progressively escalating offers from the same source beginning at £500,000 and that the final 'offer' was a result of the successful auction house marketing programme drumming up interest.

The Wright of Derby rests today in a place of honour at the National Gallery. What Julian Agnew describes as 'one of the greatest British pictures to come on the market in the last twenty-five years' was pointed out in the National Gallery's press release at the time to be the first work by Wright of Derby to enter the gallery and one which draws together his oeuvre and interests. It is a fitting companion to Gainsborough's famous portrait of *Mr and Mrs Andrews*, sold by the sitters' descendants for £130,000 (according to some sources, then a record price) at public auction on 23 March 1960 to Agnews for stock. Subsequently it entered the National Gallery. Interestingly, the National Gallery Trustees' report noted that in the sale of *Mr and Mrs Andrews* an American collector generously stepped aside (one might well wonder whether this could have been Paul Mellon), knowing of the National Gallery's interest, rather than choosing to compete and drive the price yet higher at auction.[22] *Mr and Mrs Andrews* was acquired by the National Gallery with grants from the government of £75,000, £25,000 from the Pilgrim Trust, their own funds and further help from the National Art-Collections Fund and other sources.

Prior to the Wright of Derby sale, the artist's record had not exceeded £69,000 and no English painting (other than a Turner) had exceeded £1 million. The portrait record before *Mr and Mrs Coltman* had stood at £600,000, according to Robert Holden. The sale put Wright of Derby firmly up in the upper spheres of the mythic grand British portraitists, formerly the preserve of Reynolds and Gainsborough. Some market observers believe that the sale helped stimulate interest in the artist's oeuvre, which subsequently received such acclaim at the Tate Gallery's exhibition.

Mr and Mrs Coltman should therefore not be regarded as just a 'British portrait' set against the backdrop of an undervalued and isolated British portrait market, but rather in terms of the greater art market. In a sense the auction house's and consignor's marketing strategy, while resulting in the nation spending 'a great deal of money', also helped raise the National School (and British portraiture) on to a new plane of market regard. British painting (again, other than Turner) had entered the mainstream. While some members of the press wanted to make the sale a *cause célèbre*, other observers felt that, in market terms, the Coltman sale represented British painting coming out, so to speak, from the post-Duveen, post-war and all-things-French shadow into which it had fallen in market regard and thereby esteem in terms of national mythology.

The price for *Mr and Mrs Coltman* was not a lone example. It crucially provided the subsequent foundation for sales expectations and results: Johann Zoffany, group portrait of the family of John 14th Lord Willoughby de Broke in breakfast room at Compton Verney, hammer price £2.8 million, purchased by Agnews at Christie's, 17 November 1989; Zoffany, Colmore family, £2.09 million (including premium), sold at Christie's, 12 July 1990, to telephone bidder (nationality undisclosed); it had sold in 1928 for £5,000. But to some

Johann Zoffany (1733–1810), portrait of the Colmore family sold at Christie's (by the executors of the late Marquess of Cholmondeley) on 12 July 1990 to telephone bidder
Photo: Christie's

Johann Zoffany (1733–1810), portrait of the family of John 14th Lord
Willoughby de Broke in the breakfast room at Compton Verney, purchased by
Agnews at Christie's, 17 November 1989
Photo: Christie's

such prices were not the grist of national pride. Godfrey Barker in
the *Daily Telegraph* of 16 July 1990 cited Susan Morris of the
Antique Collector asking 'if the art market has taken leave of its
senses or has seen things in Zoffany finer than in the languid beauties, the subtle observation and the tenderness and magic of Reynolds
and Gainsborough'.

When high prices are now paid, the immediate assumption in the
press is that the portrait will be 'lost' to the nation. When Agnews
purchased Zoffany's *Willoughby de Broke family* and the Tate
Gallery expressed interest, Antony Thorncroft's article in the
Financial Times (21 November 1989) was entitled 'Zoffany masterpiece may stay'. (The Tate Gallery had tried to negotiate with the
owner before the sale and their post-sale appeal, resting on the portrait's importance as a supreme conversation piece and the idea that
it 'says so much about our past', had not yet been successful as of

June 1991.) No matter that Agnews had *actually* bought the painting for stock (and, as of March 1992, there it remained). According to market mythology (at least as presented to the public through the press), if the price is high, it must be going abroad – usually to those heritage-hungry Americans. In comparison, repatriated portraits make for less exciting copy.

And whose 'rightful' heritage are certain 'British' portraits? In November 1990 at Christie's, Benjamin West's portrait of General Monckton, which had remained in the sitter's family, failed to sell against an estimate of £1–1.5 million. To the scoffing of some members of the trade, Christie's had toured the painting in Canada, believing, along with the consignor's agent, Robert Holden, that its ultimate rightful home would be there, given that the artist (who arrived in London in 1763 with considerable reputation) was North American by birth and that the General's fame rested on his exploits against the French in Canada. Was the nationalistic pull among Anglo-Canadians not strong enough? Or was the general American absence from the marketplace during the autumn because of the Gulf War and general economic conditions to blame? (And indeed, what of the strong sentiments among French separatists claiming a different national heritage?) By June 1991, some private moves were still being made by a group of Canadians to buy the portrait for their nation. Had the portrait sold and an export licence been sought, would a British appeal have been launched? The saga of another portrait with British Empire associations and art-historical importance may prove enlightening.

At Sotheby's 11 March 1987 sale of British paintings in London, two Australians' bids competed for Benjamin West's portrait of the naturalist Sir Joseph Banks (who accompanied Captain Cook on his first voyage of 1768–71). Against an estimate of £600,000–£800,000, the portrait fetched the extraordinary price of £1,815,000. The Australian entrepreneur Alan Bond (infamous purchaser of Van Gogh's *Irises* in November 1987 with the aid of a substantial Sotheby's loan) was eventually disclosed as the 'winner' (unsubstantiated rumour has it that Warren Anderson was the underbidder). Bond then decided to apply for an export licence, and his appeal was heard by the government's Reviewing Committee in September 1988. The Department of Trade and Industry's expert adviser, the Director of the National Portrait Gallery, objected to the export on the following grounds (among others):

> This portrait of Banks, which was begun about five months after his return on the *Endeavour*, summed up that voyage and the spirit of the

occasion more than any other picture. Banks was the public figure who ensured that Cook's achievement and the importance of the new lands were recognised. The portrait epitomised that first voyage and could also be seen as a pointer to the future. It was Banks who realised the potential of the newly discovered lands and set out to promote the concept of settlement and colonisation. It would be a tragic loss if a portrait so closely associated with one of the greatest events in the history of the British Empire were to be separated from the collections which it commemorated. Benjamin West's best portraits stood apart from the society images of Reynolds, Gainsborough and Romney in their emphasis on the emblematic or iconographic importance of his sitters. Of his British portraits this was one of his finest and most

Benjamin West (1738–1820), portrait of Sir Joseph Banks wearing a New Zealand mantle, sold at Sotheby's, 8 March 1987. After a heritage tussle between Britain and Australian interests, the painting came to rest in the Usher Gallery in Lincoln.
Photo: Sotheby's

telling images and was important for the understanding of his work. Its significance, however, lay more in its importance to the study of British history and its association with the natural history and ethnological specimens brought to England by Banks [many of which are now in the British Museum].[23]

The Committee concluded that therefore the portrait satisfied the first and third Waverley Criteria introduced in 1952 (the Waverley report set up an advisory Reviewing Committee on the Export of Arts and established guidelines by which it could judge whether or not export licences should be recommended to the Secretary of State for Trade and Industry, advised by the Minister for the Arts): 'Is the object so closely connected with our history and national life that its departure would be a misfortune?' and 'Is it of outstanding significance for the study of some particular branch of art, learning or history?' (The second Waverley criterion, not cited here, was 'Is it of outstanding aesthetic importance?')

The export licence was deferred to give British institutions a chance to raise funds to purchase the painting from the owner. Entering the fray, the Usher Gallery in Lincoln decided to launch an appeal for the purchase, frantically trying to raise within six months funds equal to the price paid at auction and the valuation on the export licence (£1,922,250) to which Bond's agent had agreed. It was heralded in the press as the most ambitious appeal ever launched by a provincial museum (more accurately, it could be described as among the most ambitious appeals thus undertaken). Peter Scott Walk put the case forward in the March 1989 issue of *Lincolnshire Life*: Sir Joseph Banks was 'one of Lincolnshire's most famous sons . . . The income for his many activities largely derived from his Lincolnshire estates, based on Revesby, where he stayed almost every autumn for half a century, and he was involved in almost every facet of life in the county.' The Usher Gallery's effort, according to Walk, was intended to bring the portrait 'to the county where it should belong'. Walk concluded, 'of all our illustrious sons, Sir Joseph Banks has perhaps received least recognition in the county, despite all that he did for us. This is a chance to repair that . . .'

The *Lincolnshire Life* article drew attention to the portrait's having been exhibited at the Natural History Museum in its exhibition 'First Impressions: The British Discovery of Australia' *prior to sale*. This was not actually the case. What had in fact happened was that Dr Bob Bloomfield of the Natural History Museum had been alerted by the Banks expert, Harold B. Carter, that the portrait (which he regarded as the first authentic portrait of Banks, at any age) had publicly surfaced and been shown in January 1987 at Sotheby's exhibition, 'The Glory of the Garden' (loaned anonymously). Bloomfield then proceeded to try to negotiate with the owner, through Sotheby's, for its loan to the then impending Natural History Museum exhibition. With only vaguely positive noises in response and no firm commitment, things had ground to a halt when Sotheby's announced the portrait's forthcoming sale. Dr Bloomfield, present at the March 1987 sale, managed to catch the successful bidder (Alan Bond's agent) as he was leaving Sotheby's and to hand him a previously prepared letter requesting the loan. Bond eventually agreed to lend the portrait and it was displayed publicly for the first time following its restoration at the museum's exhibition, which opened in January 1988 and closed on 20 March 1988. Undoubtedly, Bond's willingness to lend the portrait stemmed in part from the museum's plans to tour the exhibition subsequently around Australia – a pilgrimage which continued until August 1989. (Dr Bloomfield conjectured that several of the other potential owners might not have been so acquiescent to lend to such a long and touring exhibition.) Ironically, the subsequent export stop meant that West's portrait itself was not allowed to leave Britain; Australians were left with experiencing West's Banks in the form of a photographic replica on canvas. Dr Bloomfield's quickfootedness undoubtedly helped to bring the portrait and its potential export into the open early and set off a groundswell movement for its retention long preceding the eventual appeal.

Photocalls publicizing the Usher Gallery's appeal included those showing the Keeper of Art, Richard Wood, holding a five-pound-note from an anonymous donor, and actors starring in *The Late Christopher Bean* (in which Dr Taggart's life is 'suddenly dominated by speculation on the art market': *Lincolnshire Echo*, 21 March 1989) passing a top hat to the camera with Benjamin West's portrait of Banks in Maori cloak, woven from New Zealand flax, looming over their heads in the background. The National Heritage Memorial Fund gave an extremely large block grant of £1,600,000 and the National Art-Collections Fund £100,000, to which other bodies and individuals added.

By June 1989, amidst wide press coverage along the lines of 'portrait might be lost to the nation', the export licence expired without Bond handing over the painting. Under current law, the owners have a choice whether or not to accept such an offer of purchase. The possibility was posed that Bond might wait and later reapply for a licence at a much higher valuation, which Usher, having exhausted itself in the initial appeal, would be unable to match, and by which time the original monies would have been returned. In the event, by early July Bond had bowed to pressure (possibly from a high level; details were never revealed) and surrendered the portrait. The *Lincolnshire Echo*, which campaigned vigorously (while applauding itself all along the way) for the case, proclaimed on 7 July, 'three phrases have dominated the campaign to buy the portrait of the county explorer – determination, devastation and delight'.

Reflecting the fact that the tussle had, at times, taken on a distinctly nationalistic edge, the final press release from the County Council on 6 July 1989, within which Bond made a statement (one suspects as part of the negotiated settlement), was appropriately nationalistically conciliatory. For Lincolnshire, Councillor Hoyes made naturally delighted noises, to which he added:

> We are very pleased that we shall now be able to display this wonderful portrait in his native county. We hope it will help to strengthen the already close links we have with Australia as well as being a major new attraction for all visitors to the County . . . We are also grateful to the owner for his public spirited gesture in allowing this important part of our heritage to come to a public gallery where it can be enjoyed by all.

The statement from the owner included the following:

> It is recognised that where there are strong cultural links between two competing countries, the Waverley Criteria which regulate the export of works of art from the United Kingdom may be too narrowly drawn, being concerned exclusively with the claims of the United Kingdom. Here the claims of Australia, for whom Sir Joseph Banks is rightly recognised as a founding father, are considerable. Acceptance of the offer has been made more acceptable in recognition of the particular relationship between Lincolnshire and Australia. It is hoped that the loan to Australia of the portrait will be possible from time to time, in order that the Australian public should be able to share in this magnificently symbolic portrait . . . The owner is naturally disappointed that the portrait will not be permanently available in Australia, but welcomes the opportunity of its shared enjoyment by the respective publics of the United Kingdom and Australia.

As the formulation of the final press release revealed, the Banks portrait raised the issue of just who was more entitled to West's depiction of him: the Australian private (but British-born) Bond or the British public Usher? Richard Brooks, in a heated letter to the *Lincolnshire Echo* (13 May 1989), said that Bond was welcome to the painting ('if a man who can buy a whole English village and chunks of the Australian media needs it so badly, then let him have it'), but wondered why was it that Australia had imposed export controls on 'steam machinery made here in Lincolnshire'. Underlying his response was a populist message:

> Surely the County Council will not be tempted to fork out the last £1.4m in any such elitist approach when so many grassroots artistic and historical ventures in the county struggle by on shoestring budgets and voluntary efforts? Would not the expenditure of a few thousand pounds on a first-class copy serve to show us how this distinguished son of Lincolnshire looked? Is possession of the real thing so vital?

(It is ironic, that in the end, it was the Australians who were treated to a reproduction and not the British.) 'Bakewell's View' in *The Sunday Times* (29 January 1989) pointed out that Usher receives '£3,000 a year from Lincolnshire to buy things for seven museums'. Further, 'Lincoln has kept up its Australian connections, sending the cathedral's Magna Carta over for the bicentennial. But it seems Australia wants the Banks portrait, too. Relations could get strained as the rivalry intensifies.'

The controversy even prompted a dealer to enter the fray. In April 1989 David Posnett, Managing Director of the Leger Galleries Ltd, wrote a letter to *The Times*, in which he queried whether the purchasing policy of a provincial museum was best directed in pursuit of such an aim. Posnett also drew attention to the fact that the National Portrait Gallery had recently (in 1986) purchased a portrait of Banks by Sir Joshua Reynolds.[24] Should so many public funds now be directed to securing yet another Banks portrait for Britain? Posnett observed that Bond already had 'fine historical works of Australian interest, including a portrait of Captain Cook by [John] Webber', the artist who had sailed with Captain Cook on his third voyage of 1776–80. What Posnett failed to mention was that Webber's portrait of Captain Cook had been sold for £270,000 in Melbourne, Australia, consigned by the Hull Trinity House, in whose collection it had remained since 1844. By a curious twist of fate, it was its very market and heritage value which caused the portrait to be deaccessioned, and therefore to make its way 'down under'. Hull Trinity

House (originally a guild of shipmen and mariners set up in 1517 by Henry VIII and responsible for navigation of the Humber; it continues to provide pensions to retired seafarers) had decided to sell the well-documented painting because it had become a 'liability'. According to Edward John Russell, Sotheby's valued their collection and the Cook portrait valuation 'frightened us to death': insurance costs were becoming prohibitive and the necessary security increasingly difficult to arrange. They applied for and received a licence for the work's export and possible sale, without apparent difficulty.

The National Maritime Museum in Britain had to wait until 1987 to purchase its own portrait of Cook. This portrait had been sold at Sotheby's Mount Juliet House sale in Ireland, attributed to William Hodges (who accompanied Cook on the second expedition of 1772–5), an attribution which the purchaser, Leger Galleries, was able subsequently to confirm from a related print. Leger Galleries later sold it to the National Maritime Museum, according to the *Antique Collector* for £630,000. (Another portrait of Cook, by Nathaniel Dance, was on permanent loan to the museum from the Greenwich Hospital collection.)

In 1856 the National Portrait Gallery was founded, a secular shrine for the nation. Lord Mahon, in proposing such a collection in the House of Commons on 4 June 1852 (his second attempt), pointed out that, after all, at Versailles a gallery had been devoted to 'original portraits of many of the most illustrious men whom France had produced'. By implication, should Britain be left behind? In his third and successful proposal during the Commons expenditure debate on 4 March 1856, Mahon, now Lord Stanhope, pointedly contrasted the worthy portrait gallery at Versailles, which should be emulated, with the 'errors' of of the larger, heavily decorated galleries, with their 'tawdry battle pieces and Court pageants'. The Earl of Carnarvon in the 1856 debates also pointedly observed that, during the French Revolution, memorials of France's illustrious men had been destroyed. The founding of a national gallery of historical portraits in Britain, which had not experienced such an upheaval, would instead 'tend to strengthen the interest and deepen the reverence which Englishmen felt for the history and institutions of this country'.

In true Victorian spirit, the founders and benefactors saw the Gallery as promoting the moral good of the British nation: by studying the visual embodiment of great British men, the nation's citizens would be stirred to emulation. During the March 1856 expenditure debates, Stanhope intoned: 'It would be useful as an incitement to honourable exertion . . . honourable emulation and to the performance of great deeds.' The Gallery would be open to all; portraits, a visual history lesson (helped, at least in principle, by chronological hanging, made difficult by space limitations), would no longer be enshrined exclusively in the country house, learned society or club. While the realities of funding meant that the National Portrait Gallery was initially not as open and as accessible as its founders and first director envisioned due to its many moves amongst temporary and cramped quarters until it came to rest in St Martin's Place in 1896),[25] the Gallery gradually worked itself into the national consciousness as a monument and national symbol in itself.

Institutional annual reports make notoriously tedious reading, but the early annual reports written by the National Portrait Gallery's first secretary and director, George Scharf, are filled with gems which give evidence of the seriousness with which he took to heart his role as keeper of a truly national (in its broad class sense) collection and its cohesive moral and educational ends. His report on attendance during the Easter period, a traditional working-class holiday, provided an opportunity to express his delight in seeing the Gallery's efficacy in action. In their second report (15 April 1859), the Trustees recorded their 'high gratification . . . to be informed [by Scharf] of the great numbers of intelligent visitors who come to view the pictures upon public days'.

Several themes emerge in these early years. First was Scharf's record of the orderly nature of the crowds. As with the custodians of other institutions founded in the Victorian period, whether or not 'the public' would respond appropriately was of concern, exacerbated by the extremely cramped conditions in which the portraits were initially hung in the temporary quarters on Great George Street, when opened to the public in 1859. An inadvertent elbow through a painting was a real possibility – but never a reality. Second was Scharf's concern with the educational experience for visitors. Central to his efforts was his catalogue (over which he laboured for years in those days before the *Dictionary of National Biography*), which contained biographical notices in addition to the dates of the sitters and the artists. The printed word was clearly intended to augment the visual. Scharf worried over the difficulty of achieving a chronological hanging, given the space available first at Great George Street and later (after 1870) at South Kensington: he intended history to unfold in front of the visitors' eyes. Initially the available catalogue cost one shilling. By 1866, printed lists with the names and dates of the subjects and artists were given free on the public holidays. In his 2 May 1867 report Scharf noted that some of the visitors from the previous year had brought back the lists – evidence, presumably, of the regard that they had for them as an aid to historical education. In the 30 April 1868 report, Scharf noted that 'the demeanour of those visitors who went carefully through the collection, clearly proved the truth of the observation, that objects of art connected with history become more and more interesting in proportion to the amount of knowledge brought to bear upon them.'

Particularly important to Scharf, who never married, seems to have been the impact of the gallery on the receptive young. He recorded with apparent pride: 'It is gratifying to see the interest which parents take in pointing out to their children the great celebrities and the best characters of past times, and I was much pleased to observe the large proportion of intelligent lads, apparently from the printing and large warehouse establishments.' In the 30 April 1868 report, Scharf was even more struck by those lads than previously; indeed, 'these lads' reappear with some regularity in the early reports and seem part of Scharf's concerted effort to keep the mission of the National Portrait Gallery, which might otherwise have been lost amidst monetary woes, in the minds of the Trustees.

By 1871 Scharf had found that written labels attached to frames seemed to find more ready acceptance than lengthy catalogues: 'They like that kind of ready information as distinguished from elaborate catalogues' (9 May report). Sometimes visitors seemed to go through a search-for-the-celebrity process: 'It was interesting to see how diligently the casual visitors sought out the great political characters of the day, and how delighted they were when they found that their surmises were confirmed by the key-plates'. Scharf himself was amazed by the skills which the public holiday visitors themselves brought to bear on the portraits he had assembled. The 1871 report stated, 'one roughly-dressed man surprised me by reading the older specimens of handwriting [the autographs which sometimes were displayed with the portraits themselves] to his daughter. I found out afterwards that he was a journeyman printer.' He must have found personal vindication in the reflection of another visitor, 'an ivory turner, with his three sons, [who] spoke with great enthusiasm of this *good sense kind of recreation*' (emphasis added).

In 1982, a group of old age pensioners on their day outing to London visited the National Portrait Gallery's exhibition 'Van Dyck in England'. In the packed gallery two ladies vied to outdo one another in reciting the lineages of each of the sitters. It was a memorable performance; had George Scharf's ghost been eavesdropping, one suspects that the visit and commentary would have been duly and delightedly recorded for the Trustees. The exhibition attracted an attendance of 81,267 visitors. By comparison, the exhibition 'Polite Society by Arthur Devis' (1983–4) had an attendance of 18,210, 'William Dobson: Royalists at War' (1983–4) had 13,374 visitors and 'Norman Parkinson: 50 years of Portraits and Fashion' (1981) attracted a remarkable 86,361 visitors. The relative pull of the historical Van Dyck exhibition undoubtedly had much to do with the fascination with the artist, yet still more to do with the period to whose historical image he was such a prominent contributor.

To what extent the National Portrait Gallery has shaped national ideology is difficult to gauge. However, the continued reprinting of the eminently readable survey of the history of English portraiture by the former director, David Piper (*The English Face*, first published in 1957, republished in 1978 and by 1991 anticipating a new reissue) is evidence of the continued magnetism of the subject – and this despite Piper's own doubts that there was such a thing as 'the English face'. The National Portrait Gallery's well-stocked gift shop, with a range of items from expensive monographs to inexpensive slides, postcards, pencils with logos, etc. (augmenting the gallery visit) has undoubtedly helped to create a secondary heritage market for portraits and exercises an unquantifiable impact on the national consciousness, as does its very active (and inventive) educational programme. Similarly, its popular annual portrait competition has focused contemporary interest in British portraiture and helped to maintain the continuing belief in the Britishness of portrait painting. The Gallery has also contributed in less evident ways by its archivists providing research assistance to inquisitive collectors and by its curators doing their public duty on open days, when they find themselves fielding queries regarding portraits in all shapes and colours whose owners seem, as hope springs eternal, to come up with the find of the decade. But whether or not this has any effect in the fine-art portrait market is difficult to say.

Perhaps a more reliable indicator of the market for heritage portraits can be found in the establishment of the London commercial gallery Historical Portraits in 1987 by Philip Mould. The firm's main business, according to Mould, is searching for historical portraits of individuals attached to British institutions (such as the Oxford and Cambridge colleges, the City guildhalls and army regiments, in addition to the Houses of Parliament). Their computerized lists contains some 1,000–1,500 portraits for which there are would-be owners.

(Press coverage of the portrait market *per se* often focuses on, or, to read between the lines, stems from Mould's efforts, thereby helping to keep the collectability of British portraits in the public imagination.) The Historical Portraits gallery's 'best hits' list includes royalty (Charles I and Charles II, Elizabeth I), writers and poets (Wordsworth, Shelley, Shakespeare, Chaucer, Coleridge, Milton), politicians (Fox, Pitt and George Washington – 'he was an Englishman, after all'). For his clients, Mould considers that these portraits are 'necessary luxuries', sometimes providing a missing link in an already existing collection, at other times an image of an important founder of an institution. Private clients, who account for about 25 per cent of the business, often seek to restore lost ancestors to their walls. Recently Mould notes a tendency in British viewers away from reading a portrait only in terms of who the person was; according to Mould, collectors are more willing to consider purchasing good portraits of unknown sitters (previously difficult to move on the market) as evocations of an age, rather than dismissing them on grounds that they are not historically identifiable individuals. This could also be symptomatic of collectors having been pushed away from more expensive areas of collecting, and subsequently realizing the comparative undervaluation of relatively high-quality portraits as art, rather than merely portraits valued in terms of the sitters' lineage.

To return to the broader consumers of historical portraits, in 1987 the National Portrait Gallery published results of a visitor survey which took place from May to October 1985 (executed by the Office of Population Censuses and Surveys, Social Survey Division). It revealed that 'the gallery attracted more female than male visitors'; there was a strong bias towards the 'higher social classes'; 'over one third of the visitors to the Gallery came on their own'; and 'the Gallery attracts a high proportion of specialists. Over half (52 per cent) of visitors (excluding those in full-time education) said that they had a hobby or job related to painting, drawing or history.' It concluded 'The Gallery would seem therefore to attract visitors who are interested in the portraits and sculptures themselves rather than being the venue for a more general visit as part of a family's day out.'

Aspects of the Victorian moral imperative seem, as elsewhere in society, to have taken a lower place in the *raison d'être* of the surveyors (and therefore, are we to presume, of the visitors themselves?). Absent from the survey were such loaded questions as whether visitors felt that a visit to the gallery helped to heal social class divisions or to stimulate nationalistic fervour, or indeed moral exertions – sentiments which were so fundamental to the thoughts of the Gallery's founding fathers.[26] Responding to an age in which eminence is defined more by fame than by 'worthiness' in Victorian terms, the National Portrait Gallery has tried to remain a vital institution within British society while remaining true to the original founders' intent. The directorship of Roy Strong (1967–73) has been generally acknowledged as having helped the Gallery to broaden its appeal and having lent it a much needed zest. The beginning of the contemporary portrait collection in 1972, the opening of the 'Twentieth Century' galleries and the inauguration of the annual portrait award in 1981 have stimulated attendance, and thereby interest in British portraiture and British portrait artists, both today and historically. The Gallery's ambitious fund-raising campaign for an extension received a welcome boost in the autumn of 1990 when the Pittsburgh-based Henry J. and Drue Heinz Foundation gave £2 million.

In 1990, Bodelwyddan Castle, part of the National Portrait Gallery's outreach programme, won the National Heritage Museum of the Year title. After restoration work costing £8 million, partly funded by the local council with important grants from national bodies, the Castle housed the National Portrait Gallery's collection of nineteenth-century portraits. These included G. F. Watts' Hall of Fame, a series of portraits of Victorian eminent men, begun in 1849. Because of lack of space the series, so expressive of Victorian hero-worship and the ideals of the Gallery's founders, had only once before, in a 1975 Laing Art Gallery exhibition, been shown together. Yet despite the award and the warm critical reception given to the Castle's restoration and the hanging of the paintings, on 13 March 1991 the Clywd Council amazingly announced plans to sell the Castle. Its intent in so doing was to divest itself of payments on loans taken out to fund its contribution to the project. The Council Labour group's press statement of 20 January 1991 would have made George Scharf turn in his grave: 'Whilst the Labour Group still strongly supports the Cultural, Leisure, and Tourism aspects of the county, its priorities to fund good Education, Social Services and Highways is quite clear. Our service priorities must now lie elsewhere – capital for new schools and local roads, year on year money for home helps, protecting consumers, providing comprehensive nursery education and community care.' The Labour Council clearly saw tourism, leisure and cultural experiences as divorced from the social and educational good of the community.

In the view of the national bodies involved in funding the restoration and lending portraits, the Council's plans reneged on prior commitments and agreements. It is to be regretted that the loaded rhetoric of the National Portrait Gallery's founders could not be used as a counter-argument to the Council's stated position. With the newspapers full of the infamous and the two-minute fame-seekers, who will inspire the next generation's 'great and good' to exert themselves? Perhaps Lord Stanhope will deliver a blast in the ears of the Labour councillors and remind them of their moral imperative, in the more broadly defined and historically honoured sense.

Interior at Bodelwyddan Castle (St Asaph, North Wales), opened to the public 13 July 1988 as the fourth outstation of The National Portrait Gallery, in conjunction with the Clwyd County Council. The interior decoration was completed from designs and specifications by Roderick Gradidge, appointed by the National Portrait Gallery. The work was carried out under the supervision of Clwyd County Council's Department of Architecture, Planning and Estates. *The Sculpture Gallery*: loaned by the National Portrait Gallery, the portrait of John Gibson by Margaret Carpenter hangs above the fireplace. The sculptures of Cupid and Hebe by John Gibson were loaned by the Royal Academy of Arts. The Star of Brunswick Table, lent by the Trustees of the Victoria and Albert Museum, was made by H. Eyles of Bath and exhibited in the Great Exhibition of 1851. The museum won the National Heritage Museum of the Year title for 1990. In March 1991 the Labour group, which took control of the Clwyd County Council the previous May, announced its intention to sell the Castle, divesting itself of financial burdens and shifting its 'service priorities' elsewhere. Photo: Martin Trelawny, courtesy of The National Portrait Gallery.

In a sense, now is a good moment to pause and reflect on British royal portraiture and the myth of national identity, in the light of events elsewhere in the world during recent years, when newspapers have been filled with photographs of East Europeans pulling down images of former rulers and photographs of public imagery erected by Saddam Hussein (in his many guises)[27] and then subsequently riddled with bullets.

Consistently over the past twenty years royal portraiture has continued to pack in the crowds and fill the press columns in Britain. At the National Portrait Gallery, attendance for exhibitions of royal portraits, some of which the Gallery has commissioned, have been among the highest of their figures in the past two decades: 237,360 for Annigoni's 'Portrait of Elizabeth II' in 1970; 140,702 for 'Happy and Glorious: 130 years of Royal Portraits' in 1977 (the Jubilee year); and 147,496 for 'The Queen Mother: a Celebration' (1980). These may be compared with other exhibitions which would be considered successes, purely in terms of attendance: 'The Raj: India and the British, 1600–1947' (1990–1), 58,371 and 'Van Dyck in England' (1982–3), 81,267.

On 23 July 1981, a week before the Royal Wedding, the National Portrait Gallery's commissioned portrait by Bryan Organ of the Princess of Wales, seated, in trousers and a bolero jacket and white shirt, was unveiled. Within a week, 10,000 postcards (exclusively offered at the Gallery) were sold, and within two weeks 30,000 visitors had been to see the portrait. Hailed by many in the press as 'a picture of the eighties', the Princess was depicted in a 'refreshingly casual pose' and the portrayal considered 'a breakthrough in royal pictures' (*Bristol Evening Post*, 29 August 1981). The critic Brian Sewell, in his usual inimitable manner, took issue with the consensus: '*Lady Diana* was pretty enough in its way with some of the slight charm of a Thirties railway poster – and at the Festival of Britain we might have thought it daring and forward looking – but now it seems no more distinguished than a competent design for a Mills & Boon romance' (*Tatler*, December 1981).

The slashing and tearing of the painting on 29 August 1981 and the subsequent saga of its three-month restoration earned it unprecedented fame. A flurry of press articles from East Anglia, Scotland, Southampton and Liverpool to Nashville, Portland (Maine), Syracuse, Baltimore, Chattanooga, Norfolk, St Louis, Springfield (Massachusetts) and Milwaukee dwelt on the iconoclastic gesture, keeping the portrait (more than the protagonist) in the public eye. Later, the *Woman's Journal*, referring to Organ's earlier portraits of Prince

Charles and Princess Margaret, introduced its feature on the artist thus: 'Bryan Organ. Controversial Image Maker: The man who painted Prince Charles in a frame chair and Princess Margaret "behind bars" has often been a target for critics, but it was not until his portrait of the Princess of Wales was slashed that the public sat up and took notice.' Interviewed by the police, the iconoclastic Belfast student, Paul Salmon, said, '"he wanted to do something that would be well known" and the portrait was "so easy to get at"' (*Nottingham Evening Post* c.16 September 1981). His counsel was quoted in *The Times* (17 September 1981) as saying that the motivation was not political, but was instead meant to draw attention to social deprivation in Northern Ireland. (A spokeswoman for the Gallery recently noted that Royal portraits are now unveiled without glazing for the ceremony and then immediately placed behind protection for public viewing.) Photo-calls for the rehung painting featured John Bull (highly regarded by the trade as a restorer of Impressionist and Modern paintings) pointing out the damaged areas. His colleague Peter Newman was quoted saying, 'I think it is the most difficult restoration work we had done because it is such a famous painting. It was an all or nothing job' (*Daily Express*, 27 November 1981).

As often happens, the publicity rubbed off on others. The *Wolverhampton Express and Star* (n.d., around 6 September 1981) reported a brick having been thrown through a Southampton shop window, damaging a painting showing a nude model from behind, seated at a dressing table, with the Princess of Wales's face reflected in the mirror. The 35-year-old artist, Alcorn Hender, reportedly offered his painting to the National Portrait Gallery to replace Organ's while it was being restored, claiming that he had been asked by the Gallery to send colour pictures of the work. Said the artist, 'I am very upset by this vandalism because I took great care when painting the picture not to show anything which would upset the public. I know how highly they regard the Princess.' Cynics might well suggest that, given the circumstances, the Southampton brick had certainly been well timed to bring the unorthodox 'portrait' into the public gaze.

While tastefully novel approaches to portrayal might be deemed appropriate for the young Princess of Wales, views on representations of the Queen Mother were likely to be less flexible. In commissioning the young artist Alison Watt (winner of the 1987 John Player Portrait Award and graduate of Glasgow School Art in 1987), the National Portrait Gallery evidently selected an artist who would be not only strong enough to take criticism, but also daring enough to challenge public suppositions about royal visual myths. Unveiled on 3 August to coincide with the Queen Mother's 89th birthday, the portrait was described by curator Robin Gibson as intended to 'take the lid off the chocolate box' image. Recently, in June 1991, reflecting on the past controversy, he stated that when you 'add to the visual vocabulary, challenging a mental picture library established over twenty years, people are bound to get upset'. According to the *Lincolnshire Daily Echo* (3 August 1989), the painting showed 'Britain's best-loved grandmother in a singularly uncharacteristic light, hatless, wearing a simple dress and staring almost grimly out of the canvas'. What, no chiffon dress, no hat! *And* an upside down teacup at her side? Ms Watt was quoted as saying that 'I had to fight tooth and nail for her not to wear a hat' (*The Scotsman*, 4 August 1989).

The press had a field day – to the point of monotonous droning. 'Some critics' were widely quoted as saying the painting made the Queen Mother look like a 'Cabbage Patch Doll'. The *Daily Star* subtitled the painting 'Grim Gram', describing it as an 'insult to the nation's favourite gran'. 'Bung it in the Dustbin,' cried the *Daily Mirror*, citing its readers' poll for consensus opinion. The *Newcastle Evening Chronicle* (17 August 1989) published its own reader responses, under such headlines as 'we dub this daub a right royal insult,' 'It's just not her!', 'Pavement artists,' 'I hated it,' 'It should be dumped.' *Tatler* and *Evening Standard* critic Brian Sewell again rose to the occasion:

> It is absolutely terrible . . . It makes the Queen Mother look like an ancient pensioner waiting for her 100th birthday telegram from the Queen. Her hair looks like an unwashed perm and if I hadn't been told I wouldn't even know who it was supposed to be. It doesn't look like the Queen Mother and it doesn't catch at all the public image of her. Where is her sparkle and warmth? (*Evening Standard*, 3 August 1989)

The *Daily Mirror* (4 August 1989) contrasted Alison Watt's 'false impression' with 'Norman Parkinson's affectionate birthday snap . . . surrounded by flowers, beaming smile, wearing one of her fabulous over-the-top hats. That's how we are going to remember her.'

Within a week, a second portrait was unveiled which was more in line with expectations: June Mendoza painted a 'loving portrait' (*Western Independent*, Plymouth 13 August 1989) of the Queen

Mother as 'she really looks' – a commission for Queens' College, Cambridge and unveiled at Holburne Museum, Bath. Contrasting it with the Alison Watt portrait, the *Newcastle Evening Chronicle* sighed, 'Ah! this is better.'

But perhaps the prize for the worst journalism should go to the *Sunday Times* (13 August 1989). 'Watt a load of rubbish,' it intoned; 'few subjects will recognise the ham-fisted bag lady seated disconsolately before an empty grate in a bed-sit, at her elbow an inverted mug in which she has clearly read singularly inauspicious tealeaves, as Elizabeth of Glamis . . . the royal sitter appears to have been trepanned.' The commentary sunk lower still: 'Whereas she portrayed the Queen Mother as dishevelled and lank-haired, in the interests of "art" Miss Watt took care that she herself appeared impeccably groomed and made-up in all her press photographs.' No one earlier in the decade had commented on any social impropriety when Bryan Organ was photographed standing in rumpled jeans next to the informally but neatly dressed Princess of Wales.

Distinctly in the minority, Edinburgh's *Daily Record* attempted to reveal the truth (as its journalists saw it) about the character of the sitter and the portrayal. Their article, 'Real face of Supergran', reminded readers that Alison Watt's painting was, after all,

a portrait of a very Scottish matriarch. We all know one like her . . . she-who-ruled-the-family-with-a-rod-of-iron-and-took-no-nonsense . . . What everybody forgets about the Queen Mum is that she is now in well-earned retirement after maintaining Britain as a monarchy and hard-selling the First Family in a thoroughly-modern manner . . . She created the Royal family as popular soap-opera – and she's more JR than Miss Ellie . . . As the young Duchess of York, she was first to spot the potential of the mass media. In the '30s, using carefully selected writers and journals, she masterminded the first of the long line of articles about Royal babies – her own – and forever influenced popular thinking . . . Sweet she may be. But the Queen Mum is also tough, a sharp cookie, determined to do her duty as she sees it. Those chocolate box portraits of the Queen Mum don't do her justice. Alison's does.

Controversy and accompanying press coverage stimulated attendance at the National Portrait Gallery. Normal daily viewing was reported up from 500–700 a day to more than 1,000, with 4,000 on Saturdays and Sundays. The Gallery's spokeswoman was widely quoted: 'We are sorry that some people don't like it, but it has created a lot of interest . . . It is keeping alive the debate about what portraiture is or should be.'

But then there *are* limits. In April 1991 a photograph appeared in *The Times* showing entries submitted for the summer show at the Royal Academy. Centre stage, and being indecorously lifted by the porters over the heads of other sculpture, was a life-size sculpture of the Queen Mother, *Papier Mâché Lady*, leaning her head and waving. Seated on a folding chair, she was wearing a lace and chiffon dress and a fully feathered hat – the accoutrements which the press had so approvingly associated with her 'real' image. In late May, as the show was readied, a spokeswoman for the Royal Academy said that she seriously doubted that the portrayal would be accepted by judges. As it was one of the rejected works, she was unable to state who the artist was. One wonders what the press and critics *might* have made of this Royal image had it gained a coveted place in the halls of the august Academy. A spokeswoman for the National Portrait Gallery said that they receive – and reject – offers of celebrity papier maché portraits frequently. Evidently certain myths and certain truths are meant to be enshrined and others not.

NOTES

1 Sir Joshua Reynolds, *Discourses on Art*, ed. Robert R. Wark (New Haven, London, 1975), pp. 57–73. See Marcia Pointon, 'Portrait-Painting as a Business Enterprise in London in the 1780s', *Art History*, June 1984, vol. 7, no. 2, pp. 187–9.

2 In the House of Lords on 4 March 1856, Lord Ellenborough contrasted the worthy potential entrants to the proposed national portrait collection with 'the aldermen, sheriffs, railway directors, rich grocers, rich merchants, speculators, and wealthy Regent street tradesmen . . . who have their portly persons displayed upon canvas, and whose portraits illustrate or disfigure our annual exhibitions'. *Parliamentary Reports*, 31 January–11 March 1856, vol. 111, p. 1755.

3 Lionel Nathan de Rothschild (1808–79), banker and philanthropist, made it into the National Portrait Gallery in 1952, and the gift of a photographic portrait of Mrs Beeton (1836–65), author of the *Book of Household Management*, was accepted from her son (Sir Mayson Beeton) in 1932. The ten years' deceased rule was relaxed for the likes of Joseph Duveen (art dealer, d.1939, and benefactor of the National Portrait Gallery, where the Duveen galleries were opened on 3 March 1933), whose pencil portrait by Walter Tittle (signed by the artist and the sitter) was purchased in 1930. Of course, acquisitions depended, then as now, on the *availability* of a portrait of a desired sitter and of necessary purchase funds at the appropriate moment.

4 Quoted in Desmond Shawe-Taylor, *The Georgians: Eighteenth-century Portraiture and Society* (London, 1990), p. 7.

5 See Gertrude Mae Prescott, 'Fame and Photography: Portrait Publications in Great Britain, 1856–1900', PhD thesis (University of Texas at Austin, 1985).

6 For one example, see Andrew McClellan, 'D'Angiviller's "Great Men" of France and the Politics of the Parlements', *Art History*, June 1990, vol. 13, no. 2, p. 175.

7 Oliver Millar, 'Portraiture and the Country House', in *The Treasure Houses of Britain: Five Hundred Years of Private Patronage and Art Collecting* (New Haven and London, 1985), p. 32.

8 Gerald Reitlinger, *The Economics of Taste: The Rise and Fall of Picture Prices 1760–1960* (London, 1961), p. 186.

9 Ibid., p. 187.

10 Ibid., pp. 189–90.

11 S. N. Behrman, *Duveen* (London, 1986; first publ. 1956), p. 46.

12 Reitlinger, *Economics of Taste*, p. 191.

13 Reitlinger estimated that its value was £525,000 at the time when he was writing: ibid., p. 196.

14 Ibid., pp. 191–2.

15 Ibid., p. 193.

16 From Reitlinger's text (ibid., p. 193) it is unclear at which sale Leverhulme paid this price. At the time when his book was published, it remained the saleroom record for a Reynolds picture.

17 Ibid., p. 196.

18 See Gertrude Prescott Nuding, 'Selling off the Gentlemanly Image', *The Art Newspaper*, April 1991, no. 7, pp. 17–18.

19 *Private Eye*, 16 November 1984, no. 598.

20 *Apollo*, April 1991, vol. 133, no. 350, p. 291.

21 Letter to the editor, *Apollo*, April 1991, 133, no. 350, p. 291 and interviews. While John Baskett could not disclose for whom he was bidding, he did observe that Mellon had previously purchased portraits through him. Since his father had acquired such impressive full-length English portraits, Paul had tended to look elsewhere. However, Baskett noted that Paul Mellon purchased a full-length Gainsborough of Sir William Johnstone Pulteney in 1980 from a descendant of the original owner.

22 *The National Gallery*, Trustees' Report, January 1960–May 1962, p. 26. Of course, such deferral would be against the interests of the seller who had placed a work at public auction in an effort to secure the best price through open competition. Members of the trade often point out the irony that when bidders step aside for national institutions it is called 'in the nation's interest', but were dealers to step aside for each other, similarly to depress the price, their ethics are brought into question. Reserves are, after all, set not as part of a conspiracy, but to protect the seller against collusion reducing competition.

23 *Thirty-fifth Report of the Reviewing Committee on the Export of Works of Art*, 1988–89 (London, 1989), pp. 19–20.

24 Reynolds's portrait of Banks was purchased with the help of the National Heritage Memorial Fund, the National Art-Collection Fund and the Pilgrim Trust. It was offered by Thomas Agnew & Sons on behalf of Parkam Park as a Private Treaty Sale. Harold B. Carter noted that Benjamin West's portrait of Banks predates the Reynolds portrait, and therefore possesses greater historical significance.

25 See Gertrude Prescott Nuding, 'Portraits for the Nation', *History Today*, June 1989, pp. 30–6.

26 Another curious inversion of Victorian 'worthiness' was recently vocalized by the young British artist, Henry Mee, who, apparently modelling himself on G. F. Watts, put together a series of 'British Eminences: Portraits of Our Age'. Mee rented Sotheby's George Street Gallery for a two-day showing. Quoted in the *Daily Telegraph* (21 May 1990) answering Hugh Montgomery-Massingberd's question concerning what struck him about the worthies (which included Christie's chairman Lord Carrington), Sir Peter Hall, Sir Robin Day, the Archbishop of Canterbury, Sir Yehudi Menuhin, Sir Richard Attenborough and Sir Hugh Casson, among others, including the Queen, Mee said: 'That most of them were, so to speak, *interchangeable* [emphasis added]. I felt they could all have taken on each other's jobs without too much trouble.'

27 See David Keys, 'Saddam Harks Back to a Glorious Past', *Independent*, 11 August 1990, and Anthony Parsons (former British Ambassador to Iran), 'The cult of Saddam', *Independent Magazine*, 18 August 1990.

Index